SILK PURSES, RECAST DIES, AND PERIPATETIC APPLES: NARRATIVES OF RISK AND RESILIENCE FROM WITHIN THE ACADEMY

WARNIE RICHARDSON

To. Pauline,
All the very best,
Warnie

SILK PURSES, RECAST DIES, AND PERIPATETIC APPLES: NARRATIVES OF RISK AND RESILIENCE FROM WITHIN THE ACADEMY

WARNIE RICHARDSON

First published in 2013 in Champaign, Illinois, USA
by Common Ground Publishing LLC
as part of the On Diversity book series

Library of Congress Cataloging-in-Publication Data

Richardson, Warnie, 1957-
  Silk purses, recast dies, and peripatetic apples : narratives of risk and resilience from within the academy / Warnie Richardson.
     pages cm.
  Includes bibliographical references and index.
  ISBN 978-1-61229-473-5 (pbk : alk. paper) -- ISBN 978-1-61229-474-2 (pdf : alk. paper)
  1. Teacher-student relationships--Case studies. 2. Children with social disabilities--Education--Case studies. 3. Teachers--Conduct of life--Case studies. 4. Resilience (Personality trait)--Case studies. I. Title.

  LB1033.R53 2014
  371.102'3--dc23

                            2014008129

To all my former students who have looked so deeply within their hearts and souls over the last decade, this book is for you. You have definitely enriched my life!

Also, to my mother, Joyce Marie (Brown) Richardson (May 11, 1936–March 17, 2005), it's been almost ten years, but I think of you every day! And to my mother-in-law, the late Elsie Charlotte (MacDormand) MacLachlan, you loomed large in our lives and will never be forgotten (June 17, 1924–October 29, 2013).

Table of Contents

Acknowledgements

Of course this book would not have been possible without my former students, as it is their voices that speak so personally and powerfully within these pages. And although, for specific reasons related to confidentiality and anonymity, your identities cannot be publically shared, both you and I know who you are, and I want to personally thank you for seeing this ten-year project through to its successful completion. As my academic career draws to a close, I will be forever indebted to you all for letting me move forward with something I so passionately believed in.

As is the case in everything in life that I do, I also want to thank my wife, Dr. Carole Richardson, for providing both her much valued expertise on qualitative methodologies, particularly narrative, but for also trying to temper (in a proofreading capacity) my liberal expansion of all "language mechanics" boundaries.

Finally, I would like to thank my student assistant, Alexandra Rivet, for her editing prowess and for working without complaint within some incredibly challenging time constraints. I would also like to thank author/photographer Scott Liddell for kindly granting me permission to use his excellent image that now appears on the cover. From the moment I saw it, it screamed nothing but resilience and celebration. For other examples of Mr. Liddell's vast body of work, please see: http://www.scottliddell.com.

Teacher Turned around My Stormy Life

I am looking for a teacher named Michael Collins who taught at Duke of Connaught Public School in east end Toronto for a few years... In 1964 I was a very troubled young woman put into his Grade 8 class. I had just been released from the Ontario Training School for Girls in Galt, Ont., and I had a chip on my shoulder the size of an Elm tree...

I was 15 and became pregnant by my boyfriend while at Duke of Connaught. Because I was still a ward of the Government, they had the right to send me back to the training school and take my baby, no questions asked...There was nobody in my life who gave a damn about me, until Mr. Collins. He went over and above his duties as a teacher and fought the system for me, so that I wouldn't be sent back or lose my baby...Going through some family papers, I recently came across the congratulations card that Mr. Collins sent me at the East General Hospital after I had my son on Jan. 7, 1965. It was the only card I got...I realized I must try and find him. I'm praying he is still alive and I can thank him for the impact he has had on my life...I am 54 years old now, and although my life has been a hard road at times, it turned around the day he went to bat for me. I want so much to thank him, something I wish I had done years ago.

Mrs. Pat Gunson
Toronto Star Newspaper
Letter to the Editor
(Permission Granted)

Addendum

I received the book in the mail yesterday, and I want to thank you so much for the huge honour you have bestowed upon me by prefacing it with my letter to find Mr. Collins.

As I'm sure I told you, the letter did assist me in finding Mr. Collins, but he had died two years before. I was absolutely crushed that I now could not let him know what an important part he played in my life. But you have now changed that. By that letter now being printed in your book, all who read it will read his name and will see him as a teacher who was not only great at his job, and he was, but also as someone who realized that sometimes you should just remove the 'teacher hat' and put on the 'compassionate person' hat.

I may not have been able to thank him personally, but I feel that you have given me the opportunity to thank him in a different way, and for that I am forever grateful.

Chapter 1: Risk, Resiliency, and the Genesis of a Special Educational Project:

A General Overview

Human beings are not Pavlovian dogs. They don't react with conditioned reflexes to predetermined stimuli. Between stimulus and reaction, something highly specialized happens which epitomizes human consciousness and which distinguishes our species from other forms of life. Humans interpret what they perceive and on the basis of interpretation draw conclusions, make their minds, and decide what to do.

(Neitzel & Welzer, 2011, p. 8)

This book is overwhelmingly about some of my former students. It began over eleven years ago on the beaches of the Cayman Islands. I had just agreed to take a teaching job at Nipissing University in North Bay, Ontario, Canada (working with pre-service teachers), and I had just begun to piece together the preliminary draft of what my Educational Psychology/Special Education course would potentially look like. Ultimately, as one of my major assignments for the 2000/2001 academic year, I decided to have my students take an in-depth look at resilience theory, and demanded for a substantial percentage of their final mark that they review a pre-assigned book which exposed them to, and had them apply the central tenets of the aforementioned theory.

My interest in theoretical leanings as they related to both risk and resilience, without question, gestated from a very personal space. For almost 16 years of my professional teaching career, prior to taking the professorial job in Northern Ontario, I was assigned to very challenging educational environments in both Southern Ontario and the Caribbean, working with students who were overwhelmingly considered to be at-risk, marginalized, and/or delinquent. In fact, prior to being assigned to my particular educational programs (in both Southern Ontario and the Caribbean), a significant number of my students were unofficially recognized as dramatically underachieving academically, with many being officially identified as being either emotionally or behaviourally maladjusted, with some of this number being clinically diagnosed as being acutely mentally ill. This was particularly true with respect to my time spent in Southern Ontario, where, for fourteen years, I was an educational assessment teacher in a juvenile detention-centre located in downtown Toronto. It was also during this particular period, my Toronto period, that I also began my doctoral studies at the Ontario Institute for Studies in Education, an affiliate of the University of Toronto. In brief, it was while crunching numbers from the juvenile justice system (for my doctoral dissertation) that led directly to my first real exposure to some of the broader literature within the general risk/resiliency domains.

With direct reference to this early 1990's academic epiphany, I remember the trigger event very clearly. I had gone in to discuss (with one of my thesis advisors) the latest round of statistics that were being used to profile students who had been through my classroom, and under my influence, several years previous. Basically, I, as a researcher, wanted to know whether the time spent with me, in my program within the juvenile detention facility, had made any type of a significant difference with reference to their overall life trajectory, and on this particular day I had just found out that, for a fairly large longitudinal sampling, it had not. More specifically, on this particular day, I had just discovered that a great percentage of my former students had not only ultimately ended up as high school drop-outs, but a considerable number of them had gone on to chronically criminally reoffend as adults.

In understatement, these results were incredibly troubling to me at the time and, without question, negatively impacted the early stages of my meeting with my thesis advisor. When I finally expressed to him that I did not see the point in moving forward with my research given that it now seemed very obvious to me that, despite what I believed to be some considerable creative and innovative effort deployed in the design and delivery of my educational program, I was not making much of a measurable difference in their lives, he appeared quite visibly perplexed. However, after thinking about what I had said for several seconds, my academic advisor then said something that was really quite perceptive (and something that has remained with me through the passing of many years now). He said, "Why is it that you teachers always tend to fixate quantitatively on the negative?" When I asked him to explain what he specifically meant by this, he then said, "Why do you choose to focus on the large piece of your sampling that hints that you might not have made much of a difference, when you could be focusing on the smaller piece which, just maybe, suggests that you did?"

After thinking about what he had said for a very short period of time, it suddenly hit me like a ton of bricks! I remember thinking what a great deal of visceral or intuitive sense this made. What he was saying was instead of concentrating on the many that have become the prediction, thereby confirming a negative life direction, it was okay to concentrate on the few who had defied the prediction, thereby revealing a much more positive result. He was basically implying that though there were many students for whom my program (and me) may not have made much of a impact, there were some for whom it did. Hence, within a research paradigm, instead of going to one of the many who had gone on to drop out of high school and reoffend as an adult, and ask what had gone so incredibly wrong in their lives, my thesis advisor was suggesting I go to one of the few who had graduated from high school and was living a crime free life as an adult, and ask them what had gone so incredibly right.

Without question, it was from the above brief exchange on that particular day in the early 1990's that my interest in risk and resiliency was first tweaked. I desperately needed to know that the confluence of one person, arriving at a particular time in a young person's life, had the capacity to change that life in such a fashion that overall life outcome could be truly affected in a more positive or favourable way. I needed to know that one person could play a significant role in helping those most at-risk become everything they were capable of becoming, and it was in looking more closely at those working and writing within the general fields of "risk" and "resilience" that provided me with all the evidence that I needed. As a direct result, risk and resilience have since become very important influences within a great deal of my writing, and integral components of my Special Education course offering(s) at the university level; with the previously mentioned assignment overwhelmingly serving as its central ingredient. This is how it basically works.

To set up my risk/resiliency assignment, I lecture on the topic for almost two full academic periods, and then assign my students a specific reading or group of readings, authored by either Bonnie Benard, Emmy Werner, Ruth Smith, Norman Garmezy, Michael Rutter, Nel Noddings, Nan Henderson, Gina Higgins, Ann Masten, Douglas Coatsworth, Meyer Glantz, Jeannette Johnson, Edmund Gordon, Michael Ungar, Hersh Waxman, Mike Milstein, Suniya Luthar, Martin Krovetz, Howard Kaplan, etc., before freeing them up to formally review their book, and complete their assignment. My direct instruction, as far as this particular endeavour is specifically concerned has traditionally always looked something like this:

> Resilience theory is a relatively new construct. Among its central tenets, it advocates that some children demonstrate an incredible capacity to withstand quite horrendous childhoods and go on to develop completely healthy "normal" relationships, living very positive, productive lives as decent law-abiding citizens. In short, they are able to achieve much more than was predicted of them, (almost miraculously in some cases), not having been defeated by the circumstances of their birth and early childhood. In this respect, the common thread running through much of this resilience research consistently highlights some very specific characteristics of resilient children, and the significant role played by at least one caring adult, who, at some point in their lives, is not only genuinely concerned for their overall physical and spiritual well beings, but actually gives some meaning to their very troubled existences. Further, the research states that, in many instances, it has been an educator who has made the difference, enabling them to overcome tremendous odds by helping to break the cycles of poverty, addiction, abuse, neglect, physical, psychological and emotional deterioration, and anti-social, and, sometimes, very criminal behaviour.

> In this assignment you will review one book in which the author or person being profiled has seemingly transcended abysmal circumstances

and traveled far beyond the "station" for which they might have appeared to have been predestined. At minimum, you will detail the circumstances from which they came and how it was they were able to rise well above them. In summary, you will be looking at these extraordinary lives and determining what accounts for the success, instead of trying to deconstruct and explain the failure. Although this assignment will be presented to the professor for formal evaluation, be prepared to discuss your book in class.

(For a specific example of what this original book review assignment called for, and how it was supposed to look upon its successful completion, refer to **Chapter 2** (Rising From the Ashes) where the life of Frank McCourt (Angela's Ashes) is analyzed through a risk/resiliency perspective).

To summarize, within the specific parameters of my assignment, risk was identified as being any factor within the life of a child or adolescent that has a documented capacity to influence overall life trajectory or outcome in a less than favourable way. For example, within the extant literature, poverty has consistently been shown to play a significant role within a life span developmental perspective, but so too have all forms of childhood and adolescent neglect, abuse, addiction, criminality, mental illness, dislocation, abandonment, and general familial dysfunction (Richardson, Richardson & McCabe, 2004; Richardson & Paolucci, 2009; Richardson, Paolucci & Richardson, 2010). Conversely, resilience or resiliency, again for the purposes of the assignment, were terms used interchangeably to identify the specific characteristics of those individuals who appear to rise above the most negative of earliest childhood and adolescent circumstances and/or predictions (risks), with resilience theory providing the framework through which these transcendent lives could be strategically isolated and closely examined. Simply put, resilience theory provides the paradigm through which the good can be distilled from the bad.

Of note, the first year I had my students do this particular assignment, I was extremely cautious, choosing to control every aspect of it. By this, I mean I suggested/recommended all of the books that could potentially be reviewed, although I did make one concession, and that was in allowing students the option of selecting their own books, but only if they had their selected book pre-approved by me. I did this for one primary reason; when it comes to most things within the larger risk/resiliency domains, I knew that in examining some of the material that would meet the very specific conditions of the assignment, some of my students would be exposed to and required to read some profoundly disturbing narratives – and I wanted them to be well aware of that fact well before they decided to 'take on' a particular book. Most importantly, I wanted them to clearly understand that in getting to the celebration at the end of any of the recommended books, would mean, at least for some, that they would be dragged through levels/episodes of poverty, abuse (of every type), family dysfunction, addiction, incest, mental illness, criminality, neglect, hurt, shame, cruelty, and scandal, that could only be conjured up in the wildest of imaginations, and I wanted to prepare them fully for this reality.

Without exception, I always stressed the ultimate happy ending in all of the recommended books, and the importance of the intervening agents in the shaping of the ending, but I never disguised the potential ugliness in getting to the conclusion. So, for example, if I had a student who chose a book like Silent Cries by Pauline Mantley, or My Father's House by Sylvia Fraser, or Father's Touch by Donald D'Haene, or any of the trilogy of books authored by David Pelzer, I wanted them to know that they would have very little problem in identifying the resiliency within the book and within the central character, however, they would also be confronted with descriptions of childhood abuse that might, at times, make it a very difficult and deeply disturbing read. However, in my first academic year at the university (2000-2001), in assigning this scholarly task to almost 200 of my students, a funny thing happened on the way to its completion!

Almost immediately after discussing the intricacies of the assignment with all five of my classes in 2000/2001, including the two month deadline that was allocated for the essay's construction and submission, a slow trickle of my students started to schedule private office meetings with me to discuss potential modifications to the design of their individual risk/resiliency assignments. In brief, no sooner had the research begun on the core components generally falling within the larger risk/resiliency domains, before students started to request the supplanting of someone else's narrative (book review), with one emanating from their own personal set of circumstances. Between the time I had assigned the book review project and its ultimate submission two months later, 31 students had come to me claiming that they had personal stories to tell, which they truly believed met all of the criteria generally falling within the assignment's overall parameters. In the end, I agreed with all 31 of them.

From this point forward, over a span of ten years, I have designed the assignment in a very similar way, with the one major exception being that I now formally allow for the submission of personal narratives within the overall process. Thus, within the confines of the assignment as it currently exists, the exploration of pre-identified risk/resiliency principles can now be refined either through a book of my choosing, a book of the student's choosing, or from a very personal perspective. Related directly to this, in every year since the inaugural one, almost one third of all submissions have been of the personal variety, running from a low of 31% in 2004/2005, to a high of 37% in 2007/2008; and it is from this pool of narrative gold that this book draws its inspiration.

As a matter of significance, the fact that consistently around one third of my students, as identified by assignment submissions over a ten-year period, viewed themselves as being former children and/or adolescents at-risk, but now resilient adults, has been recently confirmed by two completed studies whereby at least three out of ten of all Bachelor of Education respondents surveyed saw their own lives as clearly evolving within a risk/resiliency dynamic. Even when compared to other faculties, formally surveyed education students were overwhelmingly more likely than others to view themselves as being previously at-risk, but now resilient (Paolucci & Richardson, 2009; Richardson, Paolucci & Richardson, 2010). Of course, as the two completed studies highlight, whether or not the teaching profession, in and of itself attracts more resilient candidates to this specific professional program, and if so, why, is left for future studies to more fully determine.

The Collective Literary Effort

Almost from the first personal submission way back in 2000/2001, a narrative detailing extremes of poverty and general family dysfunction that made it an extremely uncomfortable read, I knew I was onto something of real substance. I very quickly came to realize that in each and every one of my five classes, made up of approximately 35 to 40 students in each, a significant number of my students had been exposed to factors in their lives, particularly in their early childhoods and adolescences, which left them extremely vulnerable to a diminished life outcome, and yet, here they were, at minimum, working on a second degree, and about to embark on a profession, (teaching), that has a remarkable capacity to positively influence, sometimes in dramatic ways, the lives of others (Benard, 1997, 2004; Krovetz, 1999; Henderson & Milstein, 2003; Higgins, 1994; Meier, 1995; Richardson, Richardson & McCabe, 2004; Richardson, Paolucci & Richardson, 2010; Rutter,1979; Werner & Smith, 2001).

In recognizing the value of those first personal submissions, in those first years of doing the assignment, I knew almost instantaneously that I had the 'makings' of a book. I knew that I was getting some incredibly powerful narratives and that they definitely needed to be disseminated to a much wider audience. When I first discussed this possibility with my classes, that I would like some of them to consider submitting their personal stories as chapters, for inclusion in a prospective book project, the response from a large percentage of them was almost immediate. In actuality, from the very beginning of this whole endeavour, many began to write on the back of their submissions as well as contacting me both personally and electronically just after handing their reflections into me, basically indicating to me that they were indeed very interested in working with me and in seeing their very personal narratives ultimately published in a book; overwhelmingly in the hope that others of similar circumstances could draw inspiration and a degree of hope from their literary offerings. In fact, since 2000/2001, within the parameters of my risk/resiliency assignment, I have collected personal narratives from 111 individual students, all of whom have individually noted, both in person and in writing, a profound willingness to see exposed and shared a significantly challenging and sometimes deeply disturbing period in their lives. In this particular effort, I share 41 of these very personal submissions.

Of particular interest, students other than the ones I taught submitted two of the 111 personal narratives. They contacted me through some of their friends who were my students, having been made aware of the assignment through them. Both had stories that they very much wanted to tell, and felt strongly that the design of my assignment provided the perfect filter through which their very personal tales could be effectively rendered; and both wanted their stories communicated to a much broader audience. In both cases, I overwhelmingly agreed with them.

Risk, Resiliency, Schools, and Teachers: An Overview of Some Literature

One of the most important and consistent findings in resilience research is the power of schools, especially teachers, to turn a child's life from risk to resilience. While much of the recent research about effective schooling focuses on students' academic performance, the role of schools in young peoples' lives is clearly broader than pedagogy and more important than test scores. Especially in the absence of positive family relationships, schools can provide an alternative source of protective, nurturing support.

(Benard, 2004, p. 65)

As noted in two previous studies in which I played a part, risk research, at least within the humanities, has traditionally focused on individuals who appear to have factors influencing their lives in a less than constructive way. Once these troubled individuals are identified, risk researchers isolate their current set of conditions and try to locate specific correlates that appear to have a significant negative impact (Luthar & Cushing, 1999; Paolucci & Richardson, 2009; Richardson, Paolucci & Richardson, 2010; Richardson, Richardson & McCabe, 2004). These correlated factors that become clearly delineated are then known as risk factors (Garmezy, 1985; Henderson & Milstein, 2003; Losel & Bliesener, 1990; Masten, Best & Garmezy, 1990). More specifically, risk factors are defined as "those variables that have proven or presumed effects that can directly increase the likelihood of a maladaptive outcome" (Rolf & Johnson, 1990, p. 387). Or put another way, "the term at-risk is generally used to describe or identify young people who, beset by particular difficulties and disadvantages, are thought likely to fail to achieve the development in their adolescent years that would provide a sound basis for a satisfying and fulfilling adult life" (Batten & Russell in McIntyre, Freeland, Melville, & Schwenke, 1999, C:9). In brief, there remains a great deal of both historical and current evidence which suggests that the number and intensity of risk factors within one's life does indeed increase the likelihood of the outcome being shaped in a less positive way (Kirby, 1999), and certainly increases the chances that problematic and/or antisocial behaviour will ultimately ensue (Dusenbury et al., 1997; Richardson, Richardson, & McCabe, 2004; Rutter, Giller, & Hagel, 1998; Silliman, 1994).

If one closely scrutinizes the extant literature as alluded to earlier, there would appear to be many different circumstances that can help determine whether or not a child should be considered to be at-risk, with exposure to variables such as perinatal stress, physical, sexual and psychological abuse, familial dysfunction, neglect, abandonment, addiction, parental psychopathology, bullying, familial dislocation, criminality, early parental death, birth to a teenage mother, negative peers, and poverty, all measurably providing significant weight (Craig & Pepler, 1998; Dryfoos, 1990; Furstenbeg et al., 1987; Higgins & McCabe, 2000; Manning & Baruth, 1995; McCubbin et al., 1997; McWhirter et al., 2004; Mireault & Bond, 1992; Ringwalt, Greene, & Robertson, 1998; Sampson & Laub, 1993; Thornberry & Krohn, 1997; Turner, 2000). As previously mentioned, within a life-span socioeconomic analysis, poverty, in particular has been consistently shown as playing a significant role in placing some school-aged children and adolescents at considerable risk (Benard, 1997; Bradley & Corwyn, 2000; Children's Defense Fund, 2005; Dahlberg, 1998; Thornberry, Huizinga & Loeber, 1995). In fact, the latest research within the field suggests that poverty may even have a tremendous influence on how a child's brain actually develops (McIlroy, 2010), with one current study directly linking it to many lifelong problems such as learning difficulties, depression and the inability to cope with stress (Luby et al., 2013).

However, with it generally being conceded that poverty plays an impactful role within a life span developmental perspective (Garmezy in Glantz & Johnson, 1999, p. 8), the research also tells us that being poor or coming from a dysfunctional, neglectful or abusive family, by way of specific examples, does not necessarily mean that the likelihood of a negative life trajectory and/or outcome is predictably always the culminating life event (Rutter, 1990; Werner & Smith, 1992, 2001). In fact, a plethora of research within the broad risk/resiliency domain now more optimistically claims that even in the most horrendous of situations, despite the most negative of beginnings, a significant number of children and youth will eventually overcome or transcend the most unfavourable of obstacles and go on to lead completely successful and healthy lives as fully functioning adults (Benard, 1991; Chess, 1989; Dumont, Widom & Czaja, 2007; Garmezy, 1993; Levine, 2002; Rutter, 2000).

Werner and Smith (1992; 2001), in their seminal longitudinal study conducted on the Hawaiian island of Kauai, were amongst the first to formally study and quantify the risk/resilience relationship, suggesting that although some of the children they tracked, who had been exposed to multiple risk factors within their early developmental years, did indeed experience more negative psychosocial outcomes as adults (one in six), they were also pleasantly surprised to find that a far greater number of their multiply exposed subjects were able to overcome the adversity of their early childhoods and adolescences by the time they had reached their 40th birthdays. As they specifically state, "one of the most striking findings of our two follow-ups in adulthood, at ages thirty-two and forty, was that most of the high-risk youths who did develop serious coping problems in adolescence had staged a recovery by the time they reached midlife" (2001, p. 167). For Werner and Smith (1992; 2001) and many others (Benard, 2004; Garmezy, 1985; Masten, 1994; Richardson et al, 1990; Rutter 1979), there appears to be a shifting balance between stressful life events and the protective factors that greatly increase the likelihood of a child becoming resilient. Hence, for many involved in its study, resiliency is seen as not only depending on the individual and his or her upbringing, but also on the interplay of specific biological and/or environmental factors as well (Glantz & Johnson, 1999; Rutter 1979).

In looking at other factors within the literature that also appear to have the propensity to place young people at considerable risk, gender would also seem to be of serious consequence, particularly as it directly relates to perceived problematic or maladaptive behaviour (Loeber & Hay, 1996; Siegel, Welsh & Senna, 2003, p. 169; Spieker et al., 1999; Rutter & Garmezy, 1983; West, 1984). Without fail, studies consistently identify males as being unquestionably more likely to display aggressive and anti-social behaviour when compared to females, with this behaviour and societal reaction to this behaviour greatly impeding the full blossoming of potential (Barr & Parrett, 2001; Barriga el., 2001; Bennett, Elliott & Peters, 2005; Card, et al., 2008; Toro, Urberg & Heinze, 2004).

School failure would also appear to be another variable of obvious and serious relevance, especially within a framework that closely examines the concept of life trajectory and realized potential (Bersani & Chapple, 2007; Parsley & Corcoran, 2003; Waxman, Gray & Padron, 2003). Overwhelmingly, the schooling experiences of children and teenagers are seen as having profound influence upon who and what these children and teenagers become as adults (Graham, 1988). As Tilleczek, Furlong & Ferguson astutely note (2010, p. 6), "when any groups are systematically excluded from meaningful participation and achieve below their levels of competence, they become both marginalized in their current school environments and economically and socially disadvantaged over their lifetimes".

Of course, when one collectively isolates and analyses all four of the variables identified directly above (poverty, gender, problematic and/or anti-social behaviour, and school failure), race and ethnicity would also appear to enter into the equation, placing some groups at far greater risk than others (Children's Defense Fund, 2005). For example, in North America, in many studies emanating from the United States and Canada, African-American children, Latino children, and Aboriginal children would appear to be disproportionately represented in the data collected (Human Resources and Skills Development Canada, 2000; Department of Justice Canada, 2004; Manning & Baruth, 1995; McWhiter et al., 2004).

On virtually every indicator from infant mortality to shortened life expectancy, Canada's first peoples are too often the forgotten in our country and that's wrong. It's wrong morally and it's dumb economically. ....Ask the aboriginal leadership anywhere in Canada and they will tell you without hesitation that it all begins with a better education.

(Former Canadian Prime Minister Paul Martin: The Toronto Star, May 1, 2010)

It is generally accepted within the broader literature on risk/resiliency that there are four primary domains into which risk is generally clustered and investigated: family, school, community, and personal (Youth Justice Board, 2005), and three primary categories into which a person who is deemed to be at-risk can fall: low-risk, moderate-risk, and high-risk. These three general categories, first basically defined by Dr. Michael Rutter back in 1987, are delineated by the number of risk factors in a child's life, when combined with the amount of intervention needed to help overcome or transcend these risks. Quite obviously, a low-risk individual can be characterized as someone whose protective factors far outweigh his or her risk factors. A low-risk individual may experience mild problems and may even require some short term intervention, like mentoring or counseling, however, their immediate environments are relatively safe and nurturing places to be as they have access to influential people in their lives that can be consistently counted upon for nurturance and support. A moderate-risk individual is characterized as having some risk factors in their life, but having access to only a limited number of protective factors that can help see them through some of their most difficult of moments. With this identified group, their particular situations can usually be strengthened considerably merely by the introduction of other additional protective factors into their lives.

At the opposite end of the spectrum from the low-risk individual is the high-risk individual who is, quite logically, characterized as having the number of risk factors in their lives far outweighing the number of protective factors. Unfortunately, particularly with this identified group, in far too many instances, a disproportionate number of factors which place young people at incredible risk derive from within the perceived sanctity of the family unit itself so are very hard to neutralize by way of proactive intervening manipulation (Bevan & Higgins, 2002; Higgins & McCabe, 2000; Ringwalt, Green & Robertson, 1998; McWhirter et al., 2004). Irrespective of how it is specifically categorized, quantified, or framed, according to Norman Garmezy, the "peerless pioneer" of resiliency research (Masten & Coatsworth, 1998), you cannot have "resilience in the absence of stress" or risk (Gramezy in Glantz & Johnson, 1999, p. 7).

To summarize, a general examination of the literature within the risk/resiliency domains suggests that individuals who appear to rise above the most negative of earliest childhood and adolescent circumstances and/or predictions (risks), are in the possession of certain commonly shared resilient qualities (Losel & Bliesener, 1990; Masten & Coatsworth, 1998; Rutter, 1979; Ungar & Teram, 2000), while the general philosophical approach which provides the framework through which these resilient lives and qualities can be specifically targeted and analyzed, is now generally known as "resilience theory" (Glantz & Johnson, 1999; Van Breda, 2001). Restated, the terms resilience and resiliency are used interchangeably to describe a set of characteristics a person encompasses that then facilitates a process whereby successful adaptation and transformation occurs within a life span developmental perspective, despite having been exposed to profound levels of neglect, abuse, trauma, challenge, and outright hardship (Benard, 1991; Luthar, 2000; Masten, Best & Garmezy, 1990).

> Resilience often is defined in general terms of the forestalling of adverse developmental outcomes in the face of characteristics of the individual or the individual's environment that would have led to the prediction of the adverse developmental outcome.

> (Kaplan, 1999, p.23).

"Resilience theory" offers a distinctive approach to collecting, organizing, and analyzing risk data, which has increasingly been utilized within the sociological, criminological, anthropological, educational, medical, psychiatric, and psychological domains (Benard, 2004; Garmezy, 1991; Glantz & Johnson, 1999; Henderson & Milstein, 2003; Richardson, Richardson & McCabe, 2004; Rutter,

1987; Scudder, Sullivan, & Copeland-Linder, 2008; Werner, 1989). However, with very little exception, it is within the field of education that many see the utility and practicality of the theory as having significant influence, particularly in impacting in a positive, proactive way, the overall life evolution of students (Benard, 1991; Borland et al., 1998; Brown, D'Emidio-Caston & Benard, 2001; Krovetz, 2008; Milstein & Henry, 2000; Rolf & Johnson, 1999; Thomsen, 2002; Waxman, Gray & Padron, 2003), with schools, perhaps, serving "as a protective shield to help children withstand the multiple vicissitudes that they can expect from a stressful world" (Garmezy, 1991, p. 427). As Henderson & Milstein specifically state, "more than any other institution except family, schools can provide the environment and the conditions that foster resiliency in today's youth and tomorrows adults" (2003, p. 2).

> Schools build resiliency in students through creating an environment of caring and personal relationships. The foundation of this relationship begins with educators who have a resiliency-building attitude. Teachers who model the resilient behaviors they desire from their students are often called "turnaround teachers". Turnaround teachers provide and model three protective factors that buffer risk and enable positive love development by meeting students' basic needs for safety, belonging, respect, power, accomplishment, and learning. The three factors include caring relationships, high expectations, and opportunities to participate and contribute. Teachers can convey genuine support to students by listening to them and validating their feelings, and by demonstrating kindness, compassion, and respect.

> (Waxman, Gray, & Padrón, 2003, p. 12)

With very little debate, resilience research has consistently shown that the educational process is a critical component in understanding how a person realizes their full potential, particularly in overcoming the myriad negative influences of a dysfunctional or disrupted childhood or early adolescence (Benard, 1999; 2004). More precisely, it has been effectively argued that it is primarily through the schooling experience that young people (who are at serious risk) first come into potential contact with caring, supportive, nurturing others; with the concept of adult associations being advanced as one of the most important variables within the studied risk/resiliency dynamic (Noddings, 1988; Richardson, Richardson & McCabe, 2005; Turner, 2000; Werner, 1993; Werner & Smith, 2001; Wolin & Wolin, 1993). As Bonnie Benard specifically states (1991), with direct reference to the earlier work of Urie Bronfenbrenner (1983), "what is evident is that to mitigate the effect of other risks and stressful life events and to develop healthily, a child needs the enduring loving involvement of one or more adults in care and joint activity with that child".

In short, current research suggests that if a person is to become everything they are capable of becoming, thereby transcending some profound impediments of earliest childhood, it is only through the schooling experience that this positive process can be truly facilitated; a process through which the development of full potential is a most pleasant corollary.

(Richardson, Richardson, & McCabe, 2004, p. 13)

To review, the theoretical leaning as it specifically relates to the broad concept of risk and resiliency, is overwhelmingly anchored to the central notion that certain people have a greater chance of success based on the number of (both internal and external) protective factors that they have at their disposal when encountering life situations, which leaves them not only physically, psychologically, and spiritually vulnerable, but profoundly amplifies the chances of having a restricted, depleted, or diminished life outcome (Bruce, 2002; Collishaw et al., 2007; Glantz & Johnson, 1999; Werner & Smith, 1989). Quite naturally, examples of these internal and external protective factors would include such things as having a positive self-image/concept, having a self efficacious nature, having an internal locus of control, having a defined belief system, being attached to non delinquent peers, experiencing a degree of school success, and, of course, most importantly, having the unconditional support from an adult (or adults) who really matter (O'Grady & Metz, 1987; Masten & Coatsworth, 1998; Noddings, 1988, 1992, 1999, 2007; Scudder, Sullivan, & Copeland-Linder, 2008; Thomsen, 2002; Ungar & Teram, 2000; Zimmerman, 2000).

As is now well established in the literature (Paolucci & Richardson, 2009; Richardson, Paolucci & Richardson, 2010), resiliency is a process of healthy human development that grows through nurturing relationships that are grounded in an atmosphere of reciprocal trust, respect, empathy, compassion and caring (Benard, 1991, 2004; Noddings, 1992; Turner, 2000). Ideally, these relationships are usually first developed within a familial milieu, but continue to be nurtured and strengthened within the larger community, especially the school. Resiliency encompasses the idea that people can bounce back from negative life experiences and often become even stronger in the process of having faced and overcome them (Rutter, 2012). As alluded to previously, this notion has captured the attention of many social scientists and educators who are beginning to understand the need for schools to become truly resiliency-fostering bastions for all those who function within them (Henderson & Milstein, 2003; Krovetz, 2008; Waxman, Gray, & Padrón, 2003).

What began as a quest to understand the extraordinary has revealed the power of the ordinary. Resilience does not come from rare and special qualities, but from the everyday magic of ordinary, normative human resources in the minds, brains, and bodies of children, in their families and relationships, and in their communities.

(Masten, 2001, in Benard, 2004, p.iv)

According to Benard (1991; 2004), we are all born with a latent resilient drive, with this resilient drive helping us to develop problem solving skills, initiative, independence, social competence, and an overall sense of purpose. However, as many note (Scudder, Sullivan & Copeland-Linder, 2008), this internal drive has a better chance at fully blossoming if it comes under the direct influence of at least one positive, influential adult role model (Higgins, 1994; Miller, 1990; Rutter, 2012). As Ungar says (2013, p. 330), "in contexts of risk, relationships are crucial to mitigating the negative impact of toxic environments. Resilience, the capacity to overcome adversity, is facilitated by those who engage with the child". Thus, if one accepts that, within the risk/resiliency dynamic, the existence of positive relationships within the life of a child and/or adolescent is a key intervening agent within this overall process (Lerner & Overton, 2008; Masten, 2001), one must also acknowledge the importance of schools and teachers as, next to the home, it is the one place where young people spend the greatest amount of time; six to seven hours per day, 190 days per year (Benard, 1998; Borland et al., 1998; Coburn & Nelson, 1989; Geary, 1988; Henderson & Milstein, 2003; Krovetz, 2008; Richardson, Richardson, & McCabe, 2004; Rutter et al., 1977; Thomsen, 2002; Ungar, 2013).

For those of us who are involved in education on a daily basis, we know that many of the youth under our charge come to school having been exposed to many situations which place them at an incredible disadvantage. On any given day, unfortunately, for far too many of them, the time spent with us may be as good as it gets. However, within that timeframe, we need to know that we can have substantial influence, that we can help make things 'right'. The research tells us so. More specifically, the research tells us that children/youth have an abundance of ability in being able to bounce back from many of life's misfortunes, particularly if there is a significant caring adult to help them somewhere along the way. As educators, we are very well placed to be that significant caring adult.

(Richardson, Richardson, & McCabe, 2004, p. 13)

Narrative or Story as Method: Some Perspective

If we accept that one of the basic human forms of experience of the world is as story and if, further, we take the view that the storied quality of experience is both unconsciously restoried in life and consciously restoried, retold, and relived through processes of reflection, then the rudiments of method are born in the phenomenon of narrative.

(Clandinin & Connelly, 1991: 259)

Narrative inquiry begins with "experience as lived and told in stories" (Clandinin & Connelly, 2000, p. 128). It invites us to wander in amongst the words as we wend our way backwards and forwards through our storied experiences; thus enabling us to come to an understanding of what it is we know, and how we know it. In discussing the pivotal role of preservice teachers' narratives, Beattie says, "Individuals construct meaning as they live their lives, and learning involves the reconstruction of what is known in the light of new insights and understanding" (Beattie, 2001, p. v). As we move in and amongst our words and invite others to wander with us, we discover new stories, rewrite old ones and others are invited to hear this story of how we re-vision our knowledge.

"To teach should mean to offer what is personally meaningful. And teaching comes to have personal meaning only if one has reflected deeply on one's own journey so far through life" (Salmon, 1988 in Diamond, 1991, p. 16). In order to make the implicit constructs explicit, preservice teachers must engage in a more critical awareness of self; the self that they are destined to share as it is the filter through which all teaching happens. The storied life journeys that follow are stories of resiliency. These stories, by definition, chronicle myriad extraordinary and often unimaginable challenges encountered in the lives of these preservice teachers and, in the telling, when mere survival would seem to be a significant triumph, go further to become a celebration of success and joy.

Though not explicitly narratives of preservice teacher education, these stories were offered within the context of the preservice year, a year that encourages students to look deeply into their tacit understandings and to make these understandings explicit. This, then, is where one finds the collaborative aspects of these narratives. Though the tellers speak only from their perspectives, these stories are offered within the collaborative context of one specific Special Education/Educational Psychology class, during a year of intense introspection and many, many hours spent with a core group of classmates. These stories, were, then influenced, encouraged and flavored by the very context in which they were offered. The opportunity to offer their stories to others, within the context of an assignment that related directly to their life experiences, validated their voices and their seemingly isolating and sometimes tragic circumstances transformed into that which could put a personal face on the theory and nature of resiliency.

Stories of experience, then, lie at the heart of this book; waiting to be heard, to be placed in context, to become better understood as part of a continuum, as "experiences grow out of other experiences, and experiences lead to further experiences" (Connelly & Clandinin, 2000, p. 2). As with drawing

(Klee & Matisse in Montgomery-Whicher, 2002), the very act of writing our experiences changes the way in which we see things. We often do not truly understand until we see and hear our voices in our printed words. It is also true that, "A story, once told, no longer belongs solely to the storyteller... Others may see in it what the storyteller does not," (Novak, 1975: 199).

Ultimately, the concept of voice in narrative inquiry is collaborative. Though told by individuals, stories are never lived alone, and those to whom the stories are told play a pivotal role in valuing and holding sacred the stories told to them.

> In listening to people, we demonstrate to them and others that they are worth caring for and about, and in valuing the stories of their lives, we assure them that their voices sing for us and tell authentic and meaningful truths as they know them. In this way, the concept of voice is again collaborative. As we do not have experiences which are free from the influences of others, our voices cannot speak authentically if we value only our own words. It is in the silences and the resonances, amongst the harmony and the discord that we find parts of ourselves in the lives of others. In doing so, we rediscover the universality of lives lived and the human need for story to share them.
>
> (Richardson, 2008, p. 154)

An Introduction to the Narratives: Reader Beware

As mentioned previously, I had 111 narratives from which to choose, which means that 70 of my students, who wanted nothing more than to share their stories of resilience with a much wider reading audience, are not represented within these pages, and for this I apologize. All believed very strongly that their narratives had something of real substance to offer within the boundaries of my risk/resiliency assignment, as did I. However, with everything being equally considered, for this first volume I was forced to choose approximately 40 stories, and in doing so opted for nothing more than to just provide a very eclectic approach to overall selection. Although, I must say, I purposely held back a large number of stories falling within the large "special educational" sphere, only because I believe there is a completely separate book to be written within this particular risk/resiliency area. The same could be said of the large number of selections remaining who tell the story of a parent, grandparent or sibling.

As certainly alluded to previously, the stories that follow are not only very personal, some of them are also deeply disturbing. That is the curse of reading and writing within this particular area. I have come to discover that getting at the good may demand, at least for a time, that you wallow for a bit in the bad; to arrive at the happy may also require that you expend a little emotional energy sorting through the sad, and discovering the realignments that ultimately lead to the functional may drag you first through all that which is recognized as being completely dysfunctional. In the end, to reiterate what Norman Garmezy so astutely observed in the early years of risk/resiliency research (1971), you clearly cannot have one without the other. Or again, as he more specifically states, "it seems to me that you can't talk about resilience in the absence of stress" (Gramezy in Glantz & Johnson, 1999, p. 7).

Thus, what immediately follows are 41 stories, which, although all very resilient in overall orientation, are also deeply steeped in stress; certainly, some more than others. Although issues relating to poverty, abuse (sexual, physical, psychological, self), neglect, premature death, suicide, teenage pregnancy, single parenting, bullying, body image, date rape and sexual assault, mental illness, addiction, physical and neurological exceptionality, familial dysfunction, etc. are all fully represented in the narratives to come, it is incumbent upon the reader to always keep in mind the ending, and the view of those doing the sharing, that the story is truly one of celebration; emphasizing the transcending of the sometimes quite incredible circumstances and/or challenges in the sometimes earliest of years. Nonetheless, be prepared to shed a tear, and be prepared to experience a little heartache. Be prepared to be made a little uncomfortable, and be prepared to get angry. But most of all, be prepared to rejoice!

> I could not stop talking because now I had started my story, it wanted to be finished. We cannot choose where to start and stop. Our stories are the tellers of us.

> (Cleave, 2009, p. 131)

Significance of the Title

"Silk purses, recast dies, and peripatetic apples" is the title of the first lecture that I give on risk and resiliency. It is an inversion of the commonly applied idioms, particularly within the self-fulfilling prophecy domain, of "you can't make a silk purse from a sow's ear, the die is cast, and the apple doesn't fall far from the tree". Of course, the latter, all being expressions of a very negative variety that infer that fate can somewhat be determined and/or predicted based on circumstances that are completely beyond the control of the person for whom the prognostications have been made. Related directly to this, research within the risk/resiliency sector continually reinforces the fact that you can indeed make a silk purse from a sow's ear, the die can most certainly be recast, and the apple has a tremendous capacity to travel a very great distance from the tree – as some of the following chapters (3 through 43) very effectively illustrate.

The language and history purists will no doubt notice the incongruity between the utterance by Julius Caesar, "the die is cast" and the way it is referenced in the title of the book. Within the context that Caesar apparently used it, die refers to the gaming cube popular within Roman society at the time (but still popular today). Thus, the plural of die within this context would be dice. However, early in this process of collecting narratives from my students, I received one that chose to use the saying "the die is cast" in a completely different way. When it came to the metaphor that she more correctly wanted to apply to her story of risk/resilience; a story detailing, as she says, "incestuous behaviour within a family; depravity, complicity, police investigations, and years and years of counseling," she chose to very effectively use the word die as it relates directly to the steel making process – "a mold into which molten metal or other material is forced." She titled her piece, *Dies Can Be Recast and Molds Can Be Broken*. And although I was not able to use her full narrative in the book for very personal and potentially legal reasons, the official title of the book is a direct concession to her in acknowledgement of her truly remarkable journey and very powerful story.

> Though we can and do reflect, somewhat sadly, on the amount of responsibility that society continues to assign to educators for the life success of our students, we must continue to accept and rise to any challenges that will enable our students to do the same, and, by doing so, empower our most vulnerable youth to reach their full potential and, reciprocally, affect positive change in the lives of others.
>
> (Richardson, Richardson & McCabe, 2004, p. 13)

> Sometimes, a student will take the time to seek out a former teacher and thank him or her for the positive impact made in the life of that student many years earlier. Such acts of gratitude often come as a surprise to teachers, who never realized what a formative role they may play in the lives of their students. Resiliency often works this way.
>
> (Hurlington, 2010, p. 4)

> Outside of the family circle......among the most frequently encountered positive role models in the lives of children, was a favorite teacher. For the resilient youngster a special teacher was not just an instructor for academic skills, but also a confidant and positive model for personal identification.
>
> (Werner, 2000, p. 126)

> One of the great joys of teaching is that we can learn as much from our students as they can learn from us. When we lift our eyes from the pacing guide long enough to observe the individuals in our classroom, they will often teach us exactly what nourishment they need to thrive.
>
> (Tomlinson & Jarvis, 2006, p. 16)

> For teachers, learning about resilience experiences and research is critical to closing the achievement gap because it provides evidence and gives hope to educators that all children and youth have the capacity to learn and that teachers and school actually do have the power to successfully educate them.
>
> (Benard, 2004, p. 115)

> It may seem a cumbersome ritual to shake each child's hand twice each day, but the teacher who makes the effort *touches* each child. How easy

it is, otherwise, to let days go by without being in touch with certain children. The quiet and "easy" child can remain untouched for quite some time.

(Van Manen, 1986, p. 21)

An important measure of a teacher is what she can tell you about her students - not their marks or behaviour, but their lives. Who lives behind the faces that look at you expectantly at the beginning of each new day? What are their challenges and their strengths; their fears, their joys and most importantly, their dreams?......Do you know why they sometimes raise their hands wanting eagerly to participate, while at other times avoiding your gaze? Do you know how they learn? Have you talked to or met their parents? What do you know about your students?.......Everyone needs a little kindness in their lives. Your smile, your gentle word, the touch of your hand on their shoulder might be the only positive human contact they have all day. Value the voices of all of your students, and when you feel like shouting, look to laughter instead. Shouting makes us defensive and laughter breaks through our defenses. If, when you leave your classroom for the day, you know you have made an honest effort to value each child for who they are and for what they bring.......then that is the definition of a successful day.

(Richardson, 2008, p. 155-156)

If I was left to say just one thing, not just with respect to Special Education, but with reference to education in general, it would be this. Good teaching can level the playing field. It is one of the very few things in a young person's life that can; I have seen it with my own eyes. You cannot necessarily intervene to immediately enhance a student's general socioeconomic status, and you may not be able to undo the ravages of neglect and abuse, but you can definitely ensure that the time spent with you, within your four walls, is as good as it can possibly be. Just by being you, and by doing the very best within the profession upon which you will now embark has the power to affect lives in a very real and profound way.

(Richardson, 2008, p. 167)

For resilient males and females, their ability to recruit substitute parents was a major feature of how they differed from those found not to be resilient. These substitute parents unconditionally accepted them as they were...Resilient adults remember one or two teachers who made a difference for them.

(Krovetz, 2008, p.9)

Chapter 2: Rising from the Ashes (Book Review)

Mark Connell

Within contemporary psychological discourse the relationship between ones childhood environment and successive social adaptation/non-adaptation has been well documented. In congruence with what common sense would predict, studies have illustrated that factors including poverty, neonatal stress, abuse, parental alcoholism, neglect, family discord and severe environmental conditions have the tendency to doom children to delinquency, psychiatric disorders and other negative life outcomes (Howard, 2000, p. 2). Nonetheless, there are a number of individuals from "high-risk" situations that demonstrate a remarkable capacity in overcoming incredible adversity. In the novel Angela's Ashes, Frank McCourt provides a first-hand account of his own process of "resilience", as he narrates his struggle to overcome the tremendous obstacles of his poverty-ridden childhood.

In the first pages of the novel McCourt quickly draws the reader into the desperate reality of his youth. He states: "When I look back on my childhood I wonder how I survived it at all... nothing can compare to an Irish childhood: the poverty; the shiftless loquacious alcoholic father; the pious defeated mother moaning by the fire; pompous priests; bullying schoolmasters; the English and all the terrible things they did to us for eight hundred long years (p. 11)." Ironically however, the reader is also aware throughout the entire novel that McCourt does overcome the threatening conditions of his childhood, as he becomes a world-renowned Pulitzer Prize winning author. Beyond being not only a wonderfully crafted novel that articulates a number of tragic aspects of the human experience, the narrative also offers considerable insight into the theory of resilience. Much of the literature on resilience identifies a number of internal and external protective factors that can exist within an individual's social context, thus allowing them to cope and transcend their sometimes very challenging environments (Howard, 2000, p. 2). Furthermore, more recent studies also suggest that resilience is not simply a static trait that children "have", but rather is a process that develops and evolves over time within the total context of both intrinsic (personal) and extrinsic (environmental) influences (Stein, 2000, p. 3; Glantz & Johnson, 1999).

This paper will initially explore the external and internal factors that seem to contribute to McCourt's resilience. It will then, within the context of Angela's Ashes, discuss the idea that resilience is inherently bound to an individual's perception of their own power/ability to influence the social setting around them (Ungar & Teram, 2000, p. 1). Ultimately, the text provides a unique insight into various theories of resilience and illustrates that it is a process bound to both environmental influences and an individual's own sense of self.

Before examining the internal and external factors supporting the theory of "resilience" in Angela's Ashes, it is important to briefly examine the relationship between resilience and the critical developmental periods during the first three years of a child's life (Stein, 2000, p. 2). Some theorists argue that the "first few years of life are crucial for establishing relational paradigms predictive of later health" (Stein, 2000, p. 2). While the narrative begins some 1 to 2 years following Frank's critical developmental period, there is some evidence within the text that allows the reader to hypothesize about the author's earliest childhood. First, as the oldest child within the family, the young Frank would not have been initially exposed to some of the later burdens of the family, as there would have been less of a strain imposed on them in providing food and other necessary familial resources. Furthermore, although there is a clear portrait drawn of McCourt's father as a tragically devout alcoholic, he is also portrayed paradoxically as being somewhat altruistic. Repeatedly throughout the novel, Malachy McCourt is reported as "drinking the tea and eating nothing" (p. 24). When not clouded by "the disease of the drink", the head of the family seems to be a man who would sacrifice anything for the 'well-being' of his children. Thus, the reader may be able to assume that as an infant Frank (unlike his sister Mary) received both the nourishment and amenities necessary for life.

Secondly, there is evidence that Frank's emotional and intellectual needs were also nurtured throughout his early years. Amidst a fairly desperate setting, the narrator describes many nights in the McCourt abode where "father would tell us stories, sing songs, and show us letters and words in the daily news" (p. 24). Young Frankie's attachment to the myth of Cuchulain, as advanced through his father's colourful descriptions, further illustrates this point (p. 25). With respect to this, Developmental Psychologist's unfailingly report that being read to as an infant/toddler is highly important for cognitive development and thus later mental health (Stein, p. 2). These nightly activities may be linked to one of Frank's central internal factors contributing to his ultimate resilience – (allowing his latent intelligence to be consistently nurtured and expanded and, of course, to be later manifested in his tremendous capacity to both read and write).

Throughout the novel it is evident that there are a number of internal factors related to Frank's personality that seems to contribute to his ability to overcome the adversity of his upbringing. As already noted, the most obvious example of this is his recognized intelligence and gift for the written word. This becomes evident very early in the text, as it is his ability to read for example, that allows him to get a job reading to an old war veteran for money (p.176). Mr. Timony himself praises the young McCourt for being " such a good reader" (p. 176). Upon hearing about Franks new job his mother revels in delight as "an extra shilling a week will make a big difference to the family" (p. 177). The reader can observe how this kind of praise could considerably contribute to McCourt's sense of self-worth. This idea is also mirrored when on a number of occasions Frank steals for the sake of his family. Although these acts did very little to undo the institutionalized violence wrought on the McCourts, the tone of these accounts accurately reflect a pride and self-satisfaction in Frank's juvenile ingenuity. Here there is a reciprocal relationship between the young Frank's sense of control over his environment and his sense of personal worth.

Similarly, the interaction with Mr. Timony in the novel also reveals how resilience is a process that evolves over time through ones interaction with outside forces. It is through the relationship with this man that Frank is initially exposed to more sophisticated literature including some of the classics written by Jonathan Swift (p.176). More importantly though, this safe relationship seems to provide a venue by which a profound desire to read is further developed within the young boy. Within a similar perspective, it is while recovering from his bout of Typhoid in the hospital, that the young Frank becomes more and more drawn to books and what they have to offer. Again, it effectively illustrates how Frank's innate internal processes are profoundly shaped by external forces; namely through his relationship with another patient. As Frank reflects, "I can't wait for the doctors and nurses to leave so that I can learn a new verse from Patricia" (p. 197). This evolving passion for literature is made further evident when Frank reflects "[reading] Shakespeare is like having jewels in my mouth when I say the words" (p. 196).

Knowing the eventual outcome of Frank McCourt's life, it is undeniable that it is his raw intelligence and feelings of self-worth, expressed through his tremendous ability to read and write, that overwhelmingly enabled him to overcome the desperate reality of his earliest childhood and adolescence. Without question, it is when these internal traits come under the direct influence of significant adults in his life, which proves most beneficial to the young (developing) McCourt. For example, this particular dynamic is seen at play when Mrs. Brigid Finucane hires the adolescent Frank to write threatening letters to her creditors. Upon reading his first attempt she decrees, "that's a powerful letter - better than anything you would read in the Limerick Leader" (p. 331). Later in the narrative, it is again Frank's intelligence that allows him to be hired for a position advertised, "Smart Boy Wanted". There are a number of important observations that need to be noted from this line of discussion. As will be discussed later, on an emotional level, it seems as though it is Frank's ability to earn a wage (and acquire food through stealing or whatever means necessary - see 161) that allows him to gain a sense of empowerment and control over his circumstances. Conversely, on a practical level, it is by earning a wage that McCourt is able to ultimately pay for his passage to America - a passage that metaphorically represents a break from the cycle of "Irish misery".

In addition to a number of internal factors, some of which have been documented above, there are also a number of external circumstances evident within the novel that seem to contribute to McCourt's resilience. On a purely surface level, the fact that McCourt was born in the United States and thus had an American passport, would certainly be an external factor contributing to his early escape from Limerick. This fact alone would make immigration a more feasible option. Within the psychological literature, analysts also note the importance of the support and love of significant people as key external factors promoting resiliency. As already noted, the short friendship between Mr. Timony fits this description. Later in the text, Frank' s "Uncle Pa" also seems to take on a similar role. As will be discussed later, it is Uncle Pa who challenges Frank not to accept the easy route of complacent passivity. While space constraints limit a fuller discussion of these secondary characters it is imperative to explore Frank's mother Angela.

Perhaps one of the most powerful images in the entire novel occurs when Frank discovers his mother begging for change outside of the church. While embarrassing for the young McCourt, it epitomizes the sacrifice Angela repeatedly makes for the sake of her children. In essence, the title of the novel metaphorically alludes to this point. It is Angela's deeds of selflessness and sacrifice that acts as an allegorical fire, providing warmth and comfort to Frank and his siblings. Again, later in the text Angela sacrifices her own body (by sleeping with Laman Griffen- p. 340) in order to ensure lodging and food for her children. Through the title of the novel however, McCourt acknowledges and sanctifies the fact that the fire of his mother's sacrifice eventually consumes her.

To conclude, a recent study, which interviewed 41 high-risk youth, makes a very effective case in explaining the link between the process of empowerment and resilience (Ungar & Teram, 2000). Essentially, the article asserts that self-empowerment and a positive self-concept are central factors - contributing to resiliency. Within Angela's Ashes, this conclusion is strongly supported. This is particularly evident at the point in the novel when Frank makes his critical decision not to take the post office exam. Urging Frank not to take the test his Uncle Pa states, "if you pass the test you'll stay nice and secure the rest of your life – but you'll be dead in your head before your thirty" (p. 334). Again, Pa urges Frank to "make up his own bloody mind and to hell with the safe shots and begrudgers" (p. 334). Reflecting on his decision not to take the test Frank discloses that, "I don't want to pass that test for if I do I'll be in Limerick forever with my head dead and my ballocks al dried up" (p. 335). During this climatic decision, McCourt both accepts and demonstrates that he has power over his particular set of unfortunate circumstances.

In the final analysis, the novel Angela's Ashes provides a first-hand account of "resilience". It documents a number of internal and external factors that could explain McCourt's ability to overcome the adversity of his childhood. More importantly however, a critical study of the novel reveals that Frank McCourt's own resiliency is not simply a stagnant trait but rather a process that evolves in congruence with his social environment and his ever-changing self-concept. As he so astutely observes, "you might be poor, your shoes might be broken, but your mind is a palace" (p. 208). However, as the research within the risk/resiliency fields consistently reinforces, the developing mind has a far greater chance at becoming the potential, when somewhere along the way it comes under the direct influence of adults who care!

References

Glantz, M. D. & Johnson, J. L. *Resilience and development: Positive life adaptations.* New York: Springer Publishing, 1999.

Howard, S. & Johnston, B. What makes the difference? Children and teachers talk about resilient outcomes for children at risk, in *Education Studies* (Carfax Publishing), September 2000. Vol.26, Issue 3, p.321.

McCourt, F. *Angela's Ashes.* New York: Touchstone, 1996.

Stein, H. Lives through time: An ideographic approach to the study of resilience, in *Bulletin of the Menninger Clinic*, Spring 2000, Vol. 64, Issue 2, p.281.

Ungar, M. & Teram, E. Drifting toward mental health, in *Youth and Society*, December 2000, Vol. 32, Issue 2, p.228.

Chapter 3: I Had a Teacher Once

Many people believe that being the only girl with three brothers would mean I got special treatment. I did, but not in the way most people would think. I was three weeks late being born and weighed only 5lbs 5oz. I was unable to breathe on my own, had liver and kidney problems, as well as severe birth defects to both legs. The doctors said my prognosis was uncertain. They told my parents I would most likely never be able to walk or talk and would never develop mentally beyond that of a three or four year old. Apparently this was all my parents, especially my mother, needed to hear. My mother left the hospital the next day without even naming me and did not come back. I spent the first six months of my life in the hospital and was "almost left completely abandoned", (so a report says), until a social worker contacted my grandparents. My grandparents, although very elderly, eventually decided to take me home. They were the ones who finally named me. They called me Caitlyn. I required several surgeries over the next couple of years, and during that time, I only saw my parents and two older brothers on the few occasions when the court ordered my parents to visit me. My younger brother was born three years after me, and though he too had some health problems after birth, my mother never left his side. For five years, I continued to live happily with my grandparents, only seeing my real family on the two, yearly court ordered visits.

Sadly, two weeks shy of my fifth birthday, my grandfather suddenly died of a heart attack. Due to my continued poor health, it became virtually impossible for my grandmother to care for me all by herself. It took my grandmother over five months, and many visits to court, to finally force my parents to take me back home.

Almost from the first day I got to my parents' home, the beatings started. My grandparents had spoken another language in their house, so, to say the least, my English was very limited. As a result, I got whipped with a belt across my back every time I didn't understand an order given to me, especially by my mother. As well, my brothers were told they had permission to hit me with a wooden rod on the legs and arms if I did not listen to them, and do as they ordered me to do.

Every morning, I was woken up at 4:00am by my father, banging on the laundry room door, as he left for work. This was my signal to get up and begin my duties, making breakfast for everybody, laying out the proper clothes for each of my brothers, and organizing my mother's files so she could quickly head to work. I then had to clean up the breakfast mess and, if I had time after cleaning the bathroom, I would grab a handful of cereal before walking to school. As soon as school finished, I had to run home as fast as I could to make sure the boys had a snack ready when they came home. After cleaning and sweeping the entire house every day, I was then permitted to start on my homework in the cement, windowless laundry room, until beckoned to assist with dinner preparation. I remember quite distinctly, that this time of day was the worst for beatings, as the orders came very fast and my English was still not very good. After being at home with my parents for seven months, I was finally permitted to sit at the table while the family ate dinner, probably because it was easier for me to serve everyone's food and promptly clear the plates once the boys had finished. Only after I had fed the dog and cleared the entire table, was I allowed to eat the scraps off the plates. I then methodically washed, dried and put all the dishes away.

My father worked late every night and my mother would leave after dinner to go drinking with friends several nights of the week. My brothers were left in the care of an older teenage boy who lived across the street. During these episodes, I obediently did as I was told, remaining in the laundry room, doing laundry and trying to complete my homework before I had to draw baths for the boys and get their night clothes ready. After the boys were in bed, the sitter would always come down into the basement to find me. At first he would stroke my hair, usually as I used a flashlight to read my books. Very quickly, the touching became sexual. He would tell me to take off my clothes and put them into the washing machine. He would tell me how pretty the body of a little girl was and then he would begin to touch me all over. A couple of months after this started, he told me to put his clothes in the washing machine along with mine. He forced me to do very bad things; and he did very bad things to me. The first morning after this happened, I told my mother. She screamed at me calling me "a little whore".

She then beat me so bad, I couldn't go to school for several days. She said if I ever told another living soul, she would see to it I never left the basement. Life went on like this for about a year and a half. It was absolute hell!!

A turning point came when my grade one teacher basically forced the school to give me an intelligence test. This teacher thought I was a really smart little girl, and this made me feel really good. At the time, I didn't understand what being "gifted" meant, but I thought it was the best thing in the world, because my teacher worked with me for hours after school, to not only get me caught up, but to move me beyond all of the other kids. To this day, I still do not understand how the teacher got permission from my mother, but I was completely overjoyed, (mainly because I didn't have to endure the beatings from my brothers after school), so I dared not question why. I was very careful about what I said and how I acted during these after school sessions. For one thing, my mother used to constantly beat me if I didn't act happy, especially when I was around other people. Everyday, when my mother picked me up from school, I would wave happily and climb into the car smiling, pretending to tell her about my day – until we turned the corner, a safe distance from the school. Almost immediately, my mother would start questioning me about what I had said to the teacher, and almost daily she would slap me until I had said I had made a mistake and said something that I shouldn't have. When we got home, without fail, she would take me down into the laundry room and beat me for causing so much trouble for the family. Sometimes, I would lie and say I had cried or told the teacher I hadn't eaten in a couple of days, just so my mother would have a reason to beat me. I learned that this is what she really wanted, to beat me; it seemed to make her happy. To be completely honest, at this particular time, the beatings were almost a blessing because the boy across the street did not like touching me nearly as much if I was bruised all over.

Although I was very good at covering my bruises and hiding my feelings, (particularly my sadness), I think my teacher knew something was not right, from the beginning. For one thing, she started picking me up at my home in the mornings. Although I really liked this, and I knew she was trying to help, it also meant I had to get up even earlier, at 3:00 am, to ensure all of my chores were done before I left the house. After a couple of days of falling asleep in class, my teacher asked me what was going on, because I always seemed so tired. At this point, I told her my brother was constantly having nightmares, and these episodes were keeping me from sleeping through the night. She believed me and started letting me stay inside the classroom at recess, just so I could nap. School was like heaven for me. People liked me there. I remember constantly having to fight not to wince in pain when my teacher hugged me, because she would press on all my bruises. But believe me, I sure wasn't going to turn down all the hugs!

The weekends; oh how I feared the weekends! Being locked in the laundry room was actually a relief compared to the constant beatings, or the boy across the street. On one occasion, I almost gave myself away when I went into school one Monday morning with a broken arm. Of course, my teacher was very concerned, but I told her it was just an accident from falling off my bike. When another girl in my class blurted out I didn't even have a bike, I quickly said I'd been riding a friend's bike when it happened, and that seemed to satisfy my teacher...at least for a short time.

Through most of my grade one year, I had managed to keep many secrets. Then, two days before school was over, my whole world fell apart, (or at least that's what I thought at the time). For some reason, my mother had sent the boy from across the street to pick me up from school. I do not know why, but as soon as I saw him, I just started screaming uncontrollably, claiming I wasn't going anywhere with him. My teacher's response to this, because she so desperately wanted to help, was to immediately pick up the phone and begin to dial my mother. At this particular point, I became completely hysterical shouting I would never return to my home and no one could make me. Through the sobbing, I pleaded with my teacher to please let me stay and live at the school. I promised to do all the dishes, clean every classroom, clean all the floors...absolutely anything as long as she did not make me go home. Quite naturally, my outburst had forced a gathering of the school's many other teachers, along with the principal. I felt absolute relief when my teacher said I could go back to the classroom and take a book from her personal library and start to read.

The next thing I knew, there was a lady in the room, who said her name was Connie and who started asking me a lot of questions about my mother and my family. I cried and said I was sorry and that I had lied, and everything would be all right if they just let me go home. Instead, Connie said I was going to sleep over at another house, but first we were going to go see her friend who was a doctor. The next several days were a blur of tests, needles, and people asking me many questions about my family. At first, I would not say very much, because I knew I would get the beating of my life when my mother found out. Connie and my teacher came to visit me in the hospital every day to talk to me. I still didn't say very much, but I know the nurses said a lot, (especially about my bruises and broken bones), usually when they thought I was sleeping. The whole time I was in the hospital I was petrified, anticipating the beating I knew was coming when my mother found out other people knew what a bad girl I had been.

After a couple of weeks in the hospital, Connie said it was time to go home. I remember this moment as if it were yesterday. When she said it was time to go home, I just lay on the bed paralyzed with fear. Connie and some nurses eventually dressed me, put me in a wheelchair and took me out to a waiting car. I didn't look up the whole time, even when the car eventually stopped in front of a house. As soon as the car door opened on my side, I started crying saying "I'm sorry, I'm sorry, I'm sorry" over and over...However, my crying quickly stopped when I heard my teacher's voice saying, "You have nothing to be sorry for except for not giving me a hug!" I looked at Connie and said, "I thought you said I had to go home?" My teacher said she and Connie had talked to a lot of people who thought I was a very special little girl who needed a new home. I tried to tell them my mother would not let me stay anywhere and she would eventually come and get me. Connie held up a piece of paper that had my name on it and a lot of other writing. Connie said a very important person, more important than my mother, had said I could stay with my teacher and my mother was not allowed to hurt me anymore. I didn't really understand what was going on, but I knew that if my teacher promised I never had to go home, then I knew it had to be true.

Connie still came to visit me at my new house, but I still didn't say much about what had really gone on at my old house. She and Carla (my teacher) talked a lot about how I liked to still get up early, make breakfast, clean the house, and make the lunches. Although Carla said I didn't have to do these things anymore, I really liked doing it. Besides, I remember thinking I didn't want Carla to get mad at me and perhaps make me leave. It took me a long time to realize Carla was never going to hit me or make me leave for making any type of a mistake. Carla told Connie how I loved to write stories, and Connie asked to read some. All my stories at this time were about a very bad little girl named Angela who lived in the dungeon of a castle, who had a very wicked step mother – like Cinderella. Bad things happened to Angela because she was a bad girl who nobody liked. Connie started collecting all of my stories.

It was close to Christmas when Connie had me read all my stories to Roger. I liked telling my stories to Roger. He never asked me any questions, but listened to my stories, constantly telling me how good they were. Whenever Connie and I went to visit Roger, I felt very important, because my name was written in a book of very important people Roger liked to talk to. I later came to realize Roger was a judge, and my name was written in his appointment book. At one meeting, Roger asked me if I liked living with Carla. I said I sure did, and went on to tell him that Carla had enrolled me in a new school where there were other smart kids just like me. I told Roger all about my new school and how I liked it, because nobody really knew me there and everyone there thought Carla was my real mother.

Just before I started the third grade, Roger said if I wanted, I could live with Carla forever, and she could be my new real mother. I sobbed, but this time it was for a happy reason.

Almost two years to the day, from the fit thrown in my grade one class, because the neighbourhood boy had shown up to take me home, Carla, my teacher, "officially" adopted me and became Carla, my mother.

I know my parents and the boy across the street got into a lot of trouble, but I've never had the desire to find out what really happened to them. My brothers all went to live with different relatives, but we've rarely communicated since. On the two occasions when I've talked to them over the years, all they want to do is blame me for ruining their lives. But I refuse to go there. I refuse to accept any blame, because all I remember is the cold, scared, little girl who was always locked in the laundry room, which was also her bedroom.

Oh yes, I had a teacher once, who became my mother! Thank God!!

Chapter 4: A Shifting Parental Paradigm

My story starts with my father who had a profound negative influence on my life. My father grew up in a troubled home that was plagued by physical abuse and angry outbursts. Not that he ever talked to me about any of this, I had to hear it from my mother. My father lived with constant beatings from my grandfather and my uncles. Disagreements were settled with fists. My grandfather was mean and nasty to my father. On one occasion, my parents drove the 300 miles to visit my grandpa. On getting to the farm, my dad went inside and stayed there for several hours, while our family waited in the car. He came out eventually to tell us that my grandfather would not have us in the house. We returned to our own home without ever seeing him.

One example of my grandfather's response to life's travails is the story of the drowning of my father's younger sister. I was told that when grandpa found out that his daughter had drowned while the boys were swimming with her, the boys were taken to the barn and "horsed whipped". Grandpa used the harness from the horses to administer a severe beating. Apparently his daughter, my aunt, was made pregnant by one of her brothers, and the drowning was used to cover up the whole affair.

My parents were married just as the war was drawing to a close. Over the years, our family expanded to seven children. There were five boys and two girls. I am the oldest. One of my brothers died from suicide later in life, and another has suffered from a serious mental health condition since his teenage years. Another brother was born profoundly cognitively disabled, with my mother believing this was caused by my dad, who kicked her in the stomach during this particular pregnancy. She truly believes this event caused my brother's mental retardation.

We grew up in a time when society did not interfere with family matters like spousal and child abuse. It is too bad, but nothing was done to stop dad from abusing us. Dad had an 18 inch long hockey stick, which he called the "rod of iron". He used it to keep us children "in line". I never saw it used on my mother, but he often punched her about the face, knocking out her teeth. A memorable incident occurred one winter's day during my childhood. We had all just returned from town, and my dad was in a really ugly mood. He started hitting my mother! Blood was flowing from her mouth, and down her chin. My heart cried out for her, but I was powerless to help. He was screaming and yelling she was no good.

He often told her he wished she was dead. Mother was the victim of his emotional abuse and beatings all the years of her married life.

Believe it or not, dad was a very religious man, ensuring we went to church twice on Sunday. He also went to a mid-week prayer and Bible study class. At one time, he even produced a half hour radio show, which was broadcast every Sunday. He paid for all of this out of his own pocket. He would preach a sermon from the Bible on the radio. The hypocrisy here was astonishing. He would preach from the Bible, while several times a year, my mother could not even attend church because of a black eye or a fat lip. As well, dad's religious convictions would not allow the rest of the family to watch television, listen to the radio, visit with neighbourhood children, or read the comics in the paper. My mother never wore a pair of slacks all her life, and had to wear a hat to church. There were food laws too, which in- cluded no eating of pork or blood products because of Old Testament prohibitions. We essentially lived in poverty, because dad did not believe in spending money on his family. He would give money to help other families, but there was none for his own.

We depended on "hand-me-down" clothing from others. I can recall a pair of girl's rubber galoshes which had fur trim around the top of the boot. I was teased for weeks by classmates about wearing girls' boots. I was so embarrassed! My mother suggested removing the fur trim. Because both of my parents came from farm families, we supplemented our food needs by having one or two cows living in our garage, in town. Again, I was ridiculed about this during most of my childhood. At the time, I was completely embarrassed by all of this, but actually, in retrospect, it was good for all of us children, because there was always lots of milk, and we learned about the care of animals and how to work. I remember one particularly sad event from this time, when a calf succumbed to the extreme cold in the corner of our unheated garage. Dad got it breathing again but eventually it died on the floor of our kitchen, after about two days. I believed that my dad actually caused the death, because he provided absolutely no heat for the garage.

Dad gave me a memorable beating one day at supper time. He was angry because one of my brothers was late getting home. He was pacing the floor behind me and berating my mother. Suddenly he grabbed me around the neck and lifted me from the chair. Eventually, I lost consciousness from his stranglehold on my neck. I was lucky to have lived. The next day, I woke up to find that my rear end had ballooned. He had beaten me with the hockey stick as well. I never really knew why dad did this to me. My mother kept me home from school for the next few days. I think I was in Grade 3 or 4. The next day, I remember sitting outside in the sunshine on cushions by the garden. The amazing thing is I remember admiring the lilacs and new flowers.

No question, I was a dreamer type of child, always admiring flowers and birds. This interest was fostered by my mother, and she often talked to me about the flowers in our yard and out in the cow pasture. I remember she once got a supplement to a major newspaper, which was devoted exclusively to flowers and she gave it to me. One time, for her birthday, I used some of my paper route money to buy her a plate that had a porcelain bird attached to it. When I got it home and gave it to her, she was very pleased. However, I was disappointed by my father who said that I would have to take it back, as it served no practical good. He told me to buy a pair of nylon stockings, which I did. My spirit was crushed more by this single event than any of the previous beatings he had inflicted on me.

At some point in my childhood, as I got older, I started to have some insight into my father's behaviour. I initially saw him as a strong individual, who knew how to handle women and children. At the time, I thought that when I grow up, I want to be just like him, because he really knows how to make women tow the line, and I was going to do the same. Luckily, this foolish idea lasted only a few weeks, but it startled me by its strength. Eventually, some years later, I made a vow to myself never to lay a finger on my future wife, and this is a promise I have kept.

A lot of bad things happened to me while growing up. I could go on, but instead want to comment on what I think made a difference for me in making a success of my life. I believe one factor is my faith. At one time, I was prepared to absolutely reject everything my father stood for and believed in. But I had a Sunday school teacher who loved me. She always smiled at me, and would hug me. She would ask how I was doing, and tell me that I was great. She got me to commit my life to Jesus. Eventually, I began to understand my dad was hypocritical. He did not practice what he preached. I decided I would reject his brand of faith, and hold on to the truth as I saw it. All of my years since, I have never regretted this choice. I have a strong sense God has protected and watched over me. I attribute all of the good things in my life to God and my faith.

When I was in high school, my dad had a number of conversations with me. The intention of these talks was to let me know that as long as I was putting my feet under his table, I was to do as he directed. I had a constant anxiety he would lock me out of the house, because he threatened to do this on a number of occasions. Generally, I was a compliant child although I was starting to develop my own morality, which was at odds with his. I understood many other families got along just fine without the ugliness he brought to our family, and I longed for a time when I could get away. So, I decided to get along with dad as best I could, and keep on going to school. Without an education, I thought I would starve.

It would be putting it too strongly to say that education was seen by me as the key to escaping from the circumstances of my home. I wanted to exercise independence from my father by distancing myself emotionally and physically from him. Going to university was the avenue to make this happen. Most of my classmates were going to university, and it seemed the right thing for me to do. When I was in Grade 13, dad had talked to my mother about me going to a particular university in the southern states. I overheard some of these conversations, and did look at some of the literature he made me order. However, I did not want to go there, and waited until he left on an evangelistic trip to make application to a university in Southern Ontario. To my astonishment, this university not only accepted me, but provided me with a three year scholarship. I eventually got a BSc degree. I worked in the summers to support myself, but dad did give me $20 to help me in my first year of study.

I must also mention a significant relationship that was established with a man from our church at this time. He would invite me over for meals after church, and spend a lot of time talking with me on just about any topic under the sun. This mentor, was a practical man who taught me much about life, and developed an independent way of thinking in me. He could fix just about anything and was good with his hands. He was a self-taught musician who played two instruments most capably. He also had a violin he aspired to play, but could drive the cat out of the house if he did play. Later, I bought an instrument and learned how to play. Through his wife, I learned to drive a car, and eventually got my driver's license.

So, the big question is how did I ultimately turn out? I like to think I did okay! I married my sweetheart from university, and I truly believe she was the best thing to ever happen to me. We have been married for several decades now, and we have raised two beautiful daughters.

After completing my undergraduate degree, I desperately wanted to teach and sent applications to about 36 school boards in Ontario. However, while waiting for a response, a large multi-national company sent me a letter offering immediate employment. I accepted, because I was getting married that summer. Shortly after accepting this offer, I got a letter from a school board offering employment. My job with the multi-national company lasted a year and a half, and then I was laid off, because of a downturn with respect to their type of business.

After this, I ended up working for a large law enforcement agency. I worked for them for 30 years, and retired after being promoted on numerous occasions throughout my career. Although I started near the bottom, I ended up teaching others new to the profession. In a way, it had come full circle! It has always been my belief I did not have the typical law enforcement personality, but I survived it. It allowed me to raise a family.

Throughout the years, I have been active in my church. I have lead home groups, taught Sunday school, been treasurer, and elder. As I said earlier, my faith has sustained me through many things. My wife and I have had two pregnancies where the children were born prematurely and did not survive for more than a few days. Then in the early 1990's, my wife was diagnosed with a very serious illness. But, as I said earlier, in many other ways we have been truly blessed, like having two wonderful daughters.

Well into the 1990's, I was diagnosed with depression and lost time from work over it. Eventually, I was referred to a doctor and put on medication. Thinking back, I believe my father was a manic depressive, although he was never officially diagnosed. Nevertheless, he never would have admitted to having any mental health problem anyway!

After I retired, I returned to school and finally got my Bachelor of Education. This has been a very satisfying and rewarding experience for me. A last measure of success has been the opportunity to neutralize some of the harm caused by my father. I will tell a story about my mother, and one about my mentally challenged brother. In the late seventies, my mother was living in another country with my father. He was continuing to abuse her and make her life miserable. I found out she was thinking of killing herself to escape his influence, so I offered to bring her back home to Canada to live with family that truly loved her. She accepted, and arrived shortly after the birth of our second daughter. My father was never able to beat my mother again. I was pleased to provide sanctuary to my mother. During their childhood, our girls had the advantage of having their grandma living with them. She truly loved them, and made all our lives richer.

My brother lived most of his adult life in an institution in middle Ontario, in circumstances that could only be described as terrible. He lived on a ward with about fifty other adult males. It was a scary place, with evidence of much violence and abuse. Not long ago, I applied to have him come live in the same town as us; again closer to family who genuinely cared for him. He now lives close by and I'm officially his legal guardian. He lives in his own apartment, and is cared for by a local community organization. We visit regularly, and enjoy each others' company very much.

For many years, I saw myself as a damaged victim; not just as a person who had scars, but also one who was brave, resourceful, and determined. But, I must confess, over the years, a lot of my energy, (too much), was spent on coming to terms with the damage caused by my father. Happily though, I now understand that his legacy is not my legacy. It is most unfortunate that my dad was never able to shed the harm done to him by his father, my grandfather. With the perspective of the passing years, I now realize that dad was a product of his environment. I don't blame him as much now, but only wish he had the strength to make his life better.

Chapter 5: No Strings Attached

One of my earliest memories as a child was cleaning up the living room in our house when I got up in the morning. My mother had taught me how to gather the half-empty glasses of alcohol, wine and other spirits and take them to the kitchen to be washed. I was also taught to separate the "roaches", (the ends of the joints smoked by my parents) from the other cigarette butts in the ashtrays, before I emptied them into the garbage. If I forgot to scour each ashtray for the nights "roaches", I could expect to be in some serious trouble later that morning. It was after I cleaned up, that I was allowed to watch cartoons on the television. The volume must be low, not to disturb my sleeping parents upstairs. I got my own breakfast and ate alone facing the television. I knew no other existence; I was four years old.

There are parts of my early life that I just cannot remember. Chunks of time I simply can't recall. We moved constantly; sometimes as much as 2-3 times a year. I once counted and figured out that I went to nine public schools. I remember few and forget most. As a result, I lost chunks of time and instruction. I was an abysmal math student, but we always moved before I was identified and placed in a special program. I remember wetting my pants in the 1st and 2nd grades on a semi-regular basis. I found it hard to make friends; I wasn't in one place long enough to cultivate a lasting relationship. I looked after myself in the morning. I got myself up and dressed, made my own breakfast and lunch to take to school. Sometimes clean clothes were a scarcity. I simply wore dirty ones, went without underwear or matching socks. But if my mother caught me with mismatched clothing, I would catch hell when I got home.

School wasn't a real priority with my parents. I had a terrible attendance record in elementary school. I missed days simply because I got up late, because there was laundry and work to do around the house or on the simple whims of my mother. Mainly, when I was kept home from school, I was put to work cleaning, helping to look after my siblings or tending to my mother's needs ("Make me a pot of tea." "Do the dishes." "Put the wash in the dryer." "Go to the store and get me some cigarettes"). If she was sick, she kept me home from school to look after her. I was seven or eight. When I did attend school, teachers would phone home and ask my mother if I was smoking. Both my parents were heavy smokers, and I guess the teachers thought by the smell of tobacco on my skin, I must be smoking too.

I rarely had friends into my home. I was to ask before I brought them into the house and check to see what my parents were doing. Once I brought a friend into the foyer of the house we were living in and my parents were smoking a joint in the living room. Needless to say, I got into big trouble that day. I was often not allowed to go outside because there was work to do around the house. I became a valuable maid and babysitter. I was left alone with my infant brother at the age of six and was the only babysitter my parents ever used. I was a professional diaper changer at age six or seven and full-time nanny from that time forward as well. After school activities were absolutely not allowed, because I had to go home and tend to my siblings and the housework. When they got to be school aged, I would get them up in the morning, dress and feed them and send them off to school. My parents did not get up before 10 or 11, if they could possibly help it. Some weekends they didn't get up until two or three in the afternoon. I guess the nights of partying took their toll!

Beyond the neglect, there was physical and emotional abuse as well. My mother and father separated many times during my childhood. When they would get into arguments, they would use me as an information source. "What did your mother/father say about me?" "I'll tell you all the mean things he/she said about you, if you tell me." My parents would each quiz me on the actions of the other. My father would ask me if my mother had any men over when he wasn't there; she would ask if he had any women over. They would tell me the nasty things each one would say about me. "Your mother thinks you're stupid, lazy and fat". I remember crying over those statements. On a semi-regular basis, my parents would take me aside and tell me they thought I was too heavy or fat. I was placed on several diets starting with a 1200-calorie diet when I was eight years old. My father would tell me he couldn't see my chin and he was ashamed of me. I once told him I was happy with myself. He responded he wasn't happy with me. This continued until I was in my early teen years. In front of the borders in our house, he would announce my weight and talk about how heavy I was for my age. I was the object of familial disgust!

Physically, my mother would beat my siblings and me regularly. She would smack me in the face and around the head when I was young, until I got to be as tall as her. She stopped physically abusing me then. When she would get into a state of hysteria, she would throw things at me like laundry baskets full of clothing, toys, etc. I remember when my brother cut his bangs with his safety scissors. She beat him very badly. I distinctly remember her slapping him around the head and on the back while he was bent over his bed. I remember her screaming hysterically, "A seven dollar hair cut, a seven dollar hair cut". I can remember my brother screaming and weeping both during and long after she had finished beating him. He was four or five years old at the time. She then proceeded to pack up all of his toys in a cardboard box and moved them out of his room. This was something she had done to me as well, boxing up toys and threatening to sell them.

After I received a beating, I usually received some sort of threat as well. For example, when I was eight or nine, I accidentally left the shower curtain out of the tub when I was taking a shower. The result was a leak in the ceiling over the dining room table where we were living. After the standard slapping, my mother berated me and threatened to move out and leave me in the house all alone to fend for myself, because that is what I deserved. An accident involving my brother resulted in another harsh consequence. One afternoon, I accidentally shut the sliding glass door at the back of the house on my brother's finger. He was two or three at the time and his finger swelled up. He was crying and this sent my mother over the edge. She hit me, then grabbed me by the arms and physically dragged me outside to the front of the house. I forget what she said, but she proceeded to lock me out of the house, both at the front and the back. I remember standing there, trying to get in and crying uncontrollably. It was the middle of the afternoon, the sun was shining, and I was crying and calling into the glass of the screen door, "I'm sorry" over and over again. I remember this as if it were yesterday!

As I got older, the physical beatings slowed while the emotional abuse escalated. I remember my father bringing home a woman one night when my mother was working. I was nine years old at the time. He sent me to the store to buy her a cherry pie. I often went to the store to buy cigarettes and rolling papers for my parents, so off I went without questioning the strange request. When I returned with the cherry pie, my three year-old brother was in bed and I was told to go outside to play. I played for a while, but I returned to the house to go to the washroom. As I went upstairs, I heard my father and this woman in my parents' room having sex. I flushed the toilet, and ran out of the house, feeling sick, confused and scared. I tried going in later as my friends went inside, but the door was locked. I kept this secret for several months, until the next parental separation, when I told my mother who, in turn, immediately told my father. He proceeded to scream at me. The one phrase I do remember was, "You're not my daughter any more. You really know how to screw things up." My parents reconciled after my father told my mother I would never be believed in court. He didn't talk to me for awhile after that. This was merely one of several affairs my father had. However, the next time he had an affair, and he figured out I knew about it, he decided to try a new tactic and treat me nicely. The next time he actually took me out with his new girlfriend and bought me a new red leather Kirby Puckett baseball glove. I remember, it was even signed by Kirby Puckett! I was 12 and very into baseball at the time. Needless to say though, after this day out with my father and his new girlfriend, I came home to a severe beating from my mother. She gave me the cold shoulder for a while after that too. I guess I couldn't win.

Alcohol and drug abuse were a big part of my life with my parents. By the time I was four, I knew what a joint was. My parents smoked them right in front of me. My father kept a small propane canister beside his seat on the sofa. It was here with the aid of two knives from the kitchen that he heated up his hash, doing "hot knives". Hash oil was a favourite for a while. The oil was in small canisters, and they used darning needles to spread it onto the small white rolling papers. By the time I was eight, I could tell you how to roll a joint, do "hot knives" and smoke hash oil. I could also pour a beer from a bottle into a glass without a foamy head. These drugs were tame compared to what was to come in the future. I woke up mornings, in my teens, to find hand mirrors in the bathroom streaked with white, spoons strewn on the bathroom counter, tarnished on the bottom from the heat from a Bic lighter, syringes in drawers, magic mushrooms on the coffee table, and the list goes on. A forty-ounce bottle of Crown Royal would last a night, maybe two. A bottle of wine would not be left until morning. It was during these benders that my parents were most violent and aggressive. I would cringe when my mother started drinking, because she was the mean drunk. My father was the happy, but ridiculous drunk. My mother was mean and vindictive. She would say things that would hurt, with a look in her eye that could kill. Major holidays were disasters. They would end up drunk and fighting by the afternoon, leaving us to watch television for the rest of Christmas Day. Occasionally late at night, I would find her in the bathroom, passed out on the floor. Being in my early teens, I was able to pick her up and put her to bed. She would get drunk sometimes early in the afternoon, which meant that I would have to get dinner ready for my brother and sister.

Another major issue in our family life was the presence of mental illness. My father had been diagnosed with bi-polar disorder or manic depression. He tried to take his life several times during the time I lived with him. I remember when I was in the sixth grade, he tried to jump off the roof of our house. Another time he tried pills, but the worst time, at least where I was concerned, was the time I found him in his van after he had tried to poison himself with carbon monoxide. I woke up that morning to my mother looking for him in the house. We found his suicide note on the coffee table and a few minutes later, we found him in his van. The first thing I remember was the smell. He had defecated and urinated on himself. He had also vomited. He was all grey looking and slumped over his steering wheel. My mother and I took him out of the van. She cleaned him up and I drove him to the hospital, where he recovered. He has tried to kill himself once or twice since then. He refuses to take medication for his illness, or seek therapy. After his latest brush with death, he said he found God. I remember him telling us about his abusive relationship with his parents when I was young. I guess some things never change.

School was an outlet for me. By the time grade 10 came along, my brother and sister were old enough to be left alone. This meant I could do extra-curricular activities on a regular basis. I joined the curling team, drama club, and whatever else I could do with my time. I excelled in most areas of school, math being the exception. I did these things to get some attention from my parents. I invited them to everything I did, the plays, etc. They never came. I dreamed of going to university. My parents did not have a high school diploma. It became a dream of mine to go beyond what they had achieved. I started to talk about going to university, but my mother kept telling me I couldn't hack it in the "big city" and I would never be able to ride the subway alone. She tried to encourage me to go to the local college and stay at home. Another source of normalcy, besides school, was my mother's parents. They provided a stable home for us whenever my parents separated. There we received good care, a stable home life, and a nice place to live. I guess if I were to pinpoint the reasons why I turned out the way I did, one of those reasons would have to be the positive influence of my grandparents. They weren't perfect, but they were polar opposites of my parents. However, they turned a blind eye to things going on, and refused to see through my mother's compulsive lies. To this day, my grandmother refuses to see the woman my mother actually is. My parents found another place to live, when I was 18, and it conveniently did not include a room for me. My grandparents took me in and I lived with them until my grandfather's death three years later.

After I left home, I started college. I decided to go to college to get my Early Childhood Education Diploma. I didn't think I could handle university. I excelled in college and began to realize the dysfunction in my family life. I began to realize I had in fact been abused as a young person, and basically had lived a pretty rotten life to that particular point. The college program I chose provided me with the confidence I so desperately needed. I made friends; I started to live a normal life. After graduation, I decided to work after being accepted to university. I wanted to get my BA, then my BEd and become a teacher. But, I was afraid of failure. It was after the death of my grandfather that I decided to attend and get my degree.

As a result of my parents' abuse and our family dysfunction, I was eventually diagnosed with clinical depression. I remember telling the psychiatric intake nurse I never remembered feeling much different than I felt at that particular moment. After seeing a psychiatrist, I was treated with a drug therapy and cognitive behaviour therapy as well. Soon after, I moved away and began university. I began to deal with the abuse and issues that surrounded it. I was on anti-depressants for two years and I sought out therapy for almost another two. I am estranged from my parents now, and have a limited relationship with my siblings. But the memories don't completely go away, and the scars from the abuse don't entirely heal. For example, I have great difficulty trusting people, I have a cynical attitude, and I worry excessively. I am a type "A" personality (heavy on the "A"). But I have learned that I am worthy of happiness, love and friendship. I have learned I am a nice, intelligent, dynamic person. I have also learned that this experience has made me a far richer person for having survived it. It doesn't mean I am not angry, or don't still carry a whole lot of hurt around with me, but I am a more complete person for having experienced it. I know one day I will look into my child's eyes and know their early life will be far different than mine. I can look into my fiancée's eyes right now and know that the future is going to be far brighter than the past!

My parents still abuse everything and everyone who passes through their lives. They abuse drugs, alcohol, food, their children, their family, their animals, and each other. They live in denial. They live with bitterness, resentment and jealousy everyday. It is an intimate part of their lives. They do not know how to love. They like no one. In fact, they don't even like themselves. I am not like my parents. I live with the scars of their abuse, but I choose not to live my life like the one they modeled for me. I do not use drugs or abuse alcohol or food. I treat people with respect and care. I like people. I have learned how to love and be loved in return. I am loved and cared for by many people. I even like myself on occasion. I am not like them; they are not like me!

I grew up in fear! The fear of being smacked around, the fear of making one of them so angry they wouldn't talk to me or acknowledge my presence. The fear of being told I was fat, stupid or I simply didn't fold the laundry the right way. I just lived in fear all the time. But now I am learning not to live in fear. I am learning to live. It is not easy, but life isn't easy is it? I have made a new life for myself, a new beginning. In June, I graduated from university for a second time, with a Baccalaureate in Education (with Honours too!). I was surrounded by people who love and care for me, no strings attached!!

Chapter 6: Don't Call Me Yellowbird

I am going to share a story with you; a story that happened very early in my childhood. I grew up in a military family where we moved from city to city every three or four years. I have two caring parents whom I've always loved very much. I spent a great deal of time always trying to impress them, and was terribly afraid of disappointing them. As a direct result, this is the first time that I've shared this story with absolutely anyone.

With direct reference to our frequent moves, the first move that I remember making with my family was to a small town in Northern Ontario. When we arrived, it was time for me to start my schooling career (grade one). I remember my first day of school very well because I was extremely scared, just like every new kid who starts school. I entered the school dressed to a "T", absolutely ready to impress the teacher and all my classmates! Yet, right from the beginning, I was made "fun of" for the way I dressed. From the first day of my schooling life (at least in this particular town) I was bullied, harassed, physically beaten, and teased without mercy. Without exception, each and every day was a struggle to get out of bed and go to school; each and every day was hurtful; and each and every day was just another one that, all I wished for, was to be dead!

The kids in my class were extremely cruel to me and teased me for no apparent reason; at least that's what I thought. However, as I was to very quickly learn, I apparently dressed funny, did not have the best clothes, did not have the best school supplies, was clumsy, and was very anxious and shy.

As a result, I would get teased from the time I left my house in the morning, until the time I returned home after school. For example, I remember being made fun of because I wore "preppy" clothes and because I did not own a pair of Levi jeans. Most of my clothes were bought on sale and were not the brand everyone else was wearing and this made me an easy target.

As the weeks went on, the teasing got far worse. Everything from how I walked, to how I played sports, to how I wrote my name on the blackboard, seemed to bring nothing but ridicule from my classmates. At first I tried not to let it get to me, but after awhile it started to wear me down. I started listening to what was being said. I started hearing their voices in my head even when I wasn't at school. I never informed my parents of this constant teasing because I wanted them to think that I was doing well at school and making new friends. The teasing continued for the remainder of the grade one year.

In grade two, the teasing got far more intense, and that's when the real bullying began. On the very first day of my grade two year, the kids in my class threw me off my bike because they apparently didn't like the look of it. It was a bike that my parents had won in some type of contest but, the problem was, it had a "banana seat" and looked different from all of the other bikes. To me, it was a great bike and I couldn't understand why I was getting thrown off it, or why they were laughing at me for riding it. I was so proud of that bike! I remember this one time when they threw me off, I scraped my knee, which created a small tear in my pants. I ran home after school and changed my pants so that my mother would not see the small hole in them. I ended up hiding them in my closet. Also, that first day, I remember I wore that particular pair of pants with a Fox yellow sweater, one that my mom thought was very cute, but which the kids started teasing me about almost immediately. I remember they started calling me Foxy and Yellowbird, making fun of the way I looked and dressed. At the end of the day I took that yellow sweater and did the very same thing to it as I had done with the pants; I hid it in my closet. What's interesting about this is that both the pants and sweater were not found until many years later – after we had moved from this particular town.

After a very short while in my grade two year, the teasing eventually turned to physical beatings. For some unknown reason, the kids in my class thought it would be nice to physically hurt me. It would usually start at recess with general poking eventually turning to full fledged punching and kicking. Basically it would work like this. My classmates (at least the boys) would run ahead at recess and wait around the corner until I walked by, and then they would take turns attacking me. However, this type of abuse started to become a problem in class as well. For example, in class I sat in front of a boy named Harold, who would continually punch and pinch me when the teacher wasn't looking. He would do it, laugh, and then turn around to the rest of the boys in the class to make sure that they saw what was happening. This seemed to make Harold very happy. This routine continued for a few months until one day the group added snowballs and "face washes" to the mix; meaning they would routinely wait for me at the entrance to the school property so they could pelt me with snowballs and then throw me down and push my face forcefully into the snow. Throughout the winter, this was the ritual every single morning of my entire grade two year. Needless to say, I hated going to school.

However, the melting of the snow didn't really change things all that much. In fact, I would say it even got worse. The "leader" of the class, Harold, without fail, always waited for me to ride my bike to school so that he could push me off and throw my bike around. I remember on one occasion, he actually broke my bike which meant I had to go home and make up a story to tell my father. I certainly didn't want my parents to get involved, mainly because I was too scared to let them know what was going on, but also because I wanted them to always be proud of me. In the end, throughout this horrible year of my life, I managed to hide all of the scrapes and bruises from them. I remember throughout this year being absolutely terrified to go to school, and missing as many days as I possibly could. I remember feeling very confused and all alone. I had only one friend at this time, and it was a boy from down the street who went to another school. Of course, I kept what was going on at my school a complete secret from my friend, as I dearly wanted to hold on to the one true friend I had. I thought if I told him, he might turn against me too.

In the summertime, between the second and third grades, I distinctly remember one significant event. One morning, one of the kids from my grade two class, a boy called Jacob, approached me to go play soccer with him, and I naively agreed. We played reasonably happily for the next couple of mornings, but then one day he invited me to go play with a much larger group. However, no sooner had I joined the group when things started to quickly unravel, and the real intentions of my new found friend became abundantly clear. As soon as I started playing, everyone else stopped. Within seconds the group immediately ran towards me, grabbed me, and physically pinned me against a nearby building. Then, as if well rehearsed, everyone there took a turn kicking a soccer ball at me, consistently aiming for my very exposed pubic region, because my arms were pinned and I couldn't turn. Every kid there took at least five kicks of the ball.

Once they had finished this torture, Jacob, my supposed new found friend, calmly walked over to me and gave me a shot in the genitals just for good measure. Eventually, all of the kids left the area, leaving me lying on the ground all by myself. I remember crying and crying but, as per usual, no one heard me. I remember thinking to myself, how could I be so stupid; how could I have trusted Jacob? Eventually, as I had done many times before, I picked myself up and I limped back home. I remember not being able to wear shorts for many days after this experience, because I had too many bruises on my legs. But again, I stupidly told no one of this incident, as I wanted things to appear somewhat normal!

But it wasn't over yet. I was just starting to heal, when Jacob approached me again, claiming that he was sorry for the way I had been treated, and wanting to make up for it. He claimed that if I came back to play one more time, he would personally see that everything would be alright; besides that, they desperately needed another soccer player so I'd be really helping them out. Of course, I was extremely hesitant at first, but decided that I should give it another try, mainly because I wanted so badly to be accepted, particularly by my classmates. When I arrived at the sport's field, there was no pretend soccer playing, as Jacob was the first to grab me and walk me directly over to the building. This time when they pinned me they both kicked and threw soccer balls at all parts of my body, including my head and face. Once they were finished, Jacob, along with Harold this time, calmly walked over to me and said, "That will teach you to think you can play with us". They then both took turns kicking me in the stomach, leaving me on the ground in a heap of pain. After a time of recovery, I once again picked myself up and limped back towards home.

I spent the next few days crying and staying indoors. I didn't want to go outside because of fear of embarrassment and because I hurt so much. I lied to my parents and said I was not feeling well and that is why I was not leaving the house. The only thing good about this particular summer was when one of my family members came down to visit for a prolonged period of time, and we were able to go to the beach and get away from everything on the odd occasion. I finally had someone to have fun with. However, when she left, things quickly returned to normal as the kids kept calling for me to go out and play, but time and time again, they would turn on me whether it was throwing me off my bike, or pounding me with soccer balls, or just throwing me to the ground and kicking me. You may ask, and rightly so, why did I continually go back to these kids for more abuse? The only thing that makes any sense is that I must have been starved for acceptance. I really don't know.

The next year, my grade three year, was the hardest year of all. It started on the first day of school and never let up. My first memory of that particular year has me walking to school, but once again meeting up with Harold (not so coincidentally) who, as per usual, seemed really nice at the beginning. However, as we neared the baseball diamond, all of the other boys in the class jumped out from their hiding spaces and began to attack me. This time they not only pinned me against a fence, but they began to whip marbles at me (not soccer balls, but marbles). This left horrible welts on my chest and legs. But because I didn't want to show them that they were really starting to get to me, I went to school that morning and acted as if nothing had happened. Imagine, this was on the very first day of school, and during one of the first hours of my grade three year!

Later that day, at recess, the same group of boys decided that it would be fun to play basketball and once again they had a plan that would try to hurt me. Basically, every time they passed the ball to me, each one would come up and slap my hands as hard as they could. Finally, in pain, I decided to just walk away, but Harold just as quickly ran up behind me, first kicking me on the backside but then forcefully throwing me on the ground. The rest of the boys, one by one, methodically followed the pattern established by Harold, taking turns kicking me on the backside, as I lay prone on the ground. When it was all over, I was not only completely dejected and humiliated, but I had a hard time sitting in class for the rest of the school day because I was so bruised and sore.

But there was more to come. At the end of the school day, I discovered that my bike was gone from the racks and thrown into the middle of the field. By the time I was able get to it, my tormentors were waiting for me once again. When I got onto to my bike and tried to turn away from them, they once again grabbed me and threw me from my bike. They then took my bike and threw it over the fence. Eventually I was able to pick myself up, gather my bike, and start on my way home however, the harassment continued from the moment we left the school grounds, until we arrived at the beginning of the block where I lived. When I finally got into the house, I remember crying and crying, at least until my mom got home, then I stopped crying because I didn't want her to see me. Again, I felt so all alone. Here it was, the beginning of a brand new school year, and it had already started. I remember thinking I didn't know how I was going to survive the year. It was at this point in my life that I distinctly remember going into a shell; a shell that remained with me for a very long time.

Throughout the first half of grade three the daily routine went pretty much like this. My classmates would wait for me to come down the path leading to the school, and then do something to torment me, whether it was name calling, being thrown off my bike, being pelted with snowballs, or physically assaulting me. Recess was the same, whether it was getting a ball of some sort thrown at me (especially in the pubic region) or getting chased and then punched and/or kicked. I was so scared on most days because I had no idea what was coming next. Then, in the middle of my grade three year, things changed very dramatically, and definitely for the worse! It was in this particular year that I had an incident that changed my life at school forever. If I thought I was an outcast before, it was multiplied by one hundred after this specific event.

One day during the morning recess, I was running away from one of the kids and I jumped over a snow bank and I slipped and fell so hard that I had a bowel movement in my pants. I knew it had happened right away, and I went into the washroom and tried my best to clean it up, but I couldn't get rid of the odour completely. When I went back to class, I tried my best to hide and cover it up, but the kids began to notice the smell. When we were walking down to the gym, Harold, who was behind me said, "So you are the one who smells like poo", whereupon I quickly replied, "No it's not, so it must be you". Ultimately, I tried my best to cover it up but after we got back from the gym the teacher came up to me and asked to talk to me outside in the hall. When I followed her out, I immediately heard some of the boys come right up to the door where we were standing, and the teacher must have heard them too, but she did absolutely nothing about it. Anyway, the teacher told me that she could smell me and that she had a pretty good idea what had happened and that it was probably an accident. Well, the words were no sooner out of her mouth when I broke down sobbing, right there outside the classroom. Of course, because some of the students had crept up near the door to listen, the whole class could hear me admit that I had gone to the bathroom in my pants. Well, within seconds of my admission, the whole classroom erupted into laughter. Hearing this, I ran down the hall and into the washroom where I continued crying. The teacher came running in after me and told me she was going to call my mom, and I screamed out "No, you can't", but I was too late, she went and got the principal who immediately called my mom. My memories are vague with respect to what actually happened when my mom arrived. I think I have suppressed all the specific bad memories, so that I never have to think about them again. All I remember is that I got the rest of the day off to go home. However, I knew from that moment on, my life at school would be an absolute living hell.

To say I dreaded the next day would be a profound understatement, because when I woke up the next morning, I remembered that I did not want to go to school at all. I tried to think of something to keep me away from school, but I just went so that I wouldn't upset my parents. When I got to school, every kid in the whole school had found out what had happened, and all of the kids in my class were laughing and pointing at me. They called me names like "shithead, poo-head, stinky, and shit on a stick." During class they were all grabbing their noses and pointing at me. I just wanted to run away and hide; I desperately wanted to get out of there because I knew that at recess it was only going to get a whole lot worse.

When I first got outside, I knew something was up as all of the kids ran out before me, and I noticed it was unusually quiet in the general play area. When I walked around the corner of the school all of the boys were there, lined up, quite obviously waiting for my arrival. When I saw this I immediately started to run, but eventually they were able to run me down, and they caught me. Again, methodically, they took turns kicking me in the backside saying, "keep it up there, we don't want to smell you anymore." I remember being so scared, in fact I was petrified. Once again, I had no idea what they were going to do to me next.

All I kept thinking and saying in my head was "Why me?", "Why are they doing this to me?", "Why me?", "Why me?", "Why me?". It went on like that all day, getting kicked in the butt, all through class and especially at lunch and both recesses. That night when I got home, I cried for a very long time. I remember that I went outside and started to ride my bike. I rode and rode and rode. All I could think was "Why me?", "Why is this being done to me?", "What am I doing here?", "Why won't this all go away?", "Why me?", "Why me?", "Why me?". This was the first time that I actually thought about killing myself. I did not understand the concept of suicide, but as I reflect on it today, that is exactly what I was thinking. "Why can't I just leave this place?", that is all I kept asking myself. I must have rode for a good two hours. I remember that I could barely sit on my bike, because my backside was so sore from all the kicking. Eventually I went home and tried to put on a happy face, which, I must say, I had gotten pretty good at. From that day forward in my grade three year, everyday was an immense struggle to get up and go to school. I absolutely came to despise school. I hated going to that evil place! I hated thinking, "Why am I here?". Clearly, I was in incredible pain, and at such a young age. There is no question, as I think back, these horrible experiences effect me, even to this very day!

To claim everything was doom and gloom at this time wouldn't be completely truthful because I had one really good friend that I have previously mentioned, that I could always count on. I would never tell him what had gone on at school because I didn't want him to think badly of me. If it wasn't for him, I would have been worse off than I was. At least with him, I could escape from all my negative thoughts, at least for a while. When left all alone though, I always thought horrible things!

I also started to play hockey around this time, and that was one other thing that could help me get my mind off all the negative stuff. But even where hockey was concerned, when I played against the other kids in my class, they were always after me, either trying to injure me or call me all kinds of nasty names. It also gave them another area to criticize. They would constantly tell me how bad a player I was, and that I didn't even deserve to be on the same ice as them. I loved to play hockey (what Canadian kid doesn't) but they made it seem like I was doing something really wrong - that I shouldn't even be playing the same sport as them. It took me a very long time to get over these three years of my life...(if I've ever really gotten over them)!

As mentioned before, these horrible years of my life forced me into a shell or a type of cocoon. I retreated completely into myself. It started by me being so shy that I wouldn't talk to anybody if I didn't really know them. No matter who they were, I would not talk to them. I remember one time I had to go up and ask for badges that I had earned in "Cubs", but I refused to go on stage and ask for what I had earned because this would mean talking to a stranger. I remember my dad being really frustrated with me and he tried to force me to go up, but I just refused to go. He finally had to go up for me. I became one of the shyest kids around. I would not talk to a soul. I wanted to keep everything in. I suppressed every emotion, and tried desperately to suppress every memory.

I guess because I was suppressing so much at this time (things I couldn't really understand) I would occasionally lash out in uncontrolled anger towards those closest to me. I would just explode. Without question, the person who took the brunt of this anger was overwhelmingly my younger brother. No question, I would verbally and physically abuse him, even though I tried my best not to. Basically, I guess, I could do to him what those kids did to me. I now look back, and I feel really badly about being so mean to my brother. I also tended to block everyone out during this period. My parents would always try to talk to me, but I refused to open up to them. I was afraid to let anyone in my life get too close to me, because I was afraid they would only add to all the hurt. When my parents did try to talk with me, I would just sit there and say absolutely nothing.

If I could pick one thing in my life that initially served to turn my life completely around, it was when we moved to a new town, which, in itself was important, because I was able to get away from all of my history, my school, and all of my abusers. I also joined a large youth organization. Right away in this organization, I could see that I was accepted as an equal, something that I'd never experienced in my life before. I think it was that everyone was in the same uniform and everyone was obligated to receive formal training in citizenship and teamwork.

When I first found out that I got accepted to Teacher's College, I jumped for joy as I now knew that my life had a real purpose. I knew that I could make a difference in someone else's life. When I first went there, I was not nearly as shy as I knew that my dreams were coming true. I began to make new friends and was able to talk to people. I also met the woman of my dreams. We began to date and I saw myself open up more and more. Even though sometimes she had to force me to talk, I knew that I could absolutely trust her. We became very close and have had many in-depth conversations since. I totally opened up to her, as I knew that I could finally trust someone. Basically, the wall that had been built up all those years ago, started to come down.

So, in the end, belonging to and becoming a leader within a youth organization, forced the shyness out of me, and began a process whereby many of my bad memories and experiences were replaced by some much newer and vastly improved ones; with Teacher's College profoundly accelerating this process. I can now talk openly about my feelings with more and more people. I can give my opinion without feeling like people are going to judge, tease, or hurt me. I am no longer saying "Why me?". As far as teaching is concerned, I want nothing more than to instill good values in my students, providing them with every opportunity to fulfill their dreams. But most of all, I want all of my students to know that in my classroom there will be absolutely no bullies allowed!

Chapter 7: What If

I grew up in a white, middle class family. My parents and family have always been incredibly nurturing and supportive. From the start, I have basically had everything going for me. It was, therefore, a surprise to me that a period in my adolescent life fit the resiliency theory model. I do not presume the single situation I went through in my adolescence was more difficult than the circumstances many children face from their early childhood. I do not think it was. I simply know I was on a very scary path for a period of time, and I became resilient to this path with the help of an outstanding teacher.

My resiliency story begins on a rainy Friday night in March. I was 15 years old and had the typical teenage "I am invincible" mentality. A single moment on that Friday changed that mentality forever. My best friend and I were at my house getting ready to go out with two boys who were our respective boyfriends at the time. The boys arrived around 8 p.m. I had known Emma since I was seven, and knew she was going to be a while getting ready. I kept the boys occupied with food and TV.

Emma was finally ready around 8:30 p.m. We said goodbye to my parents and they asked the obligatory parental 20 questions, ("Where are you going?" "When will you be home?" "Who will be there?" etc.) My parents told us to be careful, as it had started raining. Payton joked about how he was an expert driver, now that he had his G2 license.

Cars bring an independence and freedom to teenagers that are undeniable. Obtaining a driver's license could be considered a North American rite of passage. We all piled into Payton's Mercury Topaz: Payton was in the driver's seat; Max was in the front passenger's seat; Emma was in the backseat behind Max; and, I was behind Payton. We decided to go for a drive north of the city where there was little traffic and winding, country roads.

Without a doubt, immense responsibility comes with the act of driving an automobile. Unfortunately, teenagers seldom fully recognize this responsibility. That night, around 9:45 p.m., Payton lost control of the car on one of the winding country roads. The car spun out on the wet pavement and the passenger's side of the vehicle hit a tree.

It is hard to describe what goes through your mind in that split second before a fatal car accident. You always hear the romanticized idea of one's life flashing before their eyes. To be completely honest, the accident itself is a blur to me, although the sounds of it still haunt me to this day. It is difficult for me to say if Payton was being reckless or if he was simply an inexperienced driver. I simply know we were four teenage kids out having a good time with the freedom and independence of driving around on our own.

After the accident, I was fully conscious along with Payton and Max. Emma had experienced the brunt of the crash. We called her name repeatedly. There was no response. I slid over to her and discovered the right side of her skull cracked open. I looked towards the tree and saw that parts of her skull and brain were stuck on the bark. The horror and chaos in the car at that moment are beyond words. I refused to let go of my friend even when the paramedics arrived. Emma was pronounced dead at the scene.

The days, weeks and months that followed the accident were difficult to say the least. I spiraled into a deep depression. I experienced overwhelming survivor's guilt along with the sometimes agonizing feeling of loss. I had never experienced anything so horrific or traumatic in my life and, as a result, was not really prepared with any coping mechanisms.

Naturally, my parents, family, and friends were extremely worried about me. They tried to distract and cheer me up in any way they could – movies, music, concerts, talking, or any kind of distraction. I refused most offers to do things I would normally have thoroughly enjoyed doing. When nothing seemed to make a difference in my mood, I was sent to a psychiatrist who tried to remedy my depression with a swarm of pills. These pills made me feel like a completely different person. I seemed to experience every single negative side effect associated with the pills such as insomnia, loss of appetite, tremors, and zombie-like state. I refused to continue taking them and, as a result, my parents decided a psychologist might be a better option. The psychologist just wanted to talk about the accident – that's it, that's all. I got extremely annoyed with this woman, as I knew when she was just trying to trick me into talking about the accident. She made no real effort to get to know me as a person. I thought I was some kind of freak experiment to this doctor, which, is basically when I refused to go back to her office. I was tired of people asking me about the accident.

When I finally went back to school, after about three weeks, I went from being a happy, social, involved, straight-A student to being a depressed, anti-social, uninvolved, failing student. My mom drove me to school and picked me up from school every day, hoping I would get back into the normal routine of life. The problem was I either simply did not go to class, or was completely unable to concentrate during the classes I did go to. I absolutely did not want to talk to anyone! I did not want to do anything! I became extremely withdrawn and lived very much inside my own head, which was not a very pretty place to be at this particular time. I stopped caring about many of the things I so deeply cared about before the accident: grades in school; going to parties; interacting with peers; and all the other activities and organizations I had been actively involved in (e.g. school clubs and sports, my job, etc.). Many people do not understand the thoughts and feelings that accompany a clinical depression like the one I experienced. I became a total recluse, trapped in my own mind.

Many of my teachers had no idea how to respond to me after the accident. I suppose their hesitant responses were natural to some degree. I had changed drastically from the happy teenager I was before the accident. People were seemingly friendly and concerned, but it was not always sincere (Note: I understand that this idea may be linked to my skewed perception of people and events at the time).

I had one teacher that was different. I knew she was different the first day I came back to school after the accident. All day, I had experienced teachers who appeared, at best, awkward. Either they did not know what to say, or asked me asinine questions like, "Are you OK?" (Uh, no?) When I went to Mrs. A's English class fifth period, I wanted to blend in and sit down as quickly as possible to avoid dealing with more teacher awkwardness. I was shocked when Mrs. A was waiting for me at my desk and gave me the most genuine hug I have ever experienced in my life. She simply held me and did not let go.

Over the next few months, Mrs. A helped me immeasurably. Since my mom was dropping me off early in the mornings (to make sure I was actually going to school), I would go and hang out in Mrs. A's class. Normally, we just talked. The remarkable thing is that Mrs. A never asked me about the accident, ever! The woman was patient beyond belief. I would ask her about her family and normal everyday things. We would talk about music, movies, history, politics, and whatever we were studying in English at the time. It was nice to talk to someone and never have to worry about him or her asking me about the accident. Eventually, I was comfortable enough with her that I opened up about the accident, on my own.

In hindsight, you always think of the "what ifs." I talked at length with Mrs. A about "what ifs." What if we decided to drive around the city instead of the dark and curving country roads? What if it was not raining? What if we were not talking and laughing so much? What if I had sat in the seat Emma sat in that night? It is natural to have these thoughts, but the truth is they do not really matter. "What ifs" are not realities! You could spend a lifetime dwelling on the "what ifs," but eventually you realize you have to live in the reality and deal with all the challenges life has to offer. Mrs. A helped me realize the accident was completely out of my control, but that I had complete control over my life in the present. She saw and encouraged me to use my inner strength to move on and reach my full potential. No more "what ifs"!

Chapter 8: Blue Clouds Allowed

In June of 1982 I was born to a mother who worked for the transit authority and a father who worked for the city in which we lived. Having only married because my mother was pregnant, theirs was a marriage that was filled with turmoil. With only a Grade II education, my mother felt that her only chance to give me a good life was to marry my father and try to make it work. However, the relationship was not meant to be and lasted only about one year. The end of the relationship was accelerated by my father's controlling and manipulative attitude and the divorce was unnecessarily drawn out, resulting in serious emotional and financial damage to my mother.

Once the divorce was final my parents were initially granted joint custody of me but the relationship between the two of them got even worse. I believe that this stemmed from the fact that my father was angry at my mother for leaving and wanted to hurt her. She very quickly started the process of becoming my sole guardian, which made him absolutely furious. He would call her at work and threaten to take me away from her or claim that he was not bringing me back at the end of the weekend. Although these comments tormented her, it did not equate to the level of suffering that I was experiencing while at his house. He had visitation rights for approximately 2 years (until I was about 4 years old). Although I was extremely young, there are situations that have been so engrained in my memory that I can vividly remember such minute details as the smell of his breath, the colour of the wallpaper, and the temperature of the room.

Going to my father's house for a weekend visit quickly became something to dread. Once I arrived at the house I was sent to my room and was forced to sit in a crib in the dark. From my room I could hear him watching television or talking with friends at his frequent parties. I remember being angry because I was not a baby and did not think it was fair that I had to be in a crib. I was lucky if the weekend only included being neglected in that bedroom. When I heard the friends talking in the other room I felt somewhat safe. It was when the other room was quiet that I became terrified. The television would be shut off and I would hear heavy footsteps coming toward the door. The light from the hallway hurt my eyes and the dark silhouette of my father appeared in the doorway. The room immediately filled with the smell of alcohol and he gruffly lifted me out of the crib. What followed was rough tickling that progressed to inappropriate touching, which made me cry. The couch felt scratchy on the soft skin of my cheek and my hot tears stung as they fell from my eyes.

My mother knew something was wrong and tried to help in every way she could. She recalls me screaming in the front hallway when I was told that my father was on his way to pick me up. Although I never told her what he was doing to me I would tell her that his house made me sad and that I did not want to go with him. In an attempt to uncover the truth I was sent to psychologists and the police became involved. In the end my mother was given sole custody of me and my father was ordered to never have contact with us. My last name was immediately changed to her maiden name because she feared that he would find us and take me away from her. To this day she lives in fear of him finding me.

We moved to Georgetown to live with my mother's new boyfriend, Tom, and for a while life was stable. I started school and was known by my teachers and neighbours as a quiet but happy child. The day that I started school proved to be a pivotal day in my life. I met my teacher, Mrs. Drexler, and decided that I wanted to be just like her. I thought that she was the smartest person I had ever met and was convinced that she knew everything. She welcomed me by name on the first day which made me feel special and she allowed me to mix the red and white paint to make pink because she knew it was my favourite colour. I have never forgotten that special interest she took in my life. She became my role model and a symbol of security for me. In fact, school quickly became my safety net. It was a place where I felt wanted, accepted, and valued. I was excited every morning to get to school and did not want to leave at the end of the day. I was allowed to be myself and be happy at school. This was a stark contrast to what was going on at home.

My mother's new boyfriend, like my father, had a drinking problem. The house was an unhappy one when he was gone but a nightmare when he came home. When he left for the bar in the evening my mother sat beside the phone crying, waiting for his return or a phone call. Then the phone would ring and no matter what day or time it was she would drop everything and go pick him up. The trips in the middle of the night are what I remember most. She would wake me up, wrap me in a big grey blanket, and put me in the backseat of our van. I usually slept on the way but when the passenger door opened I was quickly awakened. They would fight all the way home and the smell of alcohol on his breath took me back to memories that made me cry. Once at home I was allowed to go to bed but sleep would not come easily. On a good night the yelling would continue until he stormed off to bed or passed out. On a bad night we would all end up sitting in a hospital waiting room because my mom had "fallen" down the stairs and broken her collarbone. She would tell me that she was fine and that it had been an accident but her terrified cries told me a different story.

Life went on like this for almost a year and my mom became pregnant with my younger brother. That is when my life drastically changed. I came home from school one Friday afternoon to find the van packed with bags and suitcases. I was told that my mom and I were going on a trip to visit my grandparents. What I did not know was that I would end up living with them for the next year and a half. The hour-long trip to Newmarket flew by because I was so excited about seeing my grandparents. Before they had moved to Newmarket my grandmother had been my babysitter and I had developed a wonderful relationship with her. When the weekend was over my mom packed up her things and went back to Georgetown without me. I was confused, sad, and lonely. I did not understand why my mom had left without me or why I was being told that I would be going to a new school. The morning that I was supposed to start at that new school was awful. I cried all morning and would not let go of my grandmother's hand when we entered the Grade 1 class. I became even more quiet and withdrawn that year, feeling that I was different from all the other kids in my class because I did not live with my parents. I had many friends but I tried my best to hide the fact that I was different. I became really good at blending in and trying to become invisible in the classroom. I never wanted to stand out or be the centre of attention.

Living with my grandparents provided me with a level of structure, security, and stability that I had never before experienced. There was no yelling or fighting, no midnight trips to the bar or the hospital, constant healthy meals, and most importantly I was hugged and validated daily. Once I adjusted to my new surroundings the rest of my Grade 1 year was pleasant. Report card comments indicate that I was extremely shy and withdrawn. However, I only have happy memories of this period in my life.

That summer my mom came to visit me and I got to spend time with my new baby brother, Sammy. I can remember being very angry at her during this visit for two reasons. First, I had wanted a sister and had expressed this desire on numerous occasions. I thought that she had not been listening to me and so that is why she gave me a brother. It was not uncommon for me to feel ignored by her. I realize now that she had too many of her own problems to deal with and so it became increasingly more difficult to cater to the every whim of a six year old. I also felt angry because she slept and cried for most of the visit. In phone conversations prior to her arrival she had promised that we would play together but every time I made an attempt to interact with her she would tell me that it was not a good time and she would do it later. I spent much of those weeks playing alone in my grandparent's backyard, waiting for my mother to pay attention to me.

When the visit ended I was taken back to Georgetown with my mother. Things immediately went back to how they were before, accentuated by Sammy's constant crying. I was enrolled back in the neighbourhood school and began Grade 2. I was terribly unhappy during this time and had major sleep problems. I had a very hard time concentrating in class because I got very little sleep at night. When I did sleep I had terrible nightmares about people being violently murdered, which made me afraid to even close my eyes. It was during this time when I also began to sleepwalk and would wake up in strange places. Even school, which I had previously enjoyed, became an unhappy place. I did not have friends from the previous year like all of the other children and hated going outside for recess because I hated being alone. School seemed to become an extension of home where everyone had their own lives and nobody seemed to have time for me. Even the teacher seemed unaware of my existence. I remember on one occasion drawing a picture in my journal of children playing in the park. I had made the clouds blue and had left the rest of the sky white. Upon seeing my drawing my teacher commented to me that I had done it wrong because the clouds are supposed to be white, while the sky is blue. I felt crushed and remember wondering why she even cared. It really made no difference to her whether I made the clouds blue, purple, or green! I went home that day and cried in my room.

My best friend in Georgetown, Jim, lived next door to us. Jim was Tom's nephew and had a home-life exactly like mine. I remember watching Ghost Busters in Jim's living room and then, hiding under the basement stairs when his father came home from the bar. We would sit down there with a flashlight (we had both become very afraid of the dark) and would listen intently for the violence and yelling to cease. If we were lucky we would be outside when his father came home. On those occasions we would get into his Power Wheels Jeep and drive up to the top of the hill in his backyard. From there we could not hear the yelling and could continue playing – almost like normal children.

I had not been back in Georgetown very long when I was again taken out of school and sent to live with my grandparents. This was the happiest news I had been given in a very long time. My first day back at the Newmarket school happened to be picture day and I am sure that I had never had a smile so big on my face. All my friends from Grade 1 welcomed me back and my teacher, Miss Rice, was an angel. She let me read one-on-one with her at her desk and let me bring my doll in for show and tell as often as I wanted to. She gave me all kinds of praise for completing assigned tasks and I always felt like I was doing a good job.

As the end of the school year approached I learned that the entire school was planning a picnic at the nearby park on the last day. Miss Rice thought it would be fun if our class all rode our bikes over and my classmates cheered while I slipped to the back of the carpet, put my head down, and cried. With each tear my heart beat faster with anxiety. I did not own a bike, nor did I know how to ride one. More frightening than this though was the expectation that Miss Rice would ask me what was wrong in front of the whole class and they would all see me crying and learn my secret. She told the class to face the front and to be silent before she dismissed them for recess. She then dismissed them one by one until I was the only one left. To my amazement nobody had turned around and nobody knew that I was crying. When Miss Rice heard my secret she told me that it was nothing to worry about. She promised me that before the picnic I would know how to ride a bike. That night my grandparents bought me a bike and for the next few weeks I stayed after school every night while Miss Rice taught me how to ride it. She kept her promise and on the day of the picnic I rode my bike proudly to the park with the rest of my class.

At some point during the summer between Grades 2 and 3 my grandparents found my mother an apartment in Newmarket. They went to Georgetown with a moving van and moved her out of Tom's house while he was at work. The only thing she did that day was lie in the bed and cry. The new 2 bedroom apartment was inexpensive because of its location. It was surrounded by low income housing and I do not think that anyone living in our building had a legitimate job. I was sad to move back in with my mom at the end of the summer because it meant changing schools again. Sammy and I were each given our own bedrooms and my mother slept upstairs on the couch. With little education, a lack of skills, and deep depression, my mother was not able to work. Our only source of income for the next 3 years was welfare.

Despite my fears, Grade 3 ended up being excellent. In fact, every year at that school was great. I continually spent as much time as possible at school, being involved in numerous after school activities in an attempt to avoid home. I felt like I had something to offer at school and did not have to be the adult in every situation. I excelled academically and socially, although I always feared that one day someone would find out that I lived in the "rough" part of town and had no money. I learned very quickly that cleanliness was very important to my classmates and that if I wanted to continue being accepted I had to become self-reliant in this, and many other areas. Beginning in Grade 4 I made my own lunch, did my own laundry, woke up early to my alarm clock so that I could shower before school, and made my own breakfast (which I always ate alone because my mother was never awake before I left for school).

Thankfully we moved to a better neighbourhood when I was in Grade 6. I was not as ashamed to bring my friends over to this apartment. This new neighbourhood was quiet and full of families who had children around my age. At this new apartment there were never police cars in the parking lot, no drug deals in the stairwell, and nobody ever mistakenly knocked our door down in a drunken state. Although this new apartment signalled a significant positive change in my mother's life, it also assigned to me even more responsibilities. My mother had met a new man and did not cry or sleep as much anymore. She started college and although she seemed happier, she still never had time for me. If she was not in class she was doing homework or out on dates. I had to baby sit my 6 year old brother after school (and sometimes all night if my mom decided to stay at her new boyfriend's house). Along with this job came cooking and cleaning up dinner for the two of us, helping Sammy with homework (as well as doing my own), getting him ready for bed and then school the next day, and keeping the house tidy so that my mom would not get mad at me. If I failed to perform any of my duties she would scream and yell at me about how I never helped or appreciated what she did for me. Then she would give me the silent treatment for a day or two. During these years I spent extended periods of time with my grandmother. She would often pick Sammy and I up after school and care for us so that I did not have to.

Once my mom graduated from college she began working. I thought things would get better and she would be happier but she still seemed to be angry at me all the time and yelled constantly. Sammy never seemed to be disciplined though. I remember being amazed at how she could not see anything he did wrong or anything I did right. I distanced myself from her emotionally and tried to do everything she told me to in an attempt to please her. It was as though I was living two different lives. I had my life at home where I was either being yelled at or ignored and my life at school where I was adored by my teachers and laughed constantly with my friends. I was still a shy student but the happiness that I displayed at school was genuine.

I graduated Grade 8 with many awards and entered high school with a mixture of anxiety and excitement. My high school years are some of my happiest memories. I was involved in music, drama, sports, student's council, and peer mentoring. In grade nine I began working part time at a local coffee shop in order to save money for university. I knew that I had to save money if I wanted to get a post-secondary education because my mother would never be able to afford to send me. I quit that job after a year because it was awful and worked in a clothing store at the mall from Grade 10 on. I was on the honour roll every semester and had a fantastic group of friends. My confidence grew tremendously during those years and I became much more outgoing and talkative. What a difference from a few years prior when my teachers had to beg me to answer even one question the entire year!

Although things at school were fantastic, things at home remained the same. My mom broke up with her boyfriend and bounced around from guy to guy for a while. She worked full time while I was in high school and managed to save enough money to buy a house. At the time, my relationship with my mother was not good, although I would not say that it was bad either because we really did not even have a relationship at all. We lived in the same house but hardly ever saw each other. She left very early in the morning for work and I stayed after school most nights for meetings or practices or went straight to work. In the evenings when we were both home I would make myself dinner and go to my room to do my homework, while she went on dates or watched television. I suppose we were more like roommates than mother and daughter. I do not know what Sammy was doing during this time. It seems to me, in looking back, that he was generally left unsupervised. He struggled with school every year but my mom refused to take time out of her life to help him. His teachers pushed him through the grades, although they were well aware of the fact that he was not being successful. He hated school and began to hate me because I did so well. His teachers would ask him about me and it seemed to him like they were just rubbing in the fact that he was not as successful as I was.

In my final year of high school I managed to fit in time for a boyfriend. His name was Carl and we had been friends since Grade 10. He seemed to like me very much and treated me well at the beginning. A few months into the relationship he began to get upset that I was not spending as much time with him as he wanted me to. He wanted me to drop out of one of my activities and I did in order to make him happy. My sacrifice did not satisfy him though and he began to demand more and more of my time. I began to spend all my free time with him, even going to his house to do my homework. My friends resented this and I started having arguments with them about it. I had no idea how to juggle my time so that everyone was happy. There were not enough hours in the day! I tried to explain this to Carl but he did not understand. He would get mad at me if I missed his basketball games or if I did not want to go out for lunch with him. Our relationship was full of drama and fighting. His controlling nature showed itself slowly and I was in denial of his abuse. Carl would frequently spend his weekends drinking and smoking pot with his friends and would get mad at me when I expressed my negative opinion about his behaviour. I had a very negative attitude toward drugs and alcohol because of my past experiences with them. Carl did not understand my objections and I never gave him the real reasons.

Then he began to pressure me to have sex. I finally gave in one evening (I do not know why) and everything got much worse from that point forward. Carl never accepted no for an answer! The smell of alcohol on his breath always took me immediately back to very unpleasant memories of my father. The blue interior of Carl's car always smelled of dust and pot. I remember standing in the shower crying because no matter how much shampoo I used I could not seem get that smell out of my hair.

I tried to distance myself from him, hoping that he would change and stop hurting me. Instead, his alcohol and drug use escalated and his abuse toward me became more frequent. He tried to control everything I did and even tried to talk me out of going to university, claiming that we could get married and he would support me. I felt that leaving him to go to university was the only way I could truly escape him. Although I was convinced that I loved him, I desperately needed him to change his behaviour. I actually thought that things might get better if he was not able to see me whenever he wanted to.

I was delighted to be accepted into a program at a major university. Even more exciting was the fact that my best friend, Audrey, was also accepted and we were going to be roommates. Audrey and I moved to northern Ontario, terrified of leaving our families, homesick even before we said goodbye to them. Involving ourselves in residence events allowed us to make friends with the other people living on our floor. We quickly became very good friends with the three guys living in the suite across the hall from us. Carl instantly became jealous and visited me every weekend just to keep an eye on me. The weekends became opportunities for him to get me alone and do whatever he wanted to me.

I finally put a stop to his behaviour when he showed up one weekend in February. He brought his best friend (and drug dealer), Henry, with him and I would not allow them into the building because I disliked Henry, for obvious reasons. Although I thought they had left, the two of them decided to 'hot box' Carl's car and get drunk. I was on my way out of the building with a male friend when I saw them. Carl lost it because I was with another guy and I just stood there disgusted at the sight of my pathetic boyfriend. He yelled at me for what seemed like an eternity and then asked me what I had to say for myself. I told him to leave and walked away. A few weeks later I went home for Easter and he came over. I broke up with him. Through his tears he begged me to reconsider and promised he would change. I told him that his drug and alcohol use, his behaviour, and his attitude were all unacceptable and that I never wanted to see him again. Those simple words eliminated an enormous weight that had been on my shoulders for over a year. I felt empowered and like I was finally in charge of my own life. I promised myself that day that I would never let anyone take advantage of me again.

Second year felt like a fresh start for me and, until the start of the second semester, my life was really very good. Classes were challenging, but interesting. I was closer than ever with my friends, and was continually involved in residence life. To top it off, I had a new boyfriend, who made me feel very special. Then January came and everything, once again, fell apart. Audrey and I were living together for the second year and we had a huge fight. Audrey had always been very moody and fighting with her was not unusual. She frequently got mad at me and, like my mother, ignored me for a few days until she got over it. Then she would act like nothing was ever wrong and we would go on as usual. I cannot say that I enjoyed this pattern but that is how it was. But, that January something was different. I remembered the promise I had made myself when I broke up with Carl and I confronted Audrey about her attitude. She told me that she did not want to be my friend anymore because she found it too difficult. There was no explanation, no second chance, no opportunity to make anything right.

I remember sitting in my room alone after that conversation and feeling like the walls were closing in on me. I couldn't breath, think, or even cry. I had to get out of there before I went crazy. There was only one place I could think of to go where I felt safe. I ran to the other residence building where my new boyfriend lived and just lay on his bed for the rest of the night crying uncontrollably. I had known Audrey since Grade 4 and we always claimed to be best friends. I had put all my effort into that friendship and with a few hurtful words she had decided to sabotage everything we had stood for and shared in the past.

By the time I worked up enough courage to go back to my suite, Audrey had told all of our friends her side of the story (whatever that was) and they would not even speak to me. I was ignored and rejected by the people who claimed to care so much about me. I felt ashamed and betrayed. Those people were in all of my classes and lived all around me. I did not know how I would face them. They did everything they could to make my life difficult and miserable. I met with counsellors and officials from other universities, trying to convince them that I should transfer. I could not continue to live in such a hostile environment where I was continually being ridiculed. The only thing that kept me at the university at all was my new boyfriend. He stood by me and supported me throughout the entire ordeal. Through the rumours, the harassment, and even when I had to involve the police, he was right there beside me – supporting me.

Now, thanks to my grandmother, my various wonderful teachers, and my boyfriend, I have overcome all the obstacles that have been set before me and have achieved my goal of becoming a teacher. My mother and I have a better relationship now, although I would say it is anything but "normal". We finally have a mutual respect for one another. She graduated from a post secondary institution, and is now well entrenched within a professional career. Without question, she is very proud of what I have accomplished, and is the first to admit that I largely did it in her absence and without her help. On the parenting side of things, it's still very hard for me to forgive her. My brother Sammy, I am sorry to say, has become somewhat the negative prediction. At the time I write this, he is almost 18 years old and has dropped out of high school. He is currently unemployed, drinks heavily, and uses drugs on a regular basis. I often wonder if I would have turned out like him if I had not had such caring, influential people involved in my life.

My grandmother was the nurturing mother figure that my own mother was unable to be. My teachers made me feel normal, and completely accepted me despite all the turmoil that seemed to surround me. They made me feel as though I was just like everyone else in the class and did everything they could to foster my interest in learning. My new boyfriend hung in for me at a very critical time in my life, and probably saved me from destroying everything that I had worked so hard to achieve. We have been together for almost 4 years now, and he is the only other person who knows the intricate details of my life. He does not judge me based on my past, and we eventually plan to get married. We look forward to starting our own family, which will be full of love, compassion, and acceptance.

Through all the hardships I believe that I have become a very strong and independent woman. I have managed to turn a whole lot of pain into something far more positive. I have definitely learned from my experiences, and I will never return to the past! I am excited to begin teaching and to be the nurturing adult who becomes a child's safety net. Although I would not wish any child to have to live through what I experienced, I will always take that personal interest in all of my students so that they feel special and very much valued. My classroom will be one in which my students can colour their clouds any colour they want – even blue.

Chapter 9: Right Side Up

From the time I was 13 years old, until I was 18, the married male minister at my church emotionally, spiritually and sexually abused me. During those years, the minister told me there was a special, sacred bond between us; that God had blessed our 'relationship.' He also courted my parents as his dearest, most cherished friends, in order to gain their trust and have unquestioned access to me. My family, with him, his wife and three young children, shared family camping trips, Christmas dinners, and school holidays together for six years. So, he always made sure I was available to him. Also, I was their faithful babysitter, and it was always arranged that I would sleep over at his house when babysitting. This was very handy for him. He completely controlled my life, and isolated me from my peers and any social activities, to the point where his wife and children became my only friends all the way through high school. This served his purposes well, because they were the last people I would want to hurt by revealing the truth. He told me if I ever told anyone what he was doing to me, I would cause him to lose his job, his wife, his children and his future, and of course I would also cause major problems in the church if there were a scandal.

The sexual abuse began with handholding and back rubs, which I was led to believe were harmless. This soon evolved into further touching and molestation. I knew it was wrong, but as a young girl, with an adult I was supposed to trust, I was afraid to say anything that would break the special sacred bond he said we had in our friendship. He wormed his way inside my head to make me believe that his happiness and wellbeing were my responsibility, and the only way to ensure them was to do as he said. Sexual touching led to severe sexual exploitation and abuse as he continued to control and manipulate me to get what he wanted. That was always the most important thing – that he get what he wanted.

I later found out that over the years, my parents confronted him many times about how I was so wrapped up in his and his family's lives, and I had no social life of my own. They had no idea what a skilled liar he was, as he posed as their dear friend, preaching love, trust and relationships. His answer to them was always, "If we are to be Christians together we must live in trust. If we don't have trust, we have nothing."

The pressure was always on me, all those years, as I lived a double life, kept my ducks in a row, and was coached to lie. I had to appear to be the perfect teenager, so no one would question my behaviour.

The truth about my secret life was revealed in March of 2000, and he was immediately removed from ministry in the church. I made the decision to go to the police in July of 2000 and he was arrested in October of 2000, during my first year of university. There was such a huge volume of evidence (letters, e-mails, other correspondence) that it took three months for the investigation to be completed, with the police file containing over 1000 pages.

In the end, it took 15 months after the arrest for my case to get to court, where my abuser pleaded guilty to sexual exploitation, which is defined as an adult in a position of trust, abusing that trust, in order to have sexual contact with a young person turned 14 years but less than 18 years, as described in Section 153 of the Criminal Code of Canada.

Eventually, my abuser was sentenced to 12 months in prison, which is actually a strong sentence for a first offence in Ontario, 3 years of probation, 300 hours of community service, and counselling – as ordered by the court and administered by a judicially appointed probation officer. But more importantly, he is never to be alone with a female under 18 years of age, and he had to submit a DNA sample to be kept on file permanently. He now has a permanent criminal record, and is officially registered as a serious sex offender.

It was difficult at this point to deal with my secret being public knowledge, and in all the newspapers. Everyone in my small home community knew about it, and I wondered what people were thinking about me. The biggest newspaper serving the area published an article about my case the day after the completion of my court case. The headline read: "Minister Sentenced to One Year for Having Sex with Teenage Girl." Without question, it was good that I was away at university at this time and it was not in my face all the time. Nevertheless, the whole process put something of a damper on my first two years of university.

Even in court, my abuser was still preaching that everything he did was justified, because it was true love, and that he was a victim of love. The judge just sat there shaking his head in disgust as my abuser tried to justify a 40 year old, married minister of the church, initiating a sexual relationship with a 13-year-old girl. I had the opportunity in court, to give a Victim Impact Statement and the following is a quotation taken directly from it:

> In the Bible the first letter of John, chapter four, verse eighteen says, "There is no fear in love. But perfect love drives out fear, because fear has to do with punishment. The one who fears is not made perfect in love." For most of my teenage years, I lived in fear of this sick, twisted relationship, and I could not get out. The relationship could not have been love, because fear dominated it. I feared that my parents would find out, that his wife would find out, that I would make a slip, and in doing so, I would "ruin" his life. I did not love him, I feared him. It doesn't even make sense, because why would a young, pretty, intelligent teenage girl fall in love with an old, fat, controlling coward if something negative, like fear, wasn't involved? He didn't love me. If he had loved

me, if he had even cared about me, he would have walked away. He never would have touched me.

My counselling was early and intense, but not a lot of hours in total. I had a lot of important support from my parents, my assigned counsellor, as well as our Bishop. Counselling helped me to understand and own the fact that the whole situation was in no way my fault. My abuser was the adult in a position of trust and he should never have pursued anything with me. I think the counselling helped me to develop a mindset that "when it was over, it was over," which helped me to move on – to be resilient and to get on with my life, (now that I could have a life of my own, free of him). When I finally came to understand the truth, I realized I didn't have to wear a mask anymore; I could be myself.

A huge part of my healing is that, with incredible support, I have moved on, put it behind me, and do not dwell on it anymore. My abuser took six years of my life; I don't have to give up any more to him, because living well is the best revenge!

If my situation were to be applied to a school environment, (that is, if my abuser was my teacher,) I would say the following: Teachers should all be aware of a situation when a fellow teacher appears to spend too much time or attention with a particular student. There should be a procedure to follow, to address the situation without being afraid to "squeal" on a co-worker and ruin their career. If one teacher questioned another about what appears to be a risky situation, the answer should NEVER be: "You should trust me. Why would you question my ethics? Just trust me." This was my abuser's answer to my mother and father and a few other members of the community when questioned about all the time he spent with me.

When my life turned right side up, my mother and father's lives turned upside down. They feared the worst, and felt that my life was over, and that I would be a basket case with unresolved issues for the rest of my life. My uncle gave them these wise words: "Teenagers are remarkable. They are the most resilient creatures on earth." He was right, and I'm here to prove it. And my mom and dad are right side up...again!

Chapter 10: A Mother's Sorrow

As I reached for the phone, I glanced at the clock, which read 1:27 a.m. The upset voice of my seventeen-year-old daughter on the other end said, "Mom, I must have my period, there is blood all over, can you pick me up?" I answered that I would be there in a few minutes. I pulled on a pair of jeans and a sweatshirt, grabbed a towel and headed to my daughter's friend's house, where she had attended a Halloween party and was to spend the night. There were still a lot of kids there, but I didn't see my daughter. I went into the house and found one of her friends, who said she was outside and took me back out to where two friends were helping her walk to my vehicle. I was a little puzzled but got inside and put the towel on the seat. When her friends, with great effort, got her into the vehicle, I could see the blood all over her hands as she placed them on the dash. As soon as the door closed, she started to cry that a guy had sexually violated her with his fist. She kept crying and saying it hurt so bad and that she was sorry, over and over. I tried to comfort her as she was telling me what had happened.

We went straight to the hospital and into the emergency ward. The towel I had brought from home was soaked in blood, as was her clothing from the waist down. The doctor examined her and said she had lost a lot of blood and he was not prepared to deal with the possible internal injuries. She was set up on an I.V, but had consumed alcohol and therefore could not be given painkillers. Due to the extent of the injury, she was unable to urinate and the doctor was very concerned for her well-being. The police arrived and I gave them any information she had given me on the way to the hospital. After what seemed like forever, she was loaded into an ambulance and taken to another hospital where we were met by the sexual assault team and a Specialist/Surgeon. While she was in surgery, Detective L arrived and filled us in on what had been happening since receiving the call and asked a number of questions. The detective told us that the information from the kids they had interviewed, from the party, indicated that there had been around 200 in attendance throughout the evening. This was a home where my daughter and her friends spent most of their time together, because I knew it was a safe place. The friend's mom was usually home and a very nice, responsible lady.

My daughter was in surgery for over two and a half hours. Finally, the doctor came out and told us he had not encountered any major complications and she would make a full physical recovery. When my husband and I returned home later that evening, Detective L called to inform us they had charged a male with aggravated sexual assault. He was a young offender and someone our daughter knew personally. The next day, my daughter was not surprised when I told her. She had only given me clues about what he was wearing, but did not let on that she knew him. Later that day, in a flourish of friends and family, my daughter was in good spirits. In the evening, Detective L arrived to meet her and take a formal statement. When I entered the room, after an hour and a half, both my daughter and Detective L had tears in their eyes. Later that evening, we asked Detective L to come to our home so my family could talk to her. The detective was both physically and mentally exhausted when she arrived. She had also been involved in the arrest and incarceration of the offender and dealt with the emotions of his family. She came in and took off her shoes, put her feet up on a chair and let out a long sigh. After a lengthy discussion about several of our concerns, she told us she had four children of her own, the oldest almost 16, and wondered as a parent, how she would/could possibly keep them safe.

On Monday morning, I telephoned the principal of the local high school where both my daughter and the offender attended, to inform them what had happened. The principal immediately set up support services for friends of my daughter. The offender went to court that morning and was released on bail. The conditions included 10:00 p.m. curfew in the presence of his parents, no communication with my daughter and that he not attend the same high school for as long as she was enrolled there.

Three days after the assault, I brought my daughter home from the hospital. Our home was abuzz with her friends dropping in to see how she was doing, phone calls and the delivery of flowers and gifts. Reactions to the incident varied among community members, as well as within immediate family members. My initial reaction was to question what the boy had endured to be so angry to do that to an innocent human being. Police said he and his family didn't fit the criminal profiles. My daughter and I were concerned, not that he pay for what he had done, but rather make sure he received the help he needed to make sure this didn't happen to someone else's daughter.

My husband, my oldest daughter and son-in-law did not share our view of what should happen and my son just didn't talk about it. The offender was the same age as my youngest daughter, in the same school and although they traveled in different social circles, they had many of the same friends. It was extremely difficult for her over the next couple of months. Everybody was talking about what had happened.

When I returned to work, I was informed that the offender's sister was in the classroom next to where I worked as an educational assistant, with grade 8 students. She was in grade 7 and I had no idea who she was. I was a little concerned about how I would feel when I saw her – and her reaction to me as well. There was no visible initial reaction for either of us, and we have never made any reference to the incident to this day. However, over the next couple of months we both felt a need to get to know one another. For some reason it was comforting; a reassurance that she was normal and came from a normal family.

The principal asked my daughter, not to return to school until there was no physical evidence of the assault. She had trouble sitting for any amount of time due to swelling and stitches. She tried to attend after a couple of weeks, but could not finish out a full day. She also found it difficult to be at school when everyone knew what had happened. I set her up with counselling the week she came home. For four weeks, she received counselling through hospital services and the sexual assault services and then for three more months with only the sexual assault services. At our request and the insistence of the Crown Attorney, the offender was also to undergo intensive counselling with regular reporting on his progress. Then my daughter started hearing rumours that he would be returning to the high school. We called the detective and voiced our concerns, only to be told not to worry because his return would violate his bail conditions. Through our insistence, they followed up on our concerns to find out his lawyer had argued in court that the offender had a right to an education and neighbouring schools had refused to enroll him. This was when emotions really began to surface for my daughter. He would return and she would now be forced to see him, on a regular basis, while she finished high school. At this point my daughter requested, through the detective, that she be able to talk to her violator prior to his return to school. The detective contacted the lawyer personally, explained the situation, and our expectations for the visit. His lawyer had consented, but later withdrew when the Crown Attorney insisted that anything said could be used in a court of law. In essence, these were two adolescents trying to move on and put the pieces of their lives back together. The attorney did not understand how my daughter felt and didn't really care if it fell outside of the realm of the law.

We returned to the specialist five weeks after her surgery. He told us most of the swelling was gone and she still had a few internal stitches left. I was almost sick to my stomach to think that after this period of time there was still swelling. He told us he had five daughters and had been very upset in the operating room that anyone would cause this kind of damage to a young woman. He also continued to tell us he had been sexually assaulted as a child, but had been able to move on and she would need to work hard to find a way to overcome this and not to let it beat her down. All three of us were in tears as he gave her a big hug and told her to be strong.

As high school progressed, she was eventually told her marks had dropped dramatically and this would greatly affect her entrance into university. Ultimately, she decided to drop out and be taken off the register for the rest of the semester and do a course by correspondence. Every day she was away, it became harder for her to face going back, but eventually she did! She returned to school the following semester, but we quickly saw how she had changed from the once outgoing, athletic, leader to someone who now had difficulty facing people. She refused to participate in the sporting activities that had previously been the focus of her life. Her teachers were supportive and asked her if she would like to help coach if she wasn't comfortable playing. She agreed, but couldn't bring herself to show up to the practices or games because she knew that everybody there was aware of what had happened. I began to see changes in other situations as well, particularly around people she knew. If we were in the mall and someone stopped to chat with her she would appear fine, but as soon as the person left she would need to leave as well. Another time, when a store didn't have the size of her favourite pants (that were now in police custody as evidence) she just sat down and quietly started to cry. One other time, when we picked her up from a friend's birthday party, she had a flashback of being on the same road, at night, in the same vehicle, and she sobbed all the way home. For a time, it seemed like she was losing control of her world. As her mother, I felt I was doing everything I could to be supportive, but I felt absolutely helpless!

Then someone she knew from work asked her out on a date for Valentine's Day. He attended the same high school. I was terrified for her and hoped all would go well. They recently celebrated two years together. I give him credit for keeping her in school to complete her grade twelve. She says she is not prepared for the pressures of university, but maybe someday. She will attend College this fall, and I am starting to see many of her strengths and confidence returning.

Throughout our family's ordeal, there were a number of girls who told her they had been raped but they never told anybody. In the end, if not for the medical emergency, would I have ever known she had been raped? Probably not! Most likely, she would have suffered quietly with the shame.

Without doubt, I still mourn the shattered hopes and dreams of my daughter, but celebrate every day I see her alive; growing stronger by the minute. I really think she will be okay. I admire her for her strength as a survivor, and for the decisions she has made.

This incident certainly brought to light the larger issue of what society has access to on a daily basis through technology. After conversations with the detective and the Crown Attorney, I had to see how difficult it would be to access this type of pornography on the Internet. It took nothing more than a Google search for "Fisting" and I had my answer. It is no wonder sexual assault and violence against women is so high.

We still live in the same town as the offender, and I often see him because he works at a local grocery store. He will make eye contact with me, but drops his head and goes the other way when he sees my daughter. We still hope that someday he can move past the shame and simply say, "I'm sorry." I still find it very emotional when I see him, but I believe that he was also a victim, a victim of our society.

*Addendum – My daughter is now in her early twenties, and has recently graduated from College with her second professional diploma. She is stronger than ever, and her level of confidence is absolutely awe-inspiring. I truly believe treating her as a survivor, and not a victim, has made all the difference in the world.

Chapter 11: Not An Ordinary Day

I grew up in a 'normal' household. I had two parents, a sister, and a dog. Life as a child was great, but as I was to find out, life can also change drastically in a split second. We didn't have the biggest house on the block but we didn't have the smallest one either. One thing we did have was great neighbours! As a youngster, my parents both worked during the day, and went to school at nights, all in an effort to better the family's overall standing. No doubt, I missed them as a child but the time we did spend together made up for all the time we didn't. I enjoyed living in my neighbourhood because there were lots of kids my same age, and we were constantly playing together. We were particularly close to our neighbours, Felix and Audrey. They were great people, and always treated me as one of their own (like family), which of course, had its ups and downs. They had a daughter the same age as me, and for years we were absolutely inseperable (like sisters).

I was constantly over at my best friend and neighbour's house, with my parents having to drag me home for dinner and bedtime (almost every evening). At one point, something started to change, I started noticing that my friend Bethany always wanted to play at my house, and never over at hers. At the time I thought this a bit strange. It took a couple of weeks of asking but Bethany eventually told me that her parents were constantly fighting and yelling at each other, and before too long Bethany and her brother Mitchell were staying with us. At the time, my mom explained as diplomatically as she could, that our good neighbours and best friends, were working through some marital problems, and needed to be left alone to do it. I remember Bethany being really confused by this series of events, basically because her dog Rex was allowed to stay at her parents' house, but she had to leave (weird that I would remember that). I distinctly remember mom's response to Bethany, and at the time it seemed to make a lot of sense. It appeared that my mom had all the answers and explained that Rex was there to protect her parents since they were now home all alone.

I distinctly remember, one night in the middle of all this disruption and confusion, Felix and Audrey came over to our house for coffee. At some point, very early in the evening, they took Bethany and Mitchell into my parent's room for what felt like an eternity. While all of this was going on, my mom was busy getting pillows and blankets out of the closet and making the couch into a bed which, at the time, seemed very strange to me because any time previous that I had asked to sleep on the couch, my mom was always quick to respond, "A couch isn't' a place to sleep"! Needless to say, I couldn't figure out what she was doing, or what was actually going on. But this was to change, and change quite dramatically!

When Felix and Audrey came out of my parent's bedroom, I could clearly see that both were crying. I distinctly remember Felix looking at the floor, and keeping his eyes fixed to the floor all the way through, and then out of the house. He never looked up, even once! Audrey remained behind. A short time later, with respect to the incredible sadness in the house, it was finally explained that Felix and Audrey were getting a divorce..... And then the whispering began!

Although I don't remember all of the specific details, or specific timelines, from this point forward, things started to get very strange in our neighbourhood. For example, it would not be that uncommon to be awakened in the middle of the night, to hear Felix screaming, from outside the house, at Audrey sleeping inside the house. Basically, he would just stand outside and yell for Audrey to come out and talk. I remember my dad getting really upset about this and, at times, he and Felix would argue until the police were eventually called. Eventually, Felix's behaviour became so erratic that his own children, Bethany and Mitchell, started to fear that he would come for them in the middle of the night. On many occasions through this period, I remember both of them crying inconsolably, until they eventually fell asleep. Where Felix and Audrey were concerned, at the time, this is what my parents referred to as a very 'messy divorce'!

As the separation and divorce were moving forward, one day after school Bethany and I, as per usual, would stop at her house before we moved onto mine. We fell into this routine because it enabled us to take her dog Rex out for a walk. We wouldn't hang around too long because if Audrey came home and found us, she would always make both of us do our homework, right away (so we tried to avoid this). Anyway, one day, as part of our regular routine, Bethany and I walked into her house to get Rex. Only, something was really different on this particular day. On this particular day, Rex was not only at the door to greet us, he greeted us at the door in a frenzied, agitated state, barking madly, which was really weird (looking back now) because Rex was a very quiet dog and rarely barked.

Perhaps at this point we should have known something was wrong, but we didn't. All I remember is walking towards the basement, which was directly across from the front door, to get Rex's leash – (as we always did). However, this time the routine was to be very different. As soon as I turned the basement lights on, the dangling legs immediately caught my attention. They were like a rag dolls, swaying in wind. When I followed the legs up, they took me directly to Felix's face. There he was, hanging from the rafters. A red cord was tied around his neck and, I remember, he only had one shoe on. His face was charcoal black, like he had taken dirt and rubbed it on his skin, and his blue eyes were now completely red; but what I remember most was the sound. The sound was indescribable, with the cord creaking a certain way, stressed by the weight of a lifeless Felix on it. I stood there frozen, unable to speak, move or think. I just stared! The image of Felix hanging still makes me feel like I am a scared girl hoping to wake up from a really bad dream. As one can only imagine, when Bethany saw her dad, she immediately fell to the floor screaming for help, and didn't stop until her mom ran into the basement. I have no recollection of Audrey even coming into the house, I just remember the wind being knocked out of me as she grabbed me (with both arms) by the stomach, carrying me completely out of the house and setting me on the lawn. I don't remember much of the rest of the day. I do know that for the longest time I didn't want to talk about it at all. Apparently, I just sat there staring for very long periods of time. My life was about to take a 180 degree turn, and not for the better.

To say my life changed drastically that day would not be an exaggeration. My friends were no longer my friends, as I isolated myself from absolutely everyone. I turned from being an active, gregarious young girl, to someone who was reticent and withdrawn; angry at the world and all those around her. Although I never turned to self-medication, or hurting myself, my overall demeanor, mood and attitude started into a profoundly downward spiral. My parents tried their best to be patient through this period, but everything they said and did seemed to make me even more hostile and angry. For the next two years I completely lashed out, eventually being arrested for my behaviour, and put on probation as a "young offender".

In response to this downward spiral, desperate, my parents suggested that I attend a summer camp – (they didn't really know what else to do). Although, initially, there was no way I was ever going to agree to this, all my options were removed when my parents decided to involve my Child Care Worker, (assigned to me as a "young offender"), who basically said that if I didn't go to camp then she would have me arrested because she had evidence, on at least one occasion, when I had been in breach of my probation for breaking an assigned curfew. Not really knowing whether or not this was even true, or if she could even do this, I decided I was not going to take a chance, so off to camp I went! In the end, it turned out to be one of the best decisions I have ever made!

The camp itself was a world within itself. My first summer there I fell in love with something; all the kids around me. They were just like me, trying to overcome something! Almost immediately, I put my despair and anger on the back burner, discovering in the process that I had a very real ability in helping others get over their own feelings of despair and anger. At camp, I met kids who had been terribly abused and mistreated; I met kids who were completely neglected in their home lives; I met kids who had witnessed all kinds of trauma, and I met kids who were so incredibly poor they actually came to camp with no shoes at all. These kids, despite their individual backgrounds and socio-economic situations, eventually brought to me a degree of hope, and at time in my life when I thought all hope for me was gone. For nine more summers I returned to this camp, arriving each and every summer with more hope and enthusiasm than I brought the summer before. However, I must confess here, there was one person in particular at this camp that I was always able to talk to, and, more than anyone else, was responsible for my turnaround. He is now a world renown clinician, so I won't mention his real name, suffice to say his life's work has been devoted to working with kids who are "at-risk", (of which I was indeed one)! To both his colleagues and his profession, this man is known both nationally and internationally as a preeminent child psychiatrist, and a highly respected researcher and teacher. But to the thousands of children he has helped over the years, he was simply referred to as Dr. "D". To me, Dr. "D" was my savior;

without question, he saved me from my own destruction. Had I not gone to camp that one turbulent summer, I shudder to think of how different my life would be today. Kids sometimes naively think that they can get through things all by themselves (sometimes very horrible things) but in the end, they really can't, and many times these things end up consuming them. Sometimes, kids need some help to get through things they don't really understand. I was lucky, I was offered, and then took some of this help!

Eventually, after finally working my way through some of the baggage, I went on to University, got a degree, and immediately got a job with a large national children's advocacy organization. But eventually, I found my way to my real calling, which was teaching (particularly working with "at-risk" or underprivileged students). In looking back, I now know in my heart that I eventually found my way to education as a profession because I wanted to give back some of that, which was given to me at a particularly difficult and challenging time in my life. The events of that day in my neighbour's basement still linger, and, at times, still affect some aspects of my personal life. For example, there are certain movies that I will never be able to watch, and I'm still very sensitive to anyone touching my neck but, all in all, the fact I'm now in a career and working with kids who very much need me because I'm making a difference in some of their lives, keeps me moving forward—and, most times, with a smile! At minimum, I am living proof that some of life's toughest obstacles can be overcome. For the kids I have specifically chosen to work with, I will always be there!

Chapter 12: Life Is Good!

The other day, during Convocation, I sat there in amazement and reflected upon the fact that I was about to graduate and become a teacher. Without question, there was real sense of satisfaction and pride that I now had two degrees! For sure, a lot of hard work and perseverance had gone into the process. Many thoughts cycled through my head on that particular day. Thoughts of feeling very lucky in not only graduating, but in becoming a teacher, being married to a great woman, and having five wonderful children flooded through my head as I waited to go up on stage and accept my Bachelor of Education degree. I remember thinking, how could a man ask for more; a future in education and a family that loves him absolutely 100% unconditionally. Life is good, I thought!

But as I look back, I consider myself lucky because life wasn't always so good. In fact throughout the earliest part of it, I encountered many negative events during my childhood and early adolescence that could have easily led me down a very delinquent and/or destructive path. Unfortunately, memories of my childhood and early teenage years are not very pleasant ones, largely because of three significant themes: alcoholism, poverty, and abuse.

Let me clarify. Most of us have some positive memories of our father, but the majority of my memories of my father are of him drinking; and whenever my father drank he could not and would not drink just one beer. Like the saying goes, where my father was specifically concerned, "one beer was too many and twelve were not enough." It's not to say that he drank every night, but when he did, "watch out"!

When my father went on one of his drinking binges, without fail he would become (almost immediately) completely enraged and very nasty. For example, I can remember this one time when my father became so violent after drinking, that he slammed a kitchen chair right through the floor and into the basement. Another time I witnessed him throw a chair completely through the wall that separated our living room from our kitchen. However, as might be expected, not only did my father frequently break things around the house, but he would also constantly belittle and beat up my mother.

Let me give you an example. One particular day we were at one of my father's friends place and, of course, everyone started drinking very early on. Quite naturally, it wasn't long before everyone was completely drunk. As the evening wore on, as per usual, my father's behaviour became more and more erratic; on this occasion ultimately resulting in him shaving his head completely bald. When we got home later on that evening, as was always the case, my father began to immediately argue and pick a fight with my mother. Eventually, in a complete rage, he ended up breaking everything in the house, including the refrigerator, which he flipped onto the floor, naturally spilling and smashing all of the contents contained within it. But what I remember most about this particular evening, and this particular rage episode, was that there was broken glass everywhere, particularly all over the floors. But this fact didn't bother my father at all, as he still chose to walk around the house in his bare feet. I distinctly remember the terrifying sight of him, his feet cut up with many pieces of broken glass still lodged in them, bleeding profusely. It was as though in this completely enraged state he was impervious to pain. Unfortunately though, this didn't stop him from inflicting pain on others, and on this particular night he ended up breaking a beer bottle over my mother's foot, cutting her very badly in the process.

To be completely honest though, in most instances my brothers, sister and myself would only have to witness the very beginnings of most of my father's rages, because very luckily we had an older brother who tried very hard to look after us, so when my father would start to "go off", my older brother would usually begin the process of trying to shepherd us to our bedrooms.

Basically, these are the memories of the early years of my life; a drunken father who would consistently become enraged, and beat up my mother. My mother on the other hand, although she didn't drink or take drugs, had other "ghosts in her closest" that definitely played themselves out in the rearing of her children. Eventually my mother got fed up with the constant abuse she was taking from my dad, and she just took off one day. I was nine years old at the time and all I can remember is my mother telling me she was going shopping, but she never returned. She decided to leave us all alone with an out of control, alcoholic father. As a result, we did not see or talk to my mother for well over a year.

Eventually though, we were reunited with our mother, joining her to live in a rural one-bedroom mobile home where she had begun a new life with another man (not my father). What I remember most about this one-bedroom trailer and this particular time in our lives was that there was no hydro and no running water. We went to the bathroom in a bucket, and cooked whatever little food we had over a small wood burning stove. I say little food because I remember our mother actually keeping us at home from school because she had absolutely nothing to put in our lunches. Actually, I remember days where all we would get to eat was two slices of plain bread (at supper-time), that being all the food we would have to eat for an entire day. We basically went on like this, as a family, for the next two years.

My mother finally left the guy she was living with in the mobile home, and we moved to another small town. About three months after we moved to this new town, my mother met another guy, who eventually moved in with us. However, this guy was a hard working individual, who made things a whole lot better for us. We now lived in a nice warm place, where the cupboards were always filled with food. Most importantly for us though, was that the new guy didn't drink at all.

But, as we'd come to expect, the good times were not to last. Shortly after my 12th birthday, my mother's brother was allowed to move in with us. Everybody knew this individual was a hardened criminal, having already spent eight years in jail for beating his father, my grandfather, into a completely vegetative state – with a baseball bat. Apparently he did this in retribution for his father's physical and sexual abuse of him. Unfortunately, for us, my mother's brother seemed to have caught the same disease from his father, as very shortly after his arrival he turned his perverted attentions to us kids. To make a very long ugly story short, and without any specific details, during his stay at our house, I certainly did not escape his attention. The sad thing is, I told my mother all about her brother's inappropriate behaviour, but in the end she ultimately chose to do absolutely nothing about it. Her brother was allowed to stay anyway! Needless to say, it is a haunting thought/question that has remained with me all of these years, "what kind of mother lets a known pedophile stay in her home even after her very own son has told her that something ugly has happened?"

Without lingering on the very negative for too long, although the first fifteen years of my life were indeed very rough, I must confess that I too participated in some things that I'm not very proud of. I constantly stole (although mostly food), I started smoking cigarettes at the age of ten, started doing drugs and drinking alcohol at the age of twelve, and I chose to hang around with some very delinquent peers. Looking back, I think it was the only way I knew how to cope with what was going on in my life at the time. But lucky for me, things were to change, and change for the better shortly after my fifteenth year.

To conclude my story, very early on in my life, I always took part time jobs wherever and whenever I could. I would work part-time during the school year, then move to full-time work during the summer holidays. I quickly discovered that both school and work were places where I could be well away from all of the negative influences in my life, so I decided to take both environments much more seriously. I became a very hard worker, and started to receive a great deal of recognition for being this particular way. Eventually, I got completely away from the drugs, stopped smoking, and only drank occasionally. Most importantly, I started to make better choices in the things I did, and in the people I hung around with. Related directly to this pivotal change in direction at a pretty important time in my life, it's only in taking seriously this assignment on risk and resiliency that I've begun to discover some of the reasons as to why things turned out much more favourably for me, than perhaps they might have – given its early, less than positive start. Maybe as some of the literature suggests, I do possess some of the internal resilient qualities, which, when combined with meeting some pretty influential adults along the way, got me through some of my greatest challenges. If so, thank you resiliency!

As I said at the beginning, I have just graduated and I am a teacher. I have a great wife and some wonderful children. Life is good!

Chapter 13: A Little Bit of Dignity Goes a Very Long Way

I've heard it said that you can't remember things that happen to you at any early age. I disagree, for I have very vivid memories of when I was only two or three years old. My mother and father were divorced, and my mother was attempting to raise four daughters (and one on the way) by working at various low-paid jobs. We lived in a house with three walls (the fourth was just 2 by 4's and black tar paper) and all four kids slept in a double bed with two legs. I always rolled off in the night and woke up on the floor with no blankets. The year I turned three, I had pneumonia 7 times. I remember it very well, because in the hospital they made me sleep alone in a crib, which felt like a jail to me.

My sisters and I tried to supplement the family income by stealing bread from the local bakery truck. The driver always left the back doors open (looking back, I think he did it on purpose) and we would crawl in, steal whatever we could carry and hide it in the bushes. Later on we would come back and eat it. I remember once there were ants crawling all over some cinnamon buns we had stashed and we just picked them off and ate the buns anyway.

We had a big black dog that we would take with us into the grocery store and stash peanuts and bags of food in his collar. When the employees chased the dog out of the store we would go out and whistle for him, then retrieve the peanuts. We had to change churches a few times too, because once I asked what the collection plate was for and another kid said, "It's for the poor people." Since we were the poorest people I knew, I cleaned out the money and brought it home to my mother. She was very upset with me and made me give it back, but I couldn't understand why I hadn't done anything wrong - so I continued to take money from collection plates, I just didn't tell my mother.

My sister Jenny and I had a good scam going when I was about 6. We would sell Kool-Aid for five times the price of all the other kids' Kool-Aid stands. People would stop to ask us why our Kool-Aid was so expensive and Jenny would explain that we were very poor and needed the money. Of course, everyone bought a glass and just as they were about to drink it, Jenny would signal me and I would start to cry. "Why is your little sister crying?" the customer would ask. "Because she's really thirsty and we aren't allowed to drink any of the Kool-Aid", Jenny would explain. The kind customer would always give me the

Kool-Aid, and after they had left we would dump it back into the jug. We sold the same jug of Kool-Aid all summer long. When my mother found out she almost had a fit. She said that what we were doing was no better than begging and that even if we were poor we should still have some dignity and pride. Begging was definitely not allowed.

We had a lot of freedom as kids. When I was six I would take a bus downtown with Katy, who was ten, to go to the public library. We would wander all over, through the worst parts of the city, and we were never scared. We found a dead body once. We walked for what felt like miles until we found a policeman to tell and he scoffed at us and said it was probably just a drunk. We were so insulted that he would think we couldn't tell the difference between a drunk and a dead man! What did he think we were, babies or something! Shit, I'd been stepping over drunks since I could walk! We had checked to make sure he was dead before we went to all the trouble of finding a cop. But nobody ever believes kids, particularly kids like us!

It was about this time that we finally got welfare assistance. I don't know why we didn't have it before, only that we didn't. Things were a little better. We had milk for the first time and we had meat for supper once a week. The rest of the week we still ate the usual brown beans, spaghetti with tomato soup for sauce, and crackers and sardines (which were really cheap then). I started school and I loved it there. My teachers all liked me because I was very polite (my mother's influence) and an honours student. I had an English accent for the first couple of years but I worked very hard on losing it so I would fit in with the other kids. Sadly, I discovered that the reason some of the kids wouldn't play with me was because their parents wouldn't let them play with a "welfare kid" with a divorced mother. Even in the slums there is a class system. The working class poor (with two-parent families) considered themselves above the welfare class. As I became more aware of other people's prejudice, I became very self-conscious and my self-esteem suffered. It was particularly difficult when I became an adolescent. My junior-high school had students from both sides of "the tracks" so I was even more acutely aware of how I was inferior to other people. Fortunately for me, when I was twelve I met a man who had a profound effect on my life.

His name was Peter. He was in his forties and was at that time one of the most popular artists in the entire province. He painted landscapes and wildlife with astounding realism. Having been a welfare recipient himself at one time, he decided to donate some of his time to those less fortunate and volunteered to teach art to welfare kids. Katy and I rode a bus for over an hour on Saturday mornings to get to the hall where he was giving lessons. The Canadian Broadcasting Corporation heard about his classes and came to film an episode for one of their public affairs programs. Katy and I were the featured kids and were filmed drawing our pictures.

The classes weren't a great success overall I guess, because they were cancelled. Peter phoned my mother and asked if he could continue to teach Katy and me privately, because he thought we had a lot of potential. For two years, Peter would pick us up every Saturday morning and bring us to his house where we would go to his basement "studio" and paint.

One Saturday, he said we were going on a field trip instead of painting and he took us to the Provincial Art Gallery where they were exhibiting some of his works. Peter was a very scruffy looking man. He looked more like a welfare case than I did and when we were in the gallery, we got some disgusted looks from many of the patrons. I was amazed at how Peter never let it bother him. He took us to see one of his pictures and told us to listen to what people were saying. I listened to them rant and rave about the underlying message and soul of the painting, etc. When we looked at it, I was confused because it was definitely modern art- just splashes of colour- and I knew Peter hated modern art. It finally dawned on me. "That's your palette!" I said. "Yup" Peter answered with a smirk. "People like to think they're better than other people. But I guess I showed them huh?"

The lesson continued. After the gallery, Peter took us to a very prestigious private gallery with plush carpeting and expensive furniture. I was terrified. When a stylishly dressed woman approached us I felt like turning and running away, afraid she was going to throw us out, but instead she embraced Peter and asked if this was the little "protégé" -and she was looking right at me. Then they showed me one of the paintings I had done hanging right there in the gallery with a ridiculous price tag on it- probably more money than my mum got for a month from welfare. It was one I had called "Pierre" - all in blue and white and very cubist- just to tease Peter. It was the first painting I ever sold. The first money I had ever made period. Peter gave the money to mum in cash so the welfare people wouldn't know and we all got new shoes and clothes for school.

I had paintings in about three different galleries that year and I sold quite a few. Katy sold some too. We were actually sort of famous in the local art world. Peter approached someone about getting us a scholarship to an exclusive school of fine arts and we were accepted (apparently we were the youngest people they had ever accepted too). We didn't get to go because although tuition was paid, there were other expenses that my mum just couldn't afford. The next year, Peter's oldest son was diagnosed with a terminal illness and our lessons stopped. I missed him more than I can say.

I didn't paint anymore after that. Not for many years. But when I was older and my life was all messed up, I found myself sketching to relax and to get in touch with myself again. I started painting again as an adult and I still find it helps me to focus my thoughts. Painting gave me a way to feel good about myself, to feel special. And Peter taught me that no one is better than you unless you think they are.

My mother always used to say that you are no better and no worse than anyone else and Peter proved her point to me. Katy told me that of all the kids in our old neighbourhood (two-parent families included} we were the only ones who didn't end up in jail, dead or addicted to drugs (in fact, our next door neighbour came home and shot his wife and himself a week after we moved out of the neighbourhood - and a girl I used to play with was recently imprisoned in Pakistan for drug smuggling}.

Katy is a very successful professional woman now; Jenny works for the government, while my oldest sister is a financial advisor, married for over twenty years with four kids. I am happily married with two kids, a degree in psychology, and a recently completed degree in education. I am now a teacher! My youngest sister wasn't so fortunate; she is still struggling to get ahead.

When you look at what happened to all the other people in our old neighbourhood, it's pretty amazing how lucky we all were. I attribute it to my mother's insistence that we have dignity above all and, for me at least, Peter showing me in such a profound way that everyone is special, irrespective of his or her circumstances. Most importantly though, Peter helped me find that something special about myself, which gave me something powerful to cling to during those times when I doubted my own worth. As Stephen Jay Gould so astutely noted, "Few tragedies can be more extensive than the stunting of life, few injustices deeper than the denial of an opportunity to strive or even to hope, by a limit imposed from without, but falsely identified as lying within". I could not agree more!

Chapter 14: An Invincible Summer

Over the past week or so I have sat and listened to many words and terms that were apt descriptors of my youth. I never would have considered myself the resilient child, but looking back on it now it seems to fit.

My father was a 'hard' man and a bit of legend back in the small, provincial mining town that I grew up in. Not only were his exploits underground the stuff of legend, but so too was his reputation for drinking and womanizing. My mother worked out of the house, and she was a soft and tender woman—the opposite of my father.

For the most part I was brought up by my maternal grandparents, the reason being the volatile nature of my home life. Dad constantly on a tear and my mother doing her best to keep the rest of the family (my brothers and sister) safe and fed.

I am the oldest of a family of four, and I definitely was not a 'planned' baby; Mom and Dad barely knew each other when they... you know... made me, and Dad had no qualms in letting me know that. He resented me, which is why I was the only one he would beat on.

Life with my grandparents was nice. They were very devout Roman Catholics and I enjoyed the prayerful life that they brought me up in; mass in the mornings and rosary in the evenings. In their house there was a lightness that contrasted sharply with the darkness that hung over my parents' house—I hated being in my parents' house, sounds rather odd now.

My Grandmother was a saintly woman but she had her faults. She would touch me... at first it was innocent enough; drying me after a bath, but later I would have to get in bed naked and she would touch me in inappropriate ways... yes, Gran had her faults.

The only other living person that knows about what went on with my grandmother is my wife. She found this out a few years ago, after a night that I had been drinking rather heavily and all the old memories rushed back in.

However, I may be mistaken that my wife is the only person that knows about the secret. I remember a time when I was quite young, when my father came to my grandparents' house to get me to come home with him, I did not want to go. I cried, I screamed, I kicked, I put my fist through a window—my grandparents did nothing. Dad carried me home.

Life was not good in our house at this time. On top of everything else, a major labour dispute had erupted at my Dad's place of work. I remember marching to the picket line with Dad and helping him and his buddies break out the windows of the company's main office, and we set a few fires as well. I was around eight at the time and I might as well have been living in Belfast, Northern Ireland. It was a very unruly time.

My father was out of work for a long time through this particular period, hence, we were forced to go on welfare. I was spending more time in my house and not much time at my grandparents' place anymore. That is why I think I may have said something about the extra effort that my Gran was putting into drying me off after bath time—I know it is not funny, but I've personally discovered that humour is certainly a characteristic of the resilient child.

After a short little while, I eventually began visiting my grandparents' home again. Actually, the memory of going to their house still fills my heart with gladness. I do not think there were any more incidents of touching after this time; in fact, I am sure that there were not.

The years pass and I spend most of my time traveling between the two houses—the one with light and one that was dark, and of course there was school. In school I was a terribly shy and introverted child, at least that was the case at the elementary level. I would sooner wet in my pants than have to go. Among the things that absolutely terrified me there, were the big, black automatons that we had to daily deal with—the Nuns!

One day my aunt came to my classroom door to bring me home. Dad was in a blast underground, both he and his buddy were taken to the hospital—they were in a very bad way. They were drilling and hit an old long hole that contained some explosive. Dad's partner was unconscious and Dad was badly injured from all the muck and debris that cut into his face. Dad grabbed his buddy, put him on his back, and walked out half a mile of drift, and down one hundred feet of ladders. The rail haulage man found them, a blasted and bloodied heap, laying on the tracks. The legend continues!

Dad was off work for years thereafter. His drinking got worse and now he was constantly taking drugs to ease the pain in his joints, which was constant. Dad's patience for his children was nil. Still, I was the one that got most of what he wanted to dish out.

One day he beat me so bad that I had to stay out of school for two days. He used the top of a fiberglass rod, which left long welts on my back, buttocks, arms and legs. After the beating he tore off to the nearest pub. Mom came up to my bedside and put a damp cloth on the marks and tried to explain the hard time that Dad was going through, and that I cannot tell anyone what went on. Poor Mom, always trying to paint the nice picture of a perfect home life.

Later that night, as I lay in bed sobbing, Dad came up the stairs to my room, and knelt beside me. With the smell of beer on his breath he told me that he loved me and that he was very sorry for what he had done. I said that it was all right, and that I knew how tough things were. We both wept.

I still enjoyed going to my grandparents' house. The songs, stories and music that they related to me consistently lifted me out of misery. Grandpa eventually retired from his job and he and Gran moved back to their old home, closer to water. I remember spending long periods of time with them at this place and, in looking back, it was among the happiest times in my young life. Strange as it may sound, the incidents of touching never became an issue between my grandmother and me.

Their old house is still standing; it is now close to two hundred years old. When I lived with Grandpa and Gran they had no indoor toilet, they only had an "outhouse". I had to fetch water from a well. There was not even any electricity. But it was always a wonderful place to be! Full of fond memories! And, although, by times, there was indeed drinking going on at my grandparents house, it was never the dark side of drink that we had grown so accustomed to within my father's house.

One aspect of the resilient child is that of a belief system, or a notion of the spiritual; belief in something greater than you. This I did indeed have in a very powerful way. Since I was very young I would have what could be called 'spontaneous spiritual episodes'—feelings of warmth, comfort and wellbeing, associated with visions of light. The lights would encircle me; yellow, blue, red and green. They would begin gently and would increase in intensity, and it was a good thing. Even now I can achieve this sensation, usually during meditation. Many members of my family knew I had a deep spiritual leaning. I would go to the church daily and pray, but mostly I would just sit and let the 'goodness' wash over me.

How I loved being with my grandparents; life with them was so much better than going around town trying to find my father and bringing him home after one of his many binges. However, age holds still for no man, and nothing lasts forever, good or bad.

As my grandmother lay in hospital slowly dying an awful death from a virulent form of cancer, my grandfather dropped dead while out working in his garden. Thus, within the span of seven months, my grandparents were both gone, and so too was any light in my life. I can still see my grandfather in his 'big box', but as for Gran, I cannot remember her in her 'fancy box' and I honestly do not know why—(perhaps this is something for a psychologist to explain).

After my grandparents' death I was on a slippery slope; drinking and drugs were constant, my grades were slipping, I was acting out and getting into fights at school, and at home I was becoming the 'rebel child'. At this time I had started taking boxing lessons, started to run, and started to lift weights. I quickly found that all three of these activities, were great outlets for all my frustrations and anxieties.

One day in our happy home Dad, for whatever reason, was laying a real beating on one of my younger brothers. I told Dad to stop it because at this time this particular brother was just a little boy. As might be expected, Dad immediately redirected his anger toward me, however, this time I was not going to take it without a fight. I had finally reached a point where I was not going tolerate his "bullshit" anymore. When he ran at me, I merely picked him up and threw him to the ground. From this point forward, the beatings stopped. No, I did not hurt him all that bad, but things certainly changed!

Soon after this incident, Dad went away to work, and I became sort of the 'man of the house'. Although I continued to drink a lot, and edge further and further down the "slippery slope", I also met some good people along the way who helped steer me back up the hill. In no particular order, three of these people were: a substitute teacher, a Nun (they weren't all bad), and my paternal grandfather.

The Substitute

I feel badly about it now, but I actually used to make this person cry during class, that is how badly behaved I was at the time. But, I must say, to her immense credit, she never gave up on me. One day in a quiet moment she subtly told me that I "was becoming what I was brought up to be". When I pressed her on this and its true meaning, she implied that if I didn't make an effort to change my ways that I would ultimately end up just like my father, and if this is what I wanted, then by all means keep on going. As she said, "sometimes the apple doesn't fall very far from the tree". At first this made me very angry, but I knew in my heart that she was right—I could see it for myself, I was indeed well on my way to becoming my father.

Another time she arranged a meeting with just herself and me. She told me that she realized that I had just undergone a great loss with the passing of my grandparents. She said that the way I was behaving inside of school and out was probably my way of grieving. She said that I was so much better than that, and I needed to mend my ways; and that I had the potential to do so much more with my life. She finished this conversation by telling me that she cared about me and she would do anything in her power to help me succeed. Her words have lingered.

The Nun

She was very stern and could put the 'fear of Jesus' in you with just one look. One day, as I was sitting in the principal's office after another of my lunchtime frays, Sister walked in and personally led me to her room. She went up one side of me and down the other. After exorcizing my inner demons, a look of genuine compassion came upon her face. She told me that she knew I was a lot better than this; that she knew how spiritual a person I was and that I should return to the Spirit. She knew that I was capable of great things; that I was a leader because people listened when I spoke. These words have stayed with me.

The Grandfather

After the demise of my other grandparents, whom I loved deeply, my paternal-grandfather began spending a lot more time with me, especially after my father went away to work. We spent many happy days together in the woods where he was definitely in his element. Again, I lost myself in his stories about the fairies and about his time spent fishing. I looked up to him, and in many ways I wanted to be just like him—his sharp charm and wit, his gentle manner and soft-spoken demeanor, and his great love of music. No doubt my grandfather inspired me to keep our family's tradition alive, particularly through stories and music, which is why I began learning the tunes of my ancestors on a variety of instruments.

No question, these people helped contribute to me not becoming the negative prediction; to me not becoming part of the 'dark'. They helped me to step outside of the shadowy circle and into the light. I found my way through the confusion of abuse and loss. I appreciated the fact that someone cared, and I took the Sister's sage advice and began the process of revisiting my spirit again.

My grades went up and I went from just getting by in school to graduating with distinction. I became involved in a large national organization, receiving their highest award when I left. I received a scholarship upon leaving high school, which I put to good use in the achieving of my undergraduate degree. And now I am just finishing up my second degree, and embarking on a career in education. Which is really quite ironic because of all things my father really despised, teachers were always high on the list. When all is said and done, maybe the apple can indeed fall a considerable distance from the tree!

Compassion and understanding. Forgiveness and hope. Determination, faith, and a sense of humour. These are just a few aspects of my life's journey. Resiliency, like learning, is a life-long endeavour! Someone once asked me why I was not like my father? I told him that it's just this simple, I choose not to be! You have to be kind to yourself and others, go easy, and find what works best for you, and, most importantly, use it.

> In the midst of winter,
> I finally learned
> there was in me
> an invincible summer.
>
> Albert Camus

Chapter 15: What More Could a Guy Ask For?

My resiliency story is different from many of the others I have encountered this year. I have heard stories of incredible people with unbelievable strength, who have faced unimaginable hardships and tragedy. These people are true inspirations! I find it hard to consider my story worthy enough to stand up to the likes of these, but still I write, if not for anyone else but myself. I was not abused as a child, nor did I grow up in poverty or anything else I would consider a real tragedy. In fact, my home life can probably be considered as the polar opposite. I have two loving parents and two bratty, but incredible younger brothers. We have had our times of hardship, but what family doesn't? I grew up feeling loved and protected, and yet, have still had to face many challenging obstacles to get to where I am today. My story begins on September 6th, 1983.

Everybody has a birthday, and for the most part, it's just like every other day. I mean, you get the cake and the candles, but for the average person, it's just another day on the calendar. The reason that September 6th, 1983 is significant to my story is because though it is my birthday, it also happens to be two months before the day I was actually supposed to come into the world. I was a premature baby, weighing two pounds, eleven ounces. The kicker here is that on the day I was born, there was nothing wrong with me at all. I was a tiny baby, but I was healthy for the most part. The hospital staff did their job, and then stuck me in an incubator. All was well until a few days later; a nurse took me out to hold me, and while away from the incubator and the alarm system, I stopped breathing. The nurse didn't realize until it was too late, but even then, no one had any idea about what this was going to mean later on in life.

When I was about six months old, my mother took me to the family doctor, concerned that I wasn't able to sit up on my own yet. The doctor dismissed my mother's worries, attributing the problem to the fact that I was premature and that it was normal to experience a bit of a delay with these things. When I wasn't sitting up on my own at one year old, my parents knew there was a major problem. Their worries were far from being comforted by doctors. One doctor laid me out on the floor, played around with my legs for about a minute or two, turned to my mother and stated point blankly, in an insensitive manner, "This child has brain damage!" As it turned out, I did have some brain damage. About two months after that comment from the world's most tactful physician, I was diagnosed with Cerebral Palsy.

Doctors could not ensure my parents that I was ever going to walk, or be able to fully function on my own. It was my mother who was instrumental in making sure I had the best odds. Day after day, she would perform physiotherapy on me, bending my legs one after the other in an attempt to simulate walking. I started to crawl, but I tended to use my arms to propel me forward rather than my legs. When I started to walk I made use of a walker, and when I didn't have one close by, I would stay close to the wall on tiptoes. When I was four years old, doctors thought it best to put an end to my "ballerina walk" and performed a procedure to lengthen my hamstrings and some other muscles in an attempt to keep me flat-footed. I was in casts from the top of my legs all the way down to my toes for a couple of months. The procedure worked though! Now, I can't stand on my tiptoes at all!

When I came out of my casts, I wore braces for about six months. I was introduced to my first pair of crutches not long after that, and I was well into school by then. I was constantly pulled out of class a few times a week to endure periods of physiotherapy and occupational therapy. The Cerebral Palsy had its biggest affect on my walking and balance, but my fine motor skills were also an issue. I couldn't hold a pencil properly to save my life! I remember feeling like such an outcast each time I was removed from the classroom and from my friends. I just wanted to be like everybody else. I wanted to be normal! I prayed to God at night for a chance to be like everybody else. Little did I know, God was going to intervene in a very literal way!

I walked with my crutches until I was about seven years old and was now in Grade two. The day it changed was the day I was in church with the rest of my classmates, rehearsing for my First Communion. I was in line, waiting to walk down the aisle, towards the altar, when I tripped and dropped my crutch. I used to drop them all the time, and it was all good, but on that day, well, it would be the last time I ever dropped one. The crutch hit the church floor and literally snapped in half! Now, I have my faith, but I've never been an overly religious person. That experience though, is one that is going to stick with me for the rest of my life, because if you can believe it, from that day on, I've been walking with no aids. Sure, they tried to outfit me with new canes and whatnot, but this was my chance to fulfill my dream! I was going to be just like everyone else!

I still had my dark moments. It wasn't fun being accused of sexual abuse by young teenage girls on the playground, when I would lose my balance and instinctively grab onto anything to hold myself up. It was never fun to watch my friends and classmates excel in sports and other physical activities, but I made myself known in other ways. I was quick to audition for school plays, and was a staple on my high school's student council for three years. I had carved my niche in my sheltered little world where everyone knew about me and how to deal with me, but even that couldn't last forever.

The decision to go away to school was a hard one to make. I knew I wanted nothing more than to be independent, self-sufficient, and to prove to everyone around me that I was capable of anything I set my mind to. It took my parents and I a lot of time to think and plan everything out. How would I manage cooking my own meals by a hot stove everyday? Could I manage carrying my laundry to and from my room by myself? Could I walk to and from the bus stop everyday in order to get to and from school? How would I carry my groceries, and my books? I have always had to worry about simple things like these, but now, I was placing myself in a position where I was going to be without any support from family and friends. Of course, I would make friends, or at least I hoped, but for the first little while, I'd be on my own. I'd never really been on my own before, but if I was going to do it, I was going to do it right!

I made the decision not to check in with disability services. It's not that I was ashamed to identify myself as a student with a disability, but I figured I could manage well enough without any assistance, and though it may have been a gamble, I was right. It took a while for my roommates and new friends to understand how I operated, but we got into a nice groove, eventually. Similarly, it took me a while to figure out the routines for life as a full-time university student, flying solo; but I did it! Now, I'm finishing my fifth year at University. I graduated with a Bachelor of Arts in English Studies, and just recently, my Bachelor of Education. I am going to be a teacher, and work in a position where I am able to show my students, both disabled and not, that anything is possible, no matter how many obstacles life throws at you. They can and will succeed with a little bit of hard work and love along the way. Human beings are naturally resilient, and we have the potential to be able to bounce back from anything. I know this because I am living proof of that. I am a guy with brain damage, who wasn't going to walk on his own, or be able to go too far from home, but is now able not only to walk, but to drive, and live completely independently. And the icing on the cake, I now have some serious academic credentials to go along with it! What more can a guy ask for?

Chapter 16: If My Math Teacher Could Only See Me Now

The story I am about to share with you has never been documented. The only people, until now, who are aware of my childhood and adolescent experiences are my siblings who lived through it with me, and my wife, with whom I share everything! Here goes.

I grew up in a small northern community. Growing up as the youngest in a family of ten had its advantages and disadvantages. One of the good things about this was that there was always an older brother or sister around the house to play with. One of the bad things about being the youngest of ten was that I received a lot of "hand-me-down" clothing from my older brothers. No question, being from a large family with a single income was not easy for anyone, my parents included in this number. Although we did not have many luxuries, we were always fed three times a day, had clothing on our backs, and had a roof over our heads. Actually, looking back, life in my early years was pretty darned good. I had lots of friends, played many different sports, and had loads of fun. This is not to say that living in a house with ten other children was not sometimes hectic, with disagreements and fights between siblings certainly breaking out on occasion. However, when I turned eight, things took a considerable turn for the worse when my father lost his leg due to poor blood circulation and, in understatement, my mother started to act incredibly weird.

Around this time my mother became a different person. Most troublesome was the fact that she became very argumentative, particularly with my older brothers who were starting to experiment with drugs. On a few occasions things got pretty rough. For example, this one time I remember walking back from a morning church service, where my brother and I served as altar boys. As soon as we neared the house, we could distinctly hear my mother yelling and screaming. As we got a little closer, I could clearly see my mother standing on the front porch, with one of my brother's holding a knife and threatening to kill her. Eventually the situation was calmed down without anybody getting seriously injured.

On another occasion, an older brother who was no longer living at home, decided to pay the family a visit. Clearly being under the influence of a narcotic, he entered the house yelling and screaming. By the time he had finished his rampage, he had turned the whole kitchen upside down with all of the contents of the cupboards strewn all over the floor. I remember being very scared! Another episode that I distinctly remember occurred on New Year's Day, when the very same brother, again on drugs, started to argue with two other brothers over something very small, which very quickly escalated into something very big. At one particular point, my "drugged up" older brother abruptly left the room, went downstairs and managed to wrestle a gun out of the cabinet. After a whole lot of yelling and threats, with my brother threatening suicide through the whole ordeal, eventually he was forcefully disarmed.

No question, by the time I was ten years old I had seen my fair share of violence in the house. My mother in particular would go on these rampages where, through it all, she would constantly spew venom about her past. The screaming, the yelling, it all got progressively worse. Of course being the youngest, I was forced to endure all of these irrational episodes – each and every one. I remember this one time, being forced to sit on the couch in the middle of the night, having my mother ream me out for absolutely no rational reason. But worse than that, was my mother's episodes of what could only be called paranoia, where absolutely no one was allowed to go outside, and we were virtually made prisoners within our own house. Fed up with my mother's erratic behavior, many of the older siblings left the house at their first chance- eventually leaving only two of us, (the youngest), to fend for ourselves.

My father would try his very best, often taking us away to go fishing or hunting; anything to get us out of that hostile environment. No doubt, he knew that there was something horribly wrong with my mother, and he certainly tried to get her some help. But she would have nothing to do with doctors, choosing instead to completely withdraw, basically becoming a "shut in" in her own home. Even after many urgent pleas from both my father and the rest of her family to get some serious help, my mother constantly refused any type of intervention. Although the family actually discussed having her forcefully removed and medically dealt with, my father would ultimately always back down and, at least for him, for very legitimate reasons. You see, my father's mother was placed in an asylum during his youth due to a tuberculosis outbreak, and as a direct result my father never saw his mother again. Quite naturally, because of this my father had a great reluctance in having his wife removed and placed in a treatment facility for fear that he might never see his wife again, and his children might never see their mother again.

So life trudged on as per usual. Mom continued to have episode after episode, and there were many, many days when we were not allowed to leave the house at all. I continued to serve as an altar boy though, as this always gave me a chance to escape my mother's erratic behaviour and controlling grip. Both my brother and I started noticing that mom's behaviour was episodic, as there were days when she would somewhat return to normal. Quite logically, on these infrequent occasions, we took every opportunity to get out of the house, even by volunteering to do all kinds of yard work throughout the neighbourhood. Actually, we discovered that being involved in yard work was one thing that our mother consistently approved of. Consequently, we quickly learned that even when mom was going through a particularly bad patch, yard work was the one thing that could get us out of the house irrespective of her moods. In making this situation work for us in a most beneficial way, I discovered that if you dialed a certain number on the telephone you could make it ring back to your phone right away. Soon enough, we were using this technique to our advantage. I would make the telephone ring, then I would fake like I was answering the phone, always stating to my mother that someone on the other end of the phone desperately needed our assistance. This worked very well for us, as it consistently got us out of the house, even on the bad days. Mom also allowed me to take on a paper route at this time, which got me out of the house as well.

Without exception, every one of my siblings left home as soon as they reached eighteen years of age. This proved to be true with my closest sibling, my brother, as he left the madness as soon as he reached his eighteenth year. My brother and I got along extremely well together, but I could not blame him for departing the house and escaping my mother's wrath as soon as he could. Unfortunately though, this left me at home all by myself. I was thirteen years old at the time, and the only child of ten left in a house with a mother who was completely "flipped out".

Although it was very difficult without my brother, I continued to deliver newspapers and to do yard work throughout the neighbourhood. As I look back, I think it enabled me to escape all the torment and unpredictability, at least for a time. But my mother became increasingly more erratic and controlling, and soon she reached a point where she would not allow me to do anything at all.

Of course, problems in the home were eventually reflected in the school. In fact, in grade seven, with my brother now gone, my behaviour in school started to change quite dramatically. Phone calls from the principal's office were very common, and my grades started to slip, and slip quite dramatically (from the high seventies to the low sixties). I also remember being terribly uncooperative with teachers, and constantly acting out and getting into trouble in the schoolyard.

It's hard for me to now rationalize this. Going to school was my sanctuary, my only real way of truly escaping the madness of my home life, and yet, here I was screwing up profoundly. Ultimately, in this one tumultuous year, I managed to barely pass four courses out of eight, this being my first formal year of high school. To put this into some type of a perspective, I remember receiving a low of 23% in Math, and a high of 62% in one of my "shop" classes. In fact, I distinctly remember my math teacher being so upset with me and my effort that he actually told me to my face "that I'd probably never amount to anything in life".

Things started to spiral downward from this point forward, and by the time I was fourteen I started taking drugs and drinking. Basically, at fourteen years of age, all of the money that I earned from doing yard work was overwhelmingly spent on drugs and alcohol. To be completely honest though, during this period there was also the odd occasion when I was allowed to go to a hockey game, attend a school dance, or go to a house party to socialize with my friends. Hence, I remember some good times too.

However, with very little exception, my mother's torture continued throughout all of my high school years, and only really stopped after my graduation and me leaving home – for good. (Yes, after five long years, and considerable amounts of struggle, I still managed to graduate from high school). Of course, by this time I was now eighteen years of age, and like all my siblings who went before me, I couldn't wait to get out. My first stop was on a farm, where I got my first full time job. Finally I was truly free! I must say it took me an awfully long time before I went back to visit, because I really resented my mother. In essence, I think I needed some time to heal. Looking back, I can now honestly say that I hold no real anger or hatred toward my mother or any of my siblings for the way I was treated when I was growing up. I think I've learned to accept it, and certainly live with it.

As time went on I continued to work very hard at anything that I did, always managing to find work. In that respect, I have always believed that it's 100% or nothing. No question, my strong work ethic, which was basically established in trying to escape my mother's house, has carried over from adolescence into adulthood. Always in the back of mind, at least in those first years after I left home, was the thought that if I'm not able to look after myself, I might be forced into moving back home with my mother, something that made me absolutely shudder every time that I thought about it.

I think because of my early experiences, I also developed somewhat of an altruistic personality, prepared to give everyone the "benefit of a doubt". I know firsthand that good can come from bad. I have worked hard at becoming a caring individual, who tries very hard to relate to anyone or anything. I now have a wonderful wife and two great kids, all of whom I love very much. In the intervening years I have worked very hard at educating myself, culminating in finally becoming a teacher. Everyone tells me that I should be proud of my accomplishments, but I still have a very difficult time patting myself on the back.

As I take a reflective look back, I can clearly see how things could have turned out very differently for me. I realize that over the years I certainly learned to adapt to many different situations. For example, I managed to be creative by finding ways to escape from my dysfunctional household, by taking odd jobs and by using the telephone ringing technique to my distinct advantage. I also climbed out of my bedroom window on the odd occasion, just to find some peace. I discovered early on that by removing myself completely from the house allowed me, at least for a time, to feel like a normal child living in a normal house. It seemed to give me some desperately needed freedom. It served to recharge me.

Also, I have to give my brother some credit, as he and I were inseparable for twelve years. No doubt we saw each other through some very challenging times. We constantly encouraged each other, and reassured each other that nothing lasts forever; that someday we'd both get through it all. As well, for the times that I really felt as though I was imprisoned in the house all alone, my dog was an invaluable inspiration to me as he was my only true friend for the longest stretches of time, particularly after my brother left home. I remember crying and feeling extremely sad and my dog would always faithfully come over to console me, always giving me his paw and licking me on the face all in the hopes that it would make me feel better - and it did.

My father also tried his best, and his efforts on my behalf should not go unnoticed. Unquestionably, he gave me a lot of strength, providing me with many words of wisdom and always encouraging me to pursue my dreams. He always reinforced the idea of getting an education, an idea that even in the worst of times never completely abandoned me.

Without question though, the most important person in my life for many years now has been my wife. She consistently has shown me a great deal of love and care. She has always been there for me, even in the most difficult of moments. She has taught me many things in life, however, most importantly, she has taught me just to be myself. That it's good enough!

Chapter 17: Here's to a Better Life!

When I think back to my childhood, all I can remember thinking is, "Why can't my life be normal?" All I ever wanted was to have two parents that loved me more than they loved themselves; but this I quickly learned was never going to happen. After thinking long and hard about my very early years, and how I've managed to come this far, in reflection, there appear to be many things in my life that have served to counter the extreme negativity of its early beginnings. This writing endeavour has forced me to take out some of the pages from my memory, and made me realize how fortunate I was to be able to have many examples in my life of those who know what it means to do the right thing, or be responsible for another person. All of this deep contemplation has made me wonder if my story was even compelling enough to share, or if I even fit into this category generally referred to as resiliency.

From the time I was able to think about things, I have forever felt as though I didn't belong. For as much as I have overcome, I will always remember the overwhelming despair and anger that I felt as a very young girl. Going back to this place, and these feelings, has now made me realize that my story is in fact valid enough to be heard and certainly retold. Taking time to reflect on what it was that had gotten me this far, has allowed me to realize that my parents may have been of those statistics, which accurately predicted that they would never rise beyond a certain point; that they had to accept the hand they were dealt. They let their hopelessness overcome their rational thoughts, and for this, I, their child, was left to suffer. It is hard to imagine how people can do things to a person, knowing full well the tremendous damage they are causing in the process. Yet somewhere along the way, I knew that I must find that strength to carry on, so that I could break the vicious trail that was being blazed by my parents.

I think I remember the despair setting in and not leaving when I was about eight years old. Prior to this period, when my parents were together, I cannot recall all that much. I always wondered why? Yet, somewhere down deep, I'm truly afraid of the reasons why I have shut out all of those early memories. However, I do remember the beginning of my mother's cruelty to me. It all started when she picked me up from school one day and we drove to a store to get her some cigarettes. As we pulled up to the store, she casually says before she gets out of the car, "Yeah, your dad moved out, and we're breaking up". Then she goes in and gets her cigarettes and that was that! I couldn't have known it then, but that very moment would signal the start to a life of lonely desperation for me. Now, I know that loneliness may seem like a feeling that we all get over, but I can honestly say that this feeling has almost crippled me at times, and it follows me now wherever I go. Some days it takes all my strength just to ensure that it doesn't break through the "I got it together attitude", which I have created for the rest of the world to see.

The next few years of my life are a giant blur. Once my dad was gone, I didn't see him much for quite some time. Then my mom moved this boyfriend in, who, of course, was a complete "asshole". He would prove to be one person that to this very day, I despise with every ounce of my soul. I know that this is wrong to do, but my heart actually breaks all over again, each and every time I think about him. His moving in with my mother would begin a period in my life that I now refer to as the "babysitters" and "drinking" period.

Even now as a grown-up, I remember those babysitters from that time more than I actually remember my mom or dad. Don't get me wrong, some of the sitters were ok, no molestation or anything, but this would be the beginning of the decay of my self worth and the creation of a sad, lonely little girl. I remember getting up in the morning with absolutely no one being around, so I would sit completely alone. I would never dare wake my mother up because I knew this would set off a screaming, belittling rant, something I tried very hard to avoid at all possible costs. I remember constantly coming home from school only to find nobody there. Again, I would sit all alone waiting. And the weekends were no better, as my mother would constantly leave me with whomever she could find. It was as if I didn't even exist or really matter to her. She didn't even go out of her way to find adequate care for me when she left. I felt so alone!

From this period, I also remember the constant drunken fights between my mom and her new boyfriend. I remember hiding in my bedroom, wanting to completely disappear. But what I remember most of all from this particular period, is the move. This seemed to be the final straw as it absolutely broke my heart. It meant that the only stable place in my life at this time, my school, was also taken away from me as well. No matter what was going on at home, school was a safe haven for me. There I could be a completely different person. It provided me with an escape from my chaotic life. At that particular time, none of my friends had any idea how awful my home life really was, so I felt so very free at school. I felt like everyone cared for me there and, as a result, I did my very best to excel and please everyone. For me, through this particular period, I can't say it was just one teacher, but the whole place served to daily rescue me from all my loneliness and despair.

From here we moved to another place where my mom's new boyfriend was actually from. In looking back, this decision was such a "downer" for me. I was so angry at her for making such a selfish decision. Once there, of course I had to start at a new school and I remember this being very difficult for me. Eventually though, I adapted, and at least on the school front, things got a whole lot better for me. However, on the home front, life very quickly returned to normal - meaning more drinking, more fighting, and many more babysitters.

At the new place, at night, I remember being so scared wondering who was in my house, and if they were going to come into my bedroom and hurt me. The babysitters, who were always relatives of my mother's boyfriend, always appeared very scary to me. I would hear them partying and blasting music, and even though I would get mad because I really wanted to sleep, I would never dare say anything to them because I was really too terrified to do anything about it. Now that I am grown up, and I think back to this period, I now realize just how vulnerable I was as a young child, and it frightens me right to my very core.

My motto very early in life became one of just coping with what happens and moving on, so that is what I always did. We must have lived in this particular spot for less than a year, because before I knew it I was back at my old school. I can still remember walking back into my class and seeing the looks on everyone's faces. It felt so great! Although it's very hard for me to place all of these moments into their proper sequence at this particular time in my life, what I do know is that while my mother went back to live with my dad at this time, I was sent to live with my Grandma and Grandpa. Quite naturally, for the longest while I deeply resented my parents for sending me away, as I felt nothing more than a cast off. However, in now looking back at the situation, I must admit that it was the best thing that could have ever happened to me. In the end, they ended up being the happiest days of my life.

My grandparents were so wonderful to me. They enrolled me in sports and came to every one of my games. They made me breakfast every morning, and said goodnight at the end of each day. They cared if I was late for school, and showed real enthusiasm for my outstanding achievements. They taught me that there is more to a person than what you actually see, and that life is about being strong and working your way through the hardest of times. They taught me that life was more than just a fashion show. I remember so much of what they personally did for me, and constantly wonder how differently things might have turned out without their involvement in my life at this very particular time. My grandmother, in particular, was a real good person, who set a very good example for me. She was a woman who would go miles out of her way to do something good for someone, just because it was the right thing to do. She truly inspired me, and always gave me hope. Although my grandfather was always very good to me, apparently this wasn't always the case and perhaps explains why my mother turned out the way she did. Apparently my beloved Grandpa had his own problems with alcohol when his children were young, and this of course went on to affect some of them. Although several of the children grew up to be honest, hard-working and respectable people, two, one of which was my mother, turned out to be raging alcoholics themselves. But to me, my grandfather was always the best!

Anyway, at the end of grade six, sadness struck again as my grandfather's two brothers died within months of each other and this was really hard on the entire family. I remember being there with him, and it was dreadful to watch. But what I remember most of all about this time is that my mother suddenly decided it might be nice to have me around again; that it might be a perfect time for me to rejoin my real family. Although I thought it a bit weird, even a bit shady that she was making such a concerted effort to have me rejoin her, my life was once again completely disrupted, and I was shifted to where she wanted me to be (with her again). However, no sooner had I rejoined her, than the true motivations behind her actions became perfectly clear to me. By this time she'd had another baby, and there was another on the way. It seemed to me, that she only took me back because she wanted me to help her mind her kids. I was eleven years old at the time and I was about to become a full time babysitter.

Shortly thereafter, my grandfather passed away, and I was completely devastated. He meant the world to me. In essence, he was the only father that I had ever known. After he was gone, I felt so empty, so sad, and so all alone – again! Nothing was the same for me anymore. Now when I rode my bike to my soccer games, or to my baseball games, no one else ever came.

Living with my mother ended up being just more of the same. Nothing had changed! However, this time I was a little older, and although she was rarely around, when I did get glimpses of her true self, I could truly see just how hateful and self-centred she really was.

I don't remember my mom ever working when I was growing up. Yet, I do remember that she still liked to go out and get drunk, and that she always had a lot of boyfriend's. However, through it all, the same old "asshole" from my earlier years would always periodically come back into the picture. In fact, he ended up being the father to one of the two younger siblings referred to directly above. When this guy was around my mother constantly got the shit beaten out of her. When they would get together it would always be so loud; lots of smashing and screaming; lots of broken glass, and lots of blood on the floor. When they were fighting, sometimes I would just try to lie quietly in my bed and pray that they didn't wake up the two younger ones. I quickly came to realize that when these fights were underway, you never got up and said anything to either one of them because that would be it for you. The times when I actually did get up, I would try and sneak into the girls' room to make sure they didn't say anything and, of course, to console them.

No question, I was asked to rejoin my mother because she wanted a babysitter. Which, probably worked out better for the girls because in the end I probably took better care of them anyway. From this point forward, I was forced to grow up real fast because I was clearly the most responsible person in the house. Although the late night fighting continued, and the constant partying with strangers continued, it was the constant lack of money that proved to be the worse thing of all. I always envied the other kids for what they had. I really hated being the poor kid who couldn't afford new clothes or even get a decent birthday gift. As well, we were constantly having our heat or phone cut off. The phone, for me, was always the most embarrassing thing to have cut off though. If that happened then everyone around you knew that you were the poor kid. Through this period, I absolutely hated my life! One year, my mother even forgot to put the Santa gifts out because she was too drunk to do it. Although outside of my house I desperately wanted people to think I had a normal life, it was anything but normal – and getting worse by the day.

Alcoholism is something that many people have to contend with. A happy drunk is one thing, however, this was not my mother. When my mother drank she was downright mean and miserable. Always criticizing, always blaming! Always yelling, always screaming! And you learned very quickly in life never to stand up to her or challenge her, or you'd sure live to regret it. Oh I hated her then! As I look back, she was so emotionally abusive. No matter what I did for her, no matter how good I did at school, it never really mattered.

I have so many weird and hurtful memories emanating from the years spent living under her roof that I don't even know where to start. I can picture her coming home some nights all drunk and bloody because she had gotten into an altercation down at the local bar. I can hear her having relations with a man so loud that the whole house would be wakened up in the middle of the night. I can see her lying in bed, while the children constantly fended for themselves. In fact, I can remember several weekends when she didn't bother coming home at all. It was a good thing for my sisters that I learned about cooking while living with my grandparents because I always managed to feed them.

Lucky for me, at this time I'd also managed to develop some very close friendships, and some of these friends were very good to me. They could see what I was going through, and some of them did their best to help out. For example, when they knew my mom was likely gone for the weekend, some would start staying with me to keep me company and assist with the two younger girls. Through all of these rough times, where my two sisters were specifically concerned, I tried my very best to do right by them. I always wanted them to know that I loved them with all my heart.

In my early teens, my mother finally made a very wise decision on behalf her family. She moved closer to my school, which meant that I no longer had to take a bus because we now lived within district. However, to suggest that my mother did it for the good of the entire family would be far too generous. It was because the "asshole" she constantly hooked up with was finally forced out of the picture. After all of the domestic assault charges filed against him, I guess he finally got the message.

One of the questions that may arise in the reading this story is why did I never try to do anything about it? Well, on one occasion I actually did. Once, I got so fed up that I actually said something about our family's situation to a professional that had been invited to the school to talk about neglect, abuse, and domestic violence. When my mother found out, she went up one side of me and down the other, basically telling me to "keep my mouth shut next time; and just mind your own business".

Although this event signaled the start of a string of visits from the Children's Aid Society, I quickly discovered that whether or not I moved forward or worked within the system left my family with very few really good options. The best case scenario, at least the way I viewed it at the time, would be that my mother would be forced out of the family, with the three children left together to be raised within a more stable family arrangement, at least for awhile. When I figured out that this was unlikely to happen, I started to backtrack and lie to them. I made sure to tell them a good story, hoping they would eventually go away, and they did. In the end, I decided under no circumstances would I ever allow myself to be separated from my sisters!

For the next year or so, I tried really hard to keep it all together. Life pretty much went on as usual, minus the nightly brawls. Now mom just came home drunk and passed out. I still got the girls up in the morning and made their lunches (with whatever was there to make). I then would faithfully walk them to school. I continued to be an excellent student; was on all the sports teams, and was even fairly popular amongst my peers. However, none of this mattered a bit to my mother. Instead, I had to take pride in myself. I quietly celebrated my own accomplishments. I started to become very focused. When other girls were talking about fairy tales and happy endings, I was dreaming about finding a career that would pay me enough money that I would never have to worry about being poor again. I must say, throughout my most challenging years, my teachers were always very supportive, implying that I was indeed very special and would certainly amount to something - one day. Even in the toughest of times, this knowledge gave me incredible strength, and something to hold on to.

However, even at school not everything was perfect for me at this time, because my youngest sister was becoming a real handful. No matter what the teachers did to calm her, they could not. She was so aggressive and wild. I laugh thinking about it now, but it sure wasn't funny at the time. She became a little holy terror in her junior kindergarten class. By now I was in grade eight, and when she wasn't just being sent home or if they couldn't get a hold of my mother or calm her down themselves, they would call me down to the office to do it for them. All my sister ever really needed was for someone to talk to her like a real person and show her a little kindness, as there were not too many people in her immediate life who were prepared to do that much for her.

The next year, my grade nine year, I took care of the girls the best that I could. However, I was becoming more angry and resentful of my mother. Then on top of everything else, my mom links up with another new man, one who would become her future husband. And just like before, this future husband brought with him the typical profile that we as a family were very much accustomed to. However, this new man also had a son, who proved to be quite a problem for me because he was just one year older, and definitely didn't have his head quite screwed on right. As it turned out, he proved to have a very negative influence on me. He would come to introduce me to alcohol, drugs, and the opposite sex.

Eventually, in my grade nine year, my first high-school year, the two families combined and we all moved in together. We actually moved closer to my new high school. By this time my mother was completely detached from my life, so I was pretty much left on my own. I could tell her whatever I wanted about where I was or where I was going, and she could care less. She never checked up on me at all. So, taking advantage of this indifference, I stayed away from the house and my mother as much as I could. I must say, I felt a great deal of guilt at the time because I was basically staying away from my sisters as well. However, even though I wasn't around as much, I always ensured that they had a lunch, as I could buy them one at the high school and personally walk it over to them at their school on my lunch break.

It was during grade nine that I began a secret relationship with a boy, of course hiding it completely from my mom. I naively came to believe that finally someone really loved me. Of course, it quickly evolved into just being about ultimate control. We formally dated for about nine months, until it became just too bizarre. He started to stalk me, sleeping outside my house, threatening to kill himself if I kept ignoring him, and he would constantly bang his head off walls if he didn't get his own way. I could go on and on but I won't. Eventually, I realized that he was a nut job and found a way to get him out of my life. I would soon realize however, that the time spent with this boy, was about to change my life far more than I could have ever expected.

About a month later I discovered that I was pregnant. I thought to myself that this was just perfect! How could I do something so stupid? I began to think about how all my dreams were now completely crushed. What would my family say, my friends, my grandma? My world was crashing in all around me. I didn't know what to do and I didn't know whom to tell, so I did neither. The next few months of my life will show you exactly how much the people in it noticed me. It took exactly seven months for my mom to actually confront me about what was going on. Can you believe it? Anyway, I still managed to finish grade nine on the school's honour roll, spend the summer uncomfortably pregnant, and have a baby just after my fifteenth birthday (in September).

After a million conversations in which my parents proceeded to tell me how disappointed they were in me, they finally, at some point, decided to leave me alone. I really resented how rapid they were in playing the disappointment card, when they didn't so much as give a damn about me, or anything that had gone on in my life before the pregnancy. They were able to very conveniently forget about all of the good things that I'd managed to accomplish in the previous fourteen years, and under sometimes horrible circumstances, just because of one impulsive decision.

Before they had even gotten used to the idea of me being pregnant, I had the baby—prematurely, at eight months. She turned out to be a healthy baby girl. I think that I realized long before she was born, that I was definitely going to give her a better life than the one I had had. I knew that I had to do much better, for both our sakes. It's not to say that I wasn't scared, but not because I didn't think that I could be an excellent mother, because I knew that I could. I'd help raise my two sisters, and thought I'd done a reasonably good job in doing it. No, at the time, I was actually more scared of what people were going to say about me in general, and about my situation. I didn't want to hear it! I dreaded having to hear it! To this very day, when the topic of teen pregnancy comes up my stomach actually churns. It is indeed a touchy subject for me for sure. It's hard being viewed as a stereotype.

I tried living with my mother for the first year after my daughter was born and, as might be expected, this was not a very positive experience at all. I stayed home for the first semester because the baby was just born. I had nowhere else to go. Fortunately, I managed to take advantage of a number of good programs in the community for young mothers. When I think back, although it has been almost ten years, I wonder how I managed to get through it all. I was so young and had to give up an awful lot. It is so hard being a young parent. You are forced to stare into the judgmental eyes of the public. It feels like no matter how good you are, no one thinks of you that way because you're just a kid yourself!

I suspect, that if it hadn't been for a few concerned and very helpful community outreach groups, I might not have been so successful in the first few years immediately after my daughter's birth. They helped me get a daycare placement for her, and helped me get a subsidy so that I could afford to pay for it. It was an in-home daycare and it was located on the way to my high school. I ultimately formally returned to high school during the second semester of my grade ten year. I was provided social assistance, which allowed me to care for my daughter and finish high school. They arranged for me to take parenting classes, cooking classes, and provided passes for public transportation. All of this help, along with family support payments, allowed me to not only graduate high school, but also to do it at the same time as all my friends and peers.

I moved out of my mother's house when I was sixteen. In between this period, I tried living with both parents, but both situations were less than ideal. I ended up getting my own apartment right next to the high school, yet, still very close to my daughter's daycare, so things ended up working out pretty well for me. I think that keeping busy, having goals, and keeping love and positive family members in my life, has helped to create a positive environment for my daughter to grow up in. I know the value of taking advantage of those people in your life that want to help you. Above all else, I wanted to make a better life for my daughter and myself; certainly far better than the one I had as a child.

Today life is not perfect, but life is never that way. I have learned to just work hard and do good things for people, knowing that things will eventually work out. I have been able to obtain two university degrees now, and plan on being an excellent teacher who can make some kind of difference in the lives of my students. I know better than most that making a difference, no matter how small, can have such a huge impact on an individual's life.

My two younger sisters have continued to mean so much to me. They are like my own daughters too. I try my best to give them what they need, and always give them my unconditional love. My daughter will be nine this year, and is the love of my life. I truly believe that she was sent to save me from myself.

Chapter 18: Twenty-nine Years Later

I grew up in a sheltered rural household with my two parents and three siblings. My mother was a housewife and my father had a good job as a certified tradesman. During my first year of high school our lives changed forever. My very young mother became very ill. The details of my mother's illness were hidden from my siblings and myself for reasons I'll never fully understand. It was on a Monday when my mother finally succumbed to a very slow dying process due to a virulent form of cancer. Almost immediately, relatives came in and removed my mother's belongings and pictures. We carried on in silence rarely mentioning her name, and never expressing our deep sense of sorrow related to her passing. I suspect this was my dad's way of dealing with his personal suffering, as he too had just lost the love of his life. He was now the only parent to 13, 14 (me), 16 and 17 year old children. Nine months later he began to date a younger woman, and within 6 weeks they got married. Of course, she immediately moved into my mother's space. Very expeditiously, my dad had found us another caregiver.

I am telling you my story 29 years after my mother's death. My oldest sister was 17 at the time, and sadly she was generally put in charge of all her siblings. This became quite a challenge for my sister because of her unpredictable personality. Later in life she was diagnosed with depression and obsessive-compulsive disorder.

My older brother Larry had a profound learning disability, and all of his school success, up until my mother's death, was directly related to my mother's dogged determination. However, his successful high school days abruptly ended with our mother's passing. From that time forward, his life definitely took a turn for the worse, resulting in him being kicked out of the house before his 18th birthday. Among many of the issues, my brother had a very hard time getting along with my father and his new wife. He eventually ended up living in a U-Haul trailer in a parking lot. To this day I do not know why our relatives or neighbours did not try to help Larry. Returning to high school was out of the question. Looking back, I distinctly remember my brother saying he would never return to high school because the teachers there would make him read out loud in front of the class and this embarrassed him tremendously. But to his immense credit, he somehow managed to struggle through and obtain a mechanics license, through some type of an apprenticeship program. I would spend time reading to him the mechanics manual since he had such trouble reading. Over the years, although he still has some minor problems like the rest of us, Larry has managed to do very well in life, owning a fair bit of real estate and his own small business.

Ted, my younger brother, never did find out that his mother was terminally ill until after she died. He feels that he never got to say goodbye. He did not experience the struggles that the rest of us did with our stepmother. He left home right after high school, went back to college and has a successful career. He is now married with four boys; the third son suffers from Pervasive Development Disorder. Ted suffers from chronic mild depression himself.

As referred to above, I was a very young teenager when my mom died. In hindsight, I think it was incredibly damaging that we, as kids, were never invited to discuss our mother, particularly her death, with anyone. I kind of understand that my father was deeply hurt, and he was worried about raising us in my mother's absence. As a result, he would swing back and forth from being strict and then not strict when it came to our freedom.

Within a year of my mother's death, my stepmother Belinda moved into my mother's bedroom and took over my mother's house. Probably unknown to her at the time, it was the little things that she did when she first arrived that absolutely broke my heart because it consistently reminded me that I no longer had a mother. For example, she moved the pots out of the cupboard that my mother always used for pots. She put sheers up for curtains, and my mother never liked sheers.

To be quite honest, almost from the outset Belinda and I did not get along. I think we both competed for my father's affection and attention. Out of all the children, I think I posed the biggest threat to her security with my father. Consequently, Belinda and I were always constantly verbally going at one another, with my father almost always unfailingly taking Belinda's side. On these occasions despite my protestations, he would always tell me that it was a man's duty to always side with the wife over the child, irrespective of whether the child was right or wrong. Needless to say, this angered me greatly and seemed to intensify my sadness due to the loss of my mom. After a year of marriage, my dad and Belinda had a baby of their own and decided to move the family further north. This meant that in the span of a little over two years my siblings and I had lost our mother, got a new stepmother and baby brother, and we were completely dislocated from our childhood home, friends, and school.

To quickly summarize, I spent my last two years of high school in a completely new environment. To say it was not the happiest of times would be to dramatically understate the case. Next, I left for college, footing the entire bill myself. Each summer I would return home to work at my 60 hour a week job to pay for the next year of school; forced for financial reasons to endure a summer full of chaos and turmoil. After my final year of college, I finally broke away to live completely on my own. During these years, my dad and Belinda went on to have two more children together, all of whom I grew to love with all of my heart.

After working for a few years I met a boy and together we bought a house on a lake. We eventually got married and currently have three children. Life should be great, but thoughts of my mother sometimes overwhelm me. I think of her often. I suspect it's one of the reasons I sometimes struggle at effectively mothering my own children. I occasionally revert, at least in my mind, back to the time when I was a young girl struggling with the death of her mother. In these moments, I find it is me that wishes to be nurtured. As I now reflect as an adult, I think I emotionally lost both my parents on that Monday 29 years ago.

My first child, a boy, was born a month premature, and although I was terrified of my new found responsibility, I managed not too badly. Two years later my second son was born; later to be diagnosed with an identifiable "special" need. At some point along the way I "hit a wall", probably being completely overcome with the realization that my second child might never have a totally normal life due to his exceptionality. Totally exhausted, frustrated, lonely, and very emotional, it was at this point that I decided to seek out some professional help, where it was clinically determined that I was suffering from Post Traumatic Stress Disorder (linked directly to the early death of my mother). It was in the early stages of being treated for PTSD that I also found out I was pregnant for the third time. Needless to say, given everything that was going on in my life, it was not something that I wanted to hear!

With the third pregnancy I became absolutely obsessed with the idea that it had to be a girl this time. Several therapy sessions later, I finally broke down and openly wept when it was brought to my attention that I probably wanted a girl so badly to fill the mother-daughter relationship that I so desperately longed for myself. Although initially difficult to think about, once I worked my way through a series of mostly melancholic emotions, it suddenly hit me like a bolt of lightening, and waves of relief immediately swept over me. I had so many pent up emotions connected to my mother's death, that once released, the healing could begin. Nineteen months after my second son was born, I gave birth to a beautiful baby girl.

In total I spent seven years at home having and raising my children. One day while taking my three children, ages 2, 4, and 6 to Guelph, I took the wrong highway cut off and I ended up going into Milton. I decided that since I was close to my mother's cemetery, I would take my children to see her for the first time. I had a hard time finding the tombstone since I had only visited her plot a few times previous. After 15 minutes of searching and trying to get the kids to stay off of the tombstones, I finally gave up and headed back to the car. As I was just about back to the car I happened to look down and there, lo and behold, was my mother's gravestone. Since my mother's visit was in no way planned, I didn't bring flowers, but I did have a bag of carrots in the car that I was taking to relatives. I instructed my children to place carrots on my mom's grave because they are pretty and also because small animals could eat them. As we did this, I distinctly remember a cool breeze picking up. I stood there completely transfixed, as the breeze seemed to wash through my whole body. It was the weirdest feeling! At that moment it became clear to me that my mother was at ground level, that my children were at varying heights, none higher than my waist, and that I was the tallest. This signified to me that I had to take the place of my mother; that I was no longer the 14 year old girl in need of being nurtured, but that I was the mother of three children and that it was time for me to nurture them. I have absolutely no doubt that it was on this particular day and at this particular moment that I was finally emotionally released from everything that was holding me back.

A year later I decided that for my own self-esteem that I wanted to return to the workforce, and I did. That career lasted 6 years. It was followed by several years of university ultimately resulting in me obtaining my teaching degree. During my Bachelor of Education year, I took the opportunity to go oversees to Asia for a month and teach. This trip was fantastic. Although I missed my family greatly, it was the first time in a very long time that I was able to completely relax and not worry about anybody or anything but myself.

In conclusion, I cannot figure out whom I owe my resilience to. My mother must have done a good job raising me for the short time we had together because I feel that she gave me the skills to survive. So, here's to you, mom!

Chapter 19: Thanks for Listening

One of many children, not rich, not completely poor. Nice life, finished high school, went to college, married college sweetheart, moved to northern part of province, got pregnant, had a baby, husband leaves for the love of his life that he forgot to tell his wife about. Move back home, single, with a baby, live alone 10 years, marry old friend, decide after ten years and two more children that it's not working out, tell husband we need a divorce, and decide to become a teacher (always wanted to). And here my story starts.

When I told my second husband that I wanted a divorce, I had no money, not a dime. We had invested all our savings in a small business and cash was very tight. As the marriage unraveled, I could not find money to even hire a lawyer. We owned our house and he wouldn't move out of it. I was strongly advised not to move out of the house, as my husband might sell it right from under me and keep all the money, so I decided to stay put. As a result, I endured absolute hell for the next year and a half, until the house was ultimately sold. Even then, I had to take my husband to court to force him to put the house up for sale, and six months later to have the price lowered enough so that it would finally sell. The whole time that we lived together through this ordeal, I was stalked, threatened physically, constantly intimidated, and mentally abused on almost an hourly basis.

The day the sale of the house went through, I moved my furniture to a townhouse that I had procured the month before the final sale. The proceeds from the house went into the business to pay off a loan we had with the bank. Originally, when I told my husband I wanted a divorce, I knew I would be striking out on my own and decided to go back to university to finish my undergraduate degree (having only one year completed previous to this time).

Before we sold the house my husband kept telling me that he wanted to be around the kids every day, so naturally when we went to our respective houses after the split, I assumed he would take the kids often. This, I thought, would have certainly made my life more manageable as a fully committed university student. However, probably because he saw it as something that might be helping me out, he decided that he only wanted the kids every second weekend. Needless to say, trying to balance going back to school, along with raising three kids proved to be an overwhelming challenge. At the time, I had a 20-year-old child with "special needs", a 10-year-old girl, and an 8-year-old boy. On top of this, my mother had just been informed that she had cancer. I distinctly remember hitting a wall here, and it was during this specific period that I came close to having a complete "melt-down". Luckily, I made the wise decision to go and see a university counselor, who put my life somewhat back on solid footing.

Long story short, with the incredible support of the university counselor, I not only managed to get through my undergraduate degree and raise a family, but I also did well enough to get accepted into another degree program; namely a Bachelor of Education or teacher training program. Although there were some very tense moments leading up to the start of my Bachelor of Education year in making sure that I had all the demanded prerequisite courses fully accounted for, (having to pick up a course from another university through distance education), I remember it being an incredibly proud time in my life; a feeling of great accomplishment!

One thing I forgot to mention, and it certainly needs to be, was that the Bachelor of Education was a full time program, and it was located over a one hour drive (one way) from where we lived, hence, I was going to need lots of help with daycare if I was to get through this very busy year and succeed. Fortunately, many people jumped in to help in this regard, including a very special coach who was very good in working with my oldest "special needs" child, but also not excluding the wonderful help and support of extended family and friends, who, without fail, agreed to pitch in whenever and wherever they could!

So off to school I went, full time, leaving my kids who missed me terribly, blamed me for everything wrong in their lives, argued with me when I came home in the evening after a long day because they were angry that I had left them in the first place, and yet, I managed to trudge on. I managed, somehow, to keep moving forward. I also need to mention that the two hour journey that I embarked on every day to attend school was done in my sister-in-law's car, because my husband got our vehicle in the settlement. Not that it would have been any help anyway because it was a piece of junk that would have required a lot of money, which I didn't have, to make it road worthy for the daily migrations.

I must say that when I first started my Bachelor of Education year, panic set in almost immediately, at least every time I entered a classroom. In the early days I felt utterly inadequate. I remember great moments of doubt, feeling completely overwhelmed, questioning whether or not I would be able to survive an entire year. And then, to top things off, I discovered at Christmas time that my dad had contracted a serious lung disease (another setback). As the year progressed it wasn't just the concerns of being a fulltime university student, raising a family, and worrying about sick elderly parents that preoccupied me, I was also in an on-going battle trying to get child support from my husband. Eventually I had to go to court to accomplish that as well.

In all actuality, my story really started decades ago as a young girl; somewhat beaten down within the family, (always told she was stupid, and consistently browbeaten by her siblings). I went through elementary school and high school with no confidence until my parents sent me away to a camp as a young teenager. From that time forward, the first week of each summer offered me solitary space, different people that didn't know me, peace among the trees, time for introspection, and plenty to do as this camp was a work camp. Most importantly, while there I met one lady that I really respected and grew to love. She was selfless, giving and fair in everything she did, or I observed her do. She had a common sense sort of attitude about life, didn't get riled up easily, and absolutely cared about what other people thought.

I have grown to realize that all people can offer us something, and I take away from each person I meet the things I want to carry with me into the future. It has taken me a long time to realize that teaching was something I had done all my life, and that now I wanted to make it my career – something that I will do for the duration of my working life. For several years now I have been involved with a large national organization that deals exclusively with people with profound intellectual deficits, and while I have been off this year attending to my full time studies, I have missed both the positive influence of the organization, and all of the people associated with it. Of particular significance, I have discovered that the kids there help sustain me, stabilize me, and ground me in their delight of life. When my "exceptional" daughter was growing up I learned incredible patience, but more importantly I came to understand the crippling heartache of a mother; the kind you have when you realize that your daughter will never have a normal life like everyone else around her. But somewhere along the way, I also came to make piece with my own life. I now have two degrees, one of them certifying me to teach, and I'm about to embark on a career in education. It's been one of the most challenging years in my life, and yet, one of the most rewarding. I've done it! In fact, as I write this piece, I'm currently adding more to the mix, as I'm still making the long drive everyday to university to add to my teaching qualifications, this time in Special Education. Thus, I will not only be a teacher, I will be a "special" education teacher.

As I reflect and piece together this introspective piece, I marvel each morning as I leave my house. The world is truly beautiful. I have finally reached a state of contentment. Instead of making the one hour drive every morning with feelings of tremendous anxiety welling up from deep inside me the closer I got to the university, as was the case when I first began this journey, I now make the daily drive marveling at the scenery, the slow pace of nature, and how far I've truly travelled as a person. In essence, as the year progressed, the physical journey to and from my home each and every day to university became a spiritual one. As I come out the back end of this process, I now believe fully in myself, and am truly thankful for all the people that continue to believe in me and support me unfailingly.

I will teach a Special Education class and I will be the best "special" education teacher that I can possibly be because I feel this is my calling. I want to touch people's lives positively, and make them aware of their uniqueness and their strengths. I will do my utmost to ensure that every one of my students becomes the very best that they can be. I am proof that it's never too late to pursue and realize your hopes and dreams, even though the road to getting there is chock full of many bumps, detours, and obstructions. Success can be measured in many different ways. Within the right set of parameters, everyone can experience success; everyone can be moved successfully forward.

Without question, my life has been a bit trying by times, and no doubt I have faced many challenges in getting to this point. But as I now look back, I know that the lessons I have learned will be of great value to those whose paths I cross in the future. I now set out to make a positive mark on the world. Thanks for listening

Chapter 20: Girls Can Be Bullies, Too

Imagine that you are looking at the photo album of the perfect storybook family. In the foreground of the first picture, you see a family of four. There is the mother and father who have been happily married for over thirty years. Both are professional people, attached to very respectable professions. Then there is the older daughter, the academic, and the younger brother, the athlete. They are all wearing brand-new, designer clothes. Now, pull back and look at the background of the picture. You see a big country house on a large, tree-filled yard. There are two cars in the driveway, a swimming pool in the backyard, and a dog lying at their feet. The second picture shows the inside of their house. It looks like it was taken right from a magazine. By examining other pictures in the album, there would appear to be nothing missing. Every room is spacious and looks professionally decorated. You see a picture of the kids in their rooms filled with all of the latest and the best toys. There is nothing that this family does without. You now get a chance to see their vacation pictures. There are family trips to Disney World for March break, monthly ski trips all over North America, and weeks spent at a family cottage every summer. Fast forward a few years, you see pictures from the kids' high school graduations. They get scholarships for academics or athletics, and they both set off to University to follow their dreams, with their family's complete emotional and financial support behind them. You begin to realize how fortunate that this family is and how great that their lives must be.

I can show you these photographs because this is my family album. I did have this childhood. I have lost count of the number of times that my friends have told me that I have a storybook family, how lucky I am, or how easy it must have been growing up. I come from a stable home and have loving parents. There were few problems of any nature, and we were very well off. We had everything that we ever needed or wanted; but yet we were taught respect and responsibility, so we never felt as though we were spoiled. Unfortunately, these pictures only show the superficial side of things. On the surface, I did have that perfect childhood, but underneath, it was a completely different story.

I cannot say that my entire experience at school was bad; in fact, the first few years were incredibly positive ones. I loved to go to school - to see my friends, to work at the different activity centres and to learn new things. My teachers noticed very early on that I was finishing my work very quickly and grasping new concepts with ease. My grade one teacher recommended that I be tested for placement into the gifted program, and my parents enthusiastically agreed. I was tested shortly thereafter, and scored well above the required IQ of 130 (the minimum score required to be identified as a gifted student). This meant that I was able to be placed in the program, which removed me from my regular class at least one half day a week to work with other gifted students. As a group we had so much fun when we were together. We did extra projects, brainteasers, Science Olympics, trivia games, computer work, field trips, and so much more. It allowed us to be ourselves and challenged us to work to our full potential.

There was a downside to this experience though, and it started to surface around grade four. It is here when you start to realize how different you are from the other kids. Besides being taken out of class for the program, we were also split off from the rest of the class during our normal school work. We were given harder, different or extra work than the rest of the class, and we were told that we could work in the coatroom, out in the hall or in the library (which, at age 10, is a big treat). The other kids started to realize that we were different too. We were the smart kids - the ones that you always wanted to have around when it came to doing schoolwork, even if you were not really friends. In grade five, our class was further divided. When deciding on class placements for the upcoming year, each student was evaluated on their marks from grade four. The top half of the students were placed in the French Immersion stream, and the rest were placed in the Core French stream. There were even a few students who showed enough promise in French that they were allowed to transfer into the school for the Immersion program. What you ended up with was one class of bright, well-behaved, conscientious students, and another class with behaviour problems, learning disabilities and less motivated students (thankfully, it no longer works like this!). I was placed in the Immersion program for grade five, and it is in this incredibly competitive environment that my real story begins.

I cannot remember the initial reason or event that was the catalyst, but once I hit grade five, the bullying started. It was always easy to hide the wounds, because it was never physical. I never came home with dirty clothes, scraped knees or black eyes. My schoolwork never suffered, and I still had some close friends. In my case, it was always the other girls who were the bullies, never the guys. What you begin to realize is that what girls can do to a person is often worse than what the guys can do. It is the constant verbal abuse and harassment - the teasing, the name-calling, the ridiculing - or the silent treatment that causes the wounds. They tend to hurt far worse, cut much deeper, take much longer to heal than a bruise or any other physical wound would, and they leave scars. What this kind of bullying does to you is that it calls you to question everything that you believe about yourself, especially when you are in your early teens and trying to figure out who you are and where you fit in the world. The even sadder and scarier part of this experience is that I was not alone. The girls that hurt me also hurt some of the other girls that I went to school with as well.

I can remember being laughed at or ridiculed for what I wore, what I had for lunch, what my school bag looked like or anything else that I may have done differently from the "cool" girls. I tried so hard every day not to stand out. I would follow the crowd and never did anything without making sure that it, at the least, would be the same as everyone else, or, at the best, go unnoticed. The one thing that stood out above all else and occurred the most frequently was what happened if I were to answer a question wrong in class or to make a mistake in my homework. You see, my teachers felt that a good way to get students involved in the class was to have each of us take turns marking the entire class's math homework. You would get to stay in at lunch and mark a stack of workbooks. For some reason, it was the best job you could get to do, and everyone waited anxiously for his or her turn to roll around. If I had even one answer wrong in my homework or if the answer I gave in class was incorrect, it was like the world stopped. Everyone found out if my homework was wrong, usually before I did. "Let's laugh." "She can't be wrong, she's smart." "She doesn't have the right to make mistakes, she's smart." "She's supposed to know everything." "But Miss, if she doesn't know, how am I supposed to?" I heard comments like these all of the time, and each one hurt just a little more than did the one before. I would slouch lower in my seat, look at the floor and try and fight back the tears. It took days for me to get my confidence back. If you need proof, take a look back at my report cards or parent-teacher interviews, and you would notice a change around grade five. Every year, I was told that I need to participate more in class discussions because I knew the material so well. But how could any teacher expect me to put up my hand when I knew that I would be ridiculed if my answer was not 100% correct?

It did not stop there. I remember one day in grade five when I was cornered by the group of girls while we were working on group projects. Two friends and I were working in the coatroom when the girls came in. They thought that they should be the ones that were working there. I was sitting on the floor, and they walked up to me, surrounded me, looked down and told me to move. After all, who could expect them to get any work done in the same room as a whore? I must have looked confused, because, at that point, I did not understand what that word meant. So they asked me again,

"Hey slut, I asked if you are going to move?" Then I got the picture, and since it was more trouble to stay than it was to leave, we packed up and moved back to our desks. What else could we do? A few days later, one of the girls brought in a picture from her birthday party in senior kindergarten. It was a picture taken of a group of us watching the presents being opened. Of course, in the picture, another girl and I were caught picking our noses, but at five years old, do you know a kid who does not? The other offender was one of the cool girls, so it was ignored, but it was made widely known that I was caught in this picture picking my nose. You would have thought that it happened recently, not five years before that. Everyone saw the picture ... it was the news of the week. I could not go anywhere without someone making a comment. The teacher noticed what was happening and saw that I was getting upset, so she took me aside. Do you know what she told me? "You must have an embarrassing picture of one of them. Bring it to school tomorrow and see how they like it." Sure. Like I would do that! I am trying here to fit in. Who knows what people might think if I did something like that?

I would like to say that things got better, or at least stayed constant, since I cannot remember any big events like these happening during grade six. I do remember that year, but nothing really bad stands out in my mind. Do not get me wrong, there was the normal amount of teasing and ignoring going on, but I actually had a few good friends, so I was not completely alone. It was not until the last half of grade seven that things started to fall apart. It was early on in grade seven that my best friend and I started to grow apart. We had been friends since grade one, but our lives started to head in different directions. The funny thing is that it was not an overall bad experience, and we still talk when we run into each other. We just started hanging out with different people and spending less time with each other. We still cared about each other, but we just wanted different things. I think it helped that I started hanging around new friends right away, so I never really missed her.

It seemed to be going okay after that, but a few days in January changed everything. One afternoon, I was riding home from school on the bus. Since I was in French Immersion, I was not attending the school that I was zoned for. Both schools took the same bus, but after dropping off most people at the other elementary school, there was about ten of us left that were taken to our school. We were the first ones on and last off, so we always got the back seats. Samantha, the younger sister of one of the cool girls, Carla, was sitting across from me. She grabbed my school bag and decided that she wanted to go through it, just to see what was in there. I had one pocket where I kept tampons. Now that I am 23, I have long since realized that they are a necessary part of a female's life, but at age 12, you never wanted anyone to know that you had that stuff in your bag. I told Samantha that I wanted my bag back, but she kept going through it. All I could think about was what would happen if she found them in front of everyone. I finally grabbed it back before she had the chance to get to that pocket. Of course, she tried to grab it back and kept asking me what the big deal was. I replied, in anger, "Nothing, Samantha. You're sure being a bitch today." I did not think too much of what had happened until the next morning - after all, it was my bag. I did not take the bus to school the next morning, so my mom dropped me off shortly before the bell rang. I had a welcoming party when I walked through the gate. Eight girls, some from my class and some from the other, surrounded me. They grabbed my school bag, started going through it and threw my stuff on the ground. Carla told me that I had no right to call her sister a bitch, and she wanted to make sure that I never did it again. They threw my bag on the ground and each of them called me a bitch and kicked my stuff a bit further as they walked away. Carla turned around and warned me that if I ever said anything again, they could do a whole lot worse. In tears, I managed to pick up all of my stuff and was thankful when the bell finally rang. This was the first day of many that I was afraid to go outside for recess. I never wanted to be in that situation again. The incident stayed with me for the next two years, and I would always try to make excuses to stay inside for recess. A great thing happened when I had surgery a month later, and I got to stay inside for three whole weeks. After the time was up, it was even harder to start going back out. I volunteered to work in the office, supervise younger classes, do extra work for the teacher or anything else that I could think of to avoid going outside for recess.

Grade eight was not any better. There were five of us in the class who were always the odd ones out. Three of us were in the gifted program. We began to withdraw from the class. We hung out together, which I am sure is one of the main reasons that we survived the year. We were never invited to any of the parties, always picked last for the sports teams, only had each other to do group work with, and were always teased or had comments made about us behind our backs. But at least we had each other, and we were not going through it alone. I was looking so forward to high school. I saw it as a new start, and felt like I had an advantage because my mom was on staff there and I really knew the school. There were going to be new people and new chances. I remember on the first day of school Lucy, Beth and I planned it all out. We met early on the first day of school, picked out the best lockers and found our classes together. After all, we did not want to look stupid by getting lost on the first day. It started off well. I was meeting new people, joining clubs and getting mid-90s in all of my classes. Yet, right from the start, I was still labelled as a smart kid. The cool girls from elementary school were making new friends too and passing on their labels. Even without them, just being identified as gifted meant that I was placed in a special Math class with only six other students, four of whom were from my old school. I got along well with everyone, except this one girl, Audrey. We just did not click, even at the start, but this becomes more important later. Besides having the class to single us out, teachers started posting marks, and even though it was supposed to be anonymous, we all know that it never was. We started being recognized for doing well. There were exemptions from tests, Honour Rolls, and certificates for academic achievement. We stood out even more.

Then came February. A group of us in the Immersion class had a chance to go on a four day ski trip. It started to go bad even before we left. I look back now and think that I should have spotted the signs. About a week before the trip, we had to pick our rooms. Since we had signed up, Nancy and I had talked about staying in the same room together. When I went over to ask her at the meeting, she had "forgotten" and signed up with three other girls. I had no one to room with, until I found out where the extra bed was. It was with three of the cool girls from elementary school. I could not think of anything worse than sharing a room with them, but I could not back out of the trip and there was no other choice. When the teacher tried to put us together, one of the girls told her, "Why do you think we would want to be with her?" They were told that they had no choice, and I literally ran out of the room in tears. My teacher tracked me down, and told me that it would not be that bad, as we did not spend that much time in the rooms anyways. She talked to the other girls too and warned them that they had to be nice to me until we got back from the trip. We managed to survive, although it was through a lot of politeness and fake smiles. It was not until I got back to school that my life changed forever. When I got back, none of my friends from elementary school wanted anything to do with me. They had started to hang around with Audrey and had decided that she was better than I was. Still to this day, I have no idea what happened during the four days that I was away. All I knew is that no one would talk to me, sit with me in class or at lunch, or work on any projects together. It was like I had some strange disease that you would catch if you came within ten feet of me. The talking started all over again, although it was now much worse since I had no one to turn to, and I always seemed to be the negative subject of a conversation that I was not a part of.

This is when I really started to withdraw. I came to school right at the bell and left as early as I could. Luckily, since my mom was there, I could always hide in her room and lock the door if all else failed. It was my safety net. I started to go home for lunch every day, because I had nowhere else to go. If she had a meeting and could not take me home, she would buy me lunch. I would eat in her room quickly (with the door closed, of course), then run to a study carrel in the library and do homework until class started. It was my only salvation, and it stayed like this until part way through grade ten. I began to isolate myself from everyone, and that decision started to form the divide between me and the rest of the school. From this point on, I was always by myself, either by choice or by reputation.

Something fortunate happened, purely by chance, when all of this was going on. My French teacher picked Annie, a girl who I had gotten to know in a few of my classes, and I to work together to summarize the novel that we were reading instead of having us summarize a chapter by ourselves. At least I had someone to talk to in my classes, although we did not spend much time together outside of class. When we switched from Typing to Shop, halfway through the semester, Annie invited me to sit at her table with her and her friend, Terri. As might be expected, my old friends did not like seeing me hanging out or becoming friends with anyone.

One class, we made buttons and I brought my brand new set of sixty pencil crayons to class to work with. I was sharing them with Annie and Terri when my old friends started coming over and asking to borrow them. I do not know why I said yes, but I did, until they started breaking them in half, of course, "accidentally". When I asked for them back, Lucy came over and sat down beside me. She started telling Annie and Terri that they should not hang out with me unless they wanted to lose all of their friends. I was not good enough for them. She told them that I cheated on tests and on homework, or I had my friends do my work for me. This was how I got my high marks. I would do just about anything to get out of doing my share of the work. This went on and on for the rest of the period, while I just sat there stunned, trying to keep coloring and look like I was not listening. Thankfully, Annie and Terri decided not to believe what Lucy was saying, and I still counted them among my friends when I left high school. Even though I spent time in class with Annie and Terri, I still did not have any real friends to spend my free time with for the rest of grade nine.

I met another girl, Ruthie, in my grade ten History class, who was also friends with Annie and Terri. Through the three of them, I got invited into their circle of friends, and although I did not get along with everyone, things started to get better. I had people to go places and do things with. Around the middle of grade ten, I stopped eating lunch in the library when I was stuck at school, although I would still go home whenever I could. Even if that part of my life was improving, I was still the smart girl. There was always a comment shot my way if my answer was wrong in class or if I did not get perfect on a test. There were plenty of people who would be nice to my face when they would come looking to me for help with their work, but then they would turn around and talk about me behind my back.

I could keep going on about all of the little things that happened throughout the next four years, but most of the big stuff has been covered. High school definitely had its low points, but I managed to survive. My average stayed in the mid-90s, so I was always looked at as a good student, and it gave me a reason to keep working, and expectations to live up to. I was quiet, helpful, and a good student, so the teachers liked to have me in their classes and would offer me jobs to tutor other students. I always tried hard to exceed the expectations that my teachers had for me. I played in two bands, competed in academic contests, volunteered with a local service club, stayed involved with a large national organization for girls, taught skiing lessons, and worked with special needs students. I would go to parties or out to the movies with my friends. I have to admit that things would have been considerably worse if I did not have the support of my mom at school. It gave me an out when I needed it, and it kept me up to date on what was going on within the building, so I was rarely ambushed by surprises. Our relationship grew, and we have stayed very close through the years.

Even with all of these positives, there was still a struggle every day that I had to be a part of. There was so much that chipped away at my self-esteem and my will to keep fighting. I could never let my guard down. I had to think through everything I wore, said, did, or thought. I made sure that there was nothing that would set me apart from everyone else. Even though I have been away from high school for five years now, I still carry this attitude with me. It is ingrained into who I am, and although I appear confident on the outside, I am anything but. I am still hesitant to speak out in class for fear that I might be ridiculed. If I do answer a question or make a comment in class, I spend hours going over it in my head, trying to figure out what I said and look for anything that might be used against me. I second-guess everything people say to me, as I always look for a hidden meaning. I am afraid when I think someone is ignoring me, as it is my fault and question what I must have done wrong. I will withdraw into my own world and wait for them to approach me. I do not completely trust anyone, or trust that the friendships that I now have will last. It is hard for me to accept that people are my friends because they truly like me, and not just because they want something from me. I try so hard to fit in and to be the same as everyone else. I feel like I can never be myself, because no one seems to like who I truly am. I read too deeply into everything, and I tend to see the negatives in a situation before I see the positives. I still spend a lot of time by myself, not because I have to, but because I am so used to it. Sometimes, I think that being alone gives me the chance to relax, as it is the only time when I do not have to impress anyone and can finally let my guard down. I will never again let anyone see me cry!

Each day is still a struggle against the forces holding me back, yet I still move forward and try to do my best. I want to show everyone that I can succeed and be happy, but I also feel that since I have persevered for so long, there is no way that I can give up now. As a teacher, I will be mindful of the damage children can inflict on other children. I have hopefully learned from my experiences, and will do my best to ensure that the students on my watch treat each other fairly and with respect, particularly mindful of the fact that girls can be bullies too!

Chapter 21: Please Take Some Action!

The following statement is something that took years and years to be able to admit. I developed an eating disorder in late high school and have battled it ever since. It's so odd that that one lone sentence can summarize such an epic struggle in my life; but there you have it!

I come from a great family. No question, my parents are very successful people, with both being very respected within their chosen professions. As a child and young adolescent, I was outgoing, popular, and a leader within many competitive sports. I was also a straight "A" student. Sounds pretty good doesn't it? To everyone looking in from the outside, it must have looked pretty darned good. To them, it probably appeared as though I had the world at my feet. To me, however, there was something else very different going on in my life. I was tumbling into, (particularly in mid to late adolescence), a deep, dark, bottomless pit. I was starting to enter a vortex, which, to me, at the time, seemed completely inescapable. It wasn't alcohol, it wasn't drugs, it wasn't hanging out with the wrong crowd; what it actually was, was the start of a serious eating disorder called bulimia. As I come to terms with my condition, and I look back in a reflective way, I can somewhat start to identify where things started to "come off the rails" for me. I can now see some potential moments or "triggers" where I believe things started to unravel and where, and how, my eating disorder was primarily set in motion.

Number one, as a child, I was a tad chubby – certainly not obese, but certainly not thin. Apparently, just chubby enough for other children to start calling me the mean spirited (usual) names exclusively reserved for little stout girls. Although I eventually grew taller and shed the baby fat, the feelings associated with that particular time in my life never completely abandoned me.

Number two; although I never doubted the fact that my mother loved me immensely, and faithfully did all those great motherly things for me, she was completely uncompromising when it came to her overall expectations where her children were concerned. And, although this is not necessarily a bad thing for many children, for me, given my particular makeup, I now think it had a role to play in the onset of my sickness.

Don't get me wrong, my mother has always wanted the best for me, and she always wanted me to succeed in everything I did. She wanted me to be everything

I was capable of being. No doubt, everything within this dynamic came from a very well intentioned place, however, my mother consistently kept setting the 'expectational' bar incredibly high. In fact, so high I started to believe that no matter what I did, it never was going to be good enough; that the familial standards were being set so unreasonably high that, to me, they were becoming almost unattainable. For example, if I got a 95/100 on a test, although she would always note the great achievement, in the next breath she would be voicing her concern over where the other 5 marks went. My clothes were rarely right. My room was never clean enough, the dishes weren't done properly, and on and on. From my perspective, there was very little I could do to please. Again, I want to reiterate, my mother was always unfailingly loving and caring, and she went miles out of her way to ensure that I never went without - but thinking and feeling like you never measured up, or were never really good enough, is a heart breaking conclusion for a young adolescent to arrive at.

Number 3, all my life I had excelled in sport. In fact, in one particular sport I was part of a team that competed at the national level. I loved it and thrived because I was allowed to shine with a group of girls who were very much like me. In fact, over a very short period of time I was formally recognized as being a leader within this group. In the world of competitive sport at this level, conditioning, but more particularly body weight, is always a major preoccupation. So, in the end, what you end up with is a group of girls who pretty much look the same. To maintain a collective high level of performance, we, at minimum, had 3 hour practices 4 times a week, combined with many extra hours added on to work out in a gymnasium. To monitor all this, our group was assigned a private nutritionist and trainer. As part of this overall very rigorous process, the component that really came to bother me was that our weight was consistently taken to ensure that it remained at an acceptable level. With respect to this, I will never forget, for as long as I live, the first time I was exposed to this procedure. Being new on the team, I was unaware of all the specific routines, so when I first saw the scale in the meeting room, I immediately became internally mortified, and this feeling came over me each and every week when the team was collectively "weighed in". To make matters worse, at least for me, was the fact that we were all weighed in a room together, one after the other. If your weight went up from one week to the next, you were publically scolded in front of your teammates. As I look back, I can now see how unhealthy this was for me, but because I loved the sport so much, I continued to endure the torture and potential public humiliation!

Finally, also at this particular time, my life in late high school quickly became insanely busy. Of course, I had school through the day, practices after school, competitions on weekends and, of course, lots and lots of homework. Sleep and hanging out with old friends became a real luxury. However, throughout this very busy and stressful time, I was not allowed to let my marks slip, I was not allowed to have a sub-par performance in my sport, and I had to always ensure that my bed was impeccably made before I left the house in the morning. On top of this, I started to notice some serious tension develop within my parents' relationship (either real or imagined), which had me fixating on the possible dissolution of my typical nuclear family. I now have absolutely no doubt that it was the confluence of all these things that I've previously mentioned, coming together at this specific, very vulnerable time in my life, that launched the downward spiral that saw me start to lose a significant degree of control over my life.

I was a people pleaser and a bit of a control freak and it appeared to me that everyone around me was incredibly unhappy, and situations were becoming more and more uncontrollable and chaotic. My stress level was through the roof, and I started to experience prolonged moments of extreme panic. When you factor in the typical high school stuff, where body image and teenage girls are concerned – all of a sudden, bulimia became a legitimate option for me. I almost immediately found that the binging and purging provided a release for me. Hard to believe, but it actually made me feel better! It quickly became the one thing in my life that I was completely in control of. I certainly didn't understand anything about bulimia; how harmful it was to me, or in what direction it would ultimately take me, but it fulfilled a need, and that's all that mattered. For the longest time food became my enemy; an arch nemesis that continued to taunt me. From being a very gregarious girl, who had tons of friends, belonged to a well-respected team, and had a great family—as time progressed, I started to feel more and more isolated. I started to feel as though I was all alone! It was just my 'problem' and just me!

Although, for many years of my life I waged a daily battle with bulimia, I remember one pivotal moment very early on in the evolution of my condition, when things could have very much changed dramatically for me. There was one particular day that could have pulled me back from the abyss. About one year into my 'stress relieving habit', in one of my high school classes we were examining "food from around the world" as a major curricular theme. Well, as might be expected, as soon as I saw the tables packed full of food, I panicked because I felt like people would either notice me for not eating, or eating then immediately running to the bathroom. For the first time, directly related to this period in my life, I started to completely crumble (right there in school, and in a classroom full of other students). As a defense mechanism, because I was starting to lose control, I immediately retreated to the empty hall. Quite naturally, my teacher noticed, and followed me out, asking me, "what was the matter, why are you so upset?" It's real funny because I had never even come close to confiding in anybody else before, but, for some reason, I decided that I desperately needed to "open up" to someone, and maybe this was as good a time as any. So, I did! On that day, at that particular moment, in a high school hallway, I emptied my soul to my trusted teacher.

I explained to him in great detail, what I was actually doing, why I thought I was doing it, all the while bawling my eyes out. However, throughout this whole breakdown, I never really took my eyes off him, hoping that at some point he might offer some possible answers. Here's the part I'll never forget! When I finished my full explanation and had somewhat stopped the sobbing, my trusted teacher looked away, then down at his shoes and calmly said, "Well....just do your best." He then left me standing in the hallway and went back into the classroom to rejoin the festivities. I can honestly say, until this very day, I have never in my life felt more alone or so completely abandoned!

"Just do your best!" I will never forget those four words. Here I was drowning, struggling just to get through each day, and the first time I fully recognized that something was seriously wrong and I reached out for help, what did I get, the door slammed in my face. Not one single thing ever came from the conversation I had with my teacher on that particular day. He never mentioned it again, nor did I. In my heart, I was hoping that he had secretly gone on to tell the guidance office about my situation, and for days I lived in the hope that the school counselor would knock on my classroom door and come and rescue me; but that never happened either. It was like the whole conversation never took place. No phone calls home, no meetings, absolutely nothing! In looking back, oh how I wish to God that something would have happened!

In many respects, this whole series of events, relatively early in the onset of my condition, made things a whole lot worse. Looking back, I think it gave me the impression that having bulimia was not really that big a deal. Perhaps it was completely normal, and not all that dangerous; if so, surely my teacher would have moved quickly to do something about it. Sadly, as a result, I didn't tell another soul until very late into my undergraduate year of university. Being somewhat forced to do so, basically because my body just could not take the abuse anymore. Although psychologically I was still deeply committed to the binge/purge cycles, physically my body was telling me to stop and get some help.

Eventually, I confessed to my parents, who went through all the anticipated range of emotions (with me being emotionally dragged along as well). They immediately assured me that my health was their number one concern, and they were going to do everything in their power to make things better for me. Well, to say the least, this was exactly what I wanted to hear, and my first reaction immediately after my reveal was, why did I suffer in silence for so long?

People around me rallied, and I immediately embarked on a proactive path that included both doctors and therapists. It hasn't been easy; in fact, to be honest, it's been a very long and difficult process. I still deal with it daily, but I can see myself getting stronger and better. I am well entrenched in the healing process. You just have to believe that there is light at the end of whatever tunnel you are traveling in, and you'll eventually get there. Be positive, don't lose hope, is my new mantra!

In looking back in a critical way I want to say this, specifically to teachers. You have a professional responsibility to take seriously some of the things your students tell you, even if they have absolutely nothing to do with the lesson at hand, or the particular curriculum document being advanced. If they are psychologically hurting, or physically hurting (perhaps themselves), and they ASK YOU FOR HELP, please do something (anything) about it! I continually wonder, where my own specific case is concerned, if some other teacher might have made a different decision, based on my very difficult private confession? All I know is that I went looking for help, and I chose a teacher, one whom I had known for a long time, had a great rapport with, and thoroughly trusted. And what did I get in return, nothing but let down, hurt, disappointment, and complete betrayal!

My message to teachers, who in the future think they see, or know that one of their students, male or female, are dealing with an eating disorder, is this simple, TAKE SOME ACTION. Become their advocate; become their confidante. Even if they don't seemingly want any advice or help, take it from me, one who has experienced it firsthand, deep down they really want some intervention. Trust me, initially you feel embarrassed, ashamed, weak, terrible, fat (even if you aren't') depressed, completely beyond redemption, but you also feel so very alone! The fact that you've noticed, and you want to try and make it better, may be all the incentive they need. Take it from me, it may be the greatest gift you will ever give as a teacher because it may not only change a life, it may actually end up saving a life!

Worth noting, early in my healing, I was introduced to a journal article by Sharon and Michael Omizo. It's called, Eating disorders: The school counselor's role. Although it was first published in 1992, I feel it is still very relevant. In my opinion, every school and every teacher should be made aware of this article and its contents. Most importantly, when it comes to the scourge of eating disorders, it lists ways to prevent, identify and support treatment. My high school had none of these resources around at the time, and that's a real shame. I truly believe that if I'd been caught earlier it would have saved me many years of binging, purging, losing weight, and getting weak and sick. It would have saved the enamel of my teeth, and it definitely would have saved my throat from profound scaring. Of course, it would have also saved me from the telling of thousands and thousands of lies.

Addendum

In now looking back over my completed narrative, I realize that I've talked a lot about the risk side of things but somewhat glossed over the resiliency part of my story. First off, it wasn't easy, and I wouldn't be completely honest if I didn't mention that there has been the odd slip along the way. No doubt, I'm still in the process of overcoming and recovering. I battle with it subconsciously all the time. However, when it comes to my success and my turnaround, there can be no denying the powerful role my mother has played in my "wellness" and in my life.

Early in my self-analysis, on the risk side of things, I identified my mother and the high standards that she consistently set for the family, particularly me, as perhaps contributing to my eventual turn to bulimia. Ironically, however, it was the same set of matriarchal characteristics on the resiliency side of things (related to her overall expectations), in the end, that profoundly started me on the road to recovery. In short, when it came to my "wellness", my mother's expectations always remained high, only this time I perceived it as a very positive thing.

After admitting to my parents about my problem, my mother was devastated and somewhat wracked with guilt, particularly after I tried to explain the perceived (and completely unsuspecting) role she might have played in the onset of my eating disorder. When I finally expressed to her my feelings (or interpretations of my feelings), especially with reference to never feeling good enough or never measuring up as an adolescent, she was shocked because this was clearly never her intention. Her overriding intention was to always provide me with every opportunity to become anything I wanted to become, and by "keeping the bar high", my mother was trying to convince me of my limitless possibilities. In our early conversations, immediately after my disclosures, it became instantaneously obvious that my mother and I should have had these conversations many years previous.

Without hesitation, my mother undoubtedly got me through some the toughest of times, and was absolutely instrumental in pulling me from the abyss that was an eating disorder. She expected no less!

Chapter 22: I Have a Secret

It is not something people tend to ask me about, or even notice. I am sure if they even do notice, (or if they come to their own conclusions), they wouldn't have the confidence to involve me in this overall cognitive/inquisitive process.

No one has come out directly and asked me, and I certainly prefer it that way. I have only offered up my secret to a select group of friends, and those I've told usually reply, they "already knew", or that they thought just what I wanted them to think. I have been living with my secret for a while now. I do not know when it started or how it started; it is just something I do. I grew up in a middle class home and, to most people, the fact that I even have some kind of problem would surprise, or even astound them.

I have no idea how it started; it was just something I began to do one day, and have never stopped. Revealing this secret is one of the toughest things I have ever had to do. Even as I sit here and write this, I am partaking it in my so-called "habit" …Anyway, here goes.

I suffer from a disorder known as Trichotillomania, or compulsive hair pulling. Trichotillomania or "trich" is not actually considered an Obsessive Compulsive Disorder, however, those who suffer from "trich" may also suffer from some variant of OCD. Trichotillomania is also believed to be associated with depression. Though I believe I suffer from seasonal depression, I do not believe I suffer from ongoing episodes of depression.

Some "trich" sufferers actually eat their hair and, although I do not eat my hair, I do indeed run the hair through my mouth. To my knowledge, there is no real known reason why people with "trich" do this, they just do it! "Trich", many times, is triggered in people who have poor body image, and there is no doubt that this may well have something to do with my own individual case. However, I suspect, in trying to isolate the specific causes of my ongoing problem, other negative life experiences may have played a significant role in its development as well.

I have never been thin. I was a chunky baby, and my chunky status continued into both elementary and high school, and now, well into my adult life. While I realize I really did nothing to help my image, especially when I was younger, I came to discover very early on that kids can be incredibly cruel and, as a direct result, throughout my elementary and high school days - I was teased incessantly. High school was particularly brutal, where I was bullied, teased and harassed on a daily basis. When I entered University, by the second semester of my first year I had become mildly anorexic, eating only when I felt weak. However, on the positive side, the weight certainly did come off, and I was the lightest I have ever been. There was no doubt that my mood considerably improved, and, as a direct corollary, for the first time in many years, my "hair pulling" habit became less of a concern. It definitely got better! But, near the end of my undergrad year, with more and more stress building, the "pulling" returned with a vengeance, and has continued to this very day. Over the years, my weight has fluctuated, up and down, which seems to be directly linked to my good pulling days (hardly pull) and my bad pulling days (pull until a bald spot emerges).

My hair pulling began with my eyelashes, and I really have no memory of how, or why, I specifically targeted my eyelashes, or how it moved from my eyelashes to my hair. When I "plucked", my parents became very aggravated and constantly yelled at me to stop, and, early on, I complied, but secretly snuck off to do it in a secluded space, or did it when I thought no one was paying any attention. My parents truly believed it was a "habit" that I would eventually outgrow, and I was happy to let them believe just that. Therefore, for the longest time, in fact right into my first year of University, I too believed that it was just a "habit", and I desperately needed to find some way to break my way out of it.

At the end of my first year of university, during exam time, I was sitting at my desk in residence, stressed to the max about an upcoming test. I sat for hours studying, then I looked down at my desk and realized I had spent many of those hours pulling out hundreds of pieces of my hair. It was at this point that I knew something was very, very wrong. In a bit of a panic, I did a quick Google search and was amazed at what I immediately stumbled upon. I was not alone! In fact, what I was experiencing was actually not considered a "habit" at all. It actually was a medical condition that millions of people suffer from. I was so relieved to finally have an answer for my problem, but knew that my parents would never believe me (and be of very little support). As a result, I continued to keep it from them, believing that it would have only added to their belief that I truly was the "weird" link within the family's overall chain. I think I finally confided in them (my parents) during the summer of my 3rd year at University.

My parents sat patiently and listened to my story; hence, at the time I thought I was finally making some progress. I thought, at minimum, maybe now they will stop bugging me about my condition, and actually try and help. However, no sooner had I finished my detailed explanation when my mother offered the following advice (with my father's quite obvious approval), "It's just a bad habit, so you need to get over it, and just stop doing it!" To this day they have never accepted my condition, or its potential origins. As a consequence, I tend to avoid going home for long visits because all I hear while I at home is "stop", and "please, don't do that." I tell them, "Telling me to stop it is not going to make me stop, I will still do it, don't you understand?" To that, I am generally told to remove myself from the room, "Because they do not want to see me doing that to myself." How am I suppose to stop pulling, when I am stressed out with comments like that, when I am made to feel like I am not accepted because of something I cannot help? Do they truly believe this is a personal choice; that I choose to pull out my hair?

What most people do not understand about people with Trichotillomania is that we do not want people to know we pull out our hair. I would prefer people go on thinking that I have thinning hair, or my hair falls out just because of stress; believe me, this is much easier to live with. I remember once my mother telling my neigbour of "my habit" and, at the time, this angered me considerably. I was so upset with her, and told her I didn't want other people to know; but she just didn't understand (or made no attempt to understand). Don't get me wrong, I love my mother and father deeply, and although their intentions, where I'm concerned are always honourable and commendable, the fact remains that we live in a very small town, where everyone knows your name and your personal business. I think in the end, for my parents, it's easier for them to ignore the fact that there is something wrong with their daughter, than to admitting to a very real medical condition. To admit it would mean that a "habit" would have to be replaced by a mental health illness, and I think this scares my parents profoundly, as other people in our small town may eventually find out!

Why I Pull....

I never really understood why I pulled, until I started to notice the times it got real bad; always when I was in a high stress situation. In High School, the pressure to fit in, do well in school and get into a good university may very well have trigged it. I know that my hair pulling in High School intensified when problems started to arise with the boy I was dating. Already having a body imagine problem, having a boyfriend who made it clear that I should probably lose a little weight didn't make matters any better; and having an abusive boyfriend who constantly belittled you and tried to control your every move, probably escalated things dramatically. It's only now as I reflect, that I can clearly see how my problems started to surface around this particular time in my life.

My first boyfriend told me often that I needed to lose weight; he also had no problems verbally abusing me, calling me a "bitch" and "fat." He also consistently physically abused me. I distinctly remember this one night, we had just come back to his house after a night out, and he got angry at me for something (I don't remember what specifically) and he grabbed my face and then began biting me on the cheek. I can picture that exact moment in my mind as clear as day. I was already starting to 'pick" at this time, but this incident created unneeded stress in a relationship that was already incredibly full of stress, thus, the "picking" most certainly intensified.

Looking back, I am not sure why I stayed so long in that relationship, but hindsight is definitely 20/20. I believe that because I hated myself so much, the fact that a boy actually liked me was appealing, and while he abused me both verbally and physically, the thought of not being in a relationship was far less appealing than being in an abusive relationship. In retrospect, seems very odd now, how I could be so compliant in my own abuse?

My "body image" issues continued into University, and, as mentioned previously, in my first year I started to develop an eating disorder. I soon realized that this couldn't go on. Although, I must now confess, I certainly did enjoy the weight loss, and the new clothes that I could now fit into again. Nevertheless, overall I was generally unhappy, unhealthy, and hungry most of the time, and knew for my own well-being, this type of behaviour could not be maintained. Consequently, my weight continues to fluctuate, with the "pulling" linked directly to the levels of stress in my life, and the gaining of weight.

To the outsider, "pulling" makes absolutely no sense and they always wonder how the pulling of hair, in any way, serves to relieve stress and/or tension. To that perspective, I can only say that it does....believe me, it does! I do not really have a scientific explanation for what I ultimately get out of it, however, I do know there are certain things that make me feel better when I actually do it. Let me try and briefly explain how some of this works.

When I internally hear the popping sounds of the actual hair coming out, it serves to sooth me immensely (with the tiny little white and black root of the hair actually popping). Related directly to this, the actual "plucking" process is not just something I do casually either; there is a definite process in which I go through. I don't just pull any hair out randomly; I search my head for a hair that seemingly (to me) doesn't belong. I also strategically try and limit my picking to one particular area of my head. Of course, limiting my picking to one area obviously causes other problems, in that I can create a bald spot on my head in a matter of hours. This behaviour in turn sets in motion another stress related problem as the emerging bald spot then creates a "pride/shame issue", as for women (me included), hair and hair style are generally major preoccupations (they are definitely directly related to how one feels about themselves). For me, I have certainly come to accept that given my condition and the particular way I tend to deal with stress, cute hairstyles are not something I can spend a great deal of time thinking about. In a way, it's the ultimate "Catch 22"!

In the end, I am who I am, and while I have not let Trichotillomania completely defeat me, I am not sure if this makes me in anyway resilient. I have never been able to escape the symptoms of my condition, but, on the other hand, I also haven't let it completely control my life either. In many respects, it certainly hasn't stopped me from doing the things I truly wanted to do; especially in becoming a very good teacher! I have accepted that it is just part of me, and will most likely be part of me until my dying day. I know there are options out there for me to try, however the greatest number of these options advance drug therapies as the major part of any potential solution. At this point in my life, I have decided that the pharmaceutical approach is just not for me. I have accepted that I will continue to have "good days", and I will continue to have "bad days", but medication is not something that I want to consider – at least not at this time.

As might be expected, the importance of mental health in the education system is very near and dear to me. I now know that statistically, in a High School class of thirty students, research says that up to six students will have the early onset of some type of mental health condition. Although, when I was coming through High School this research fact was not known to my teachers, hence, no general understanding or support was forthcoming, I will do my best to see that this very much changes; looking for bits of myself amongst the 30!

Chapter 23: The Summer Job

Let me take you back to the summer when I worked at a golf course. I wasn't old enough to work at the bar or on the beer cart, as I was only 15. Instead, I worked inside the clubhouse taking orders at the restaurant and serving customers their meals. It was a fun summer job; I got to meet lots of great people and best of all I got to golf for free. My family had been members at the club for several years; so getting a job there seemed like a great idea. I was familiar with the staff and many of the other members and it was very easy for me to fit in. It was my first real job (besides working where my parents did), and I thought it was great! Well, until the day that changed everything.

It started out as a usual Saturday shift at the course. I began working early in the morning to serve the morning coffee and a muffin rush and was there to fill in until the early afternoon. This particular Saturday I was asked to come back in the evening and serve at a banquet that was taking place in the golf course hall. Of course, being 15 and money hungry, I agreed, knowing that I could handle one long day of work.

Shortly after the lunchtime rush I was filling up the ice cube tray near the bar when a male member of the golf course approached the bar where I was standing. I didn't think much of it when he grabbed a cup from the tray in front of me and started to pour himself a glass of water from the pitcher on the bar. It wasn't until it was already too late that I knew something bad was going to happen.

The moments before it happened were somewhat of a blur to me, but the next thing I knew, the male member had his arm around my waist, pinning my arm at my side. He was much taller than me (about 6'3'' compared to my 5'3'', probably shorter at the time), and stronger as well. Helplessly and in a confused state, I stood there as he grabbed an ice cube from the tray I was filling and dropped it down my golf course polo shirt. As the ice cube dropped down the front of my shirt, he placed his large hand on my stomach to catch the falling ice cube in place for a moment. As I attempted to step back the ice cube fell to the floor and the man let out a disturbing laugh. He leaned towards my ear and said, "I know what will make it stay". It was at that moment that he picked up another ice cube from the tray and, while keeping my arm pinned at my side, reached his hand into my polo shirt and towards my breast. As he slid his hand into my bra, he laughed and said, "there, now it will stay". Instinctually, I tried to wriggle my arm out of his grasp and get the cold ice cube out of my bra. Almost instantly, he knocked my arm out of the way and told me that he would get the ice cube out. I don't recall whether I was actually able to get the word "NO" out of my mouth, however I do remember it resounding in my head. The man then put his hand back inside my shirt and into my bra, touching the ice cube for a moment, but instead of removing it immediately, he proceeded to massage my breast and touch my nipple. I can still remember the nauseous, scared feelings at that moment, as this man, a stranger to me, violated me and removed a large piece of my innocence. When he finally removed his hand and the ice cube from my bra and shirt he looked me in the eyes as he placed the ice cube that had touched my breast in his mouth, sucked on it for a few seconds and then placed it in his glass. The words that he said next have echoed inside my mind ever since, and haunted my dreams for a long time. Before letting me free, he leaned in towards me and said, "mmm...much better (about the ice cube he sucked on). We'll have to do this again sometime, but don't tell anyone". Then he left. Just like that he walked out the door and rejoined his friends on the patio as if nothing had happened.

I remember the tears welling inside my eyes as he walked out the door. I ran to the back of the kitchen and immediately began bawling my eyes out. As I passed the kitchen a friend of mine, a girl around the same age, saw me running past and followed me into the back office. When she reached me I was sobbing and could barely spit out what I wanted to tell her. I don't remember exactly what I told her in that moment, but I do remember asking her to get my boss. The next thing I knew I was upstairs telling my story to the owner of the golf course while someone else got my dad, who was playing golf at the time.

The rest of my day involved giving a statement to a police officer (who came to see me at the golf course), going to see my mom at her work, and then finally returning home. Although I can't recall the exact details of the whole day now, I do however know that I have never seen my parents so upset and hurt, as they were to hear what had happened to their daughter. Despite the horrible thing that happened, it was reassuring to know that in the end my parents supported and believed me, no matter what.

After this incident took place, I knew that I had a choice to make, I could either show this man, and those around him that I was scared, or stand up and be strong, for myself and to prove others wrong. I chose the second option, to be strong, mainly for myself, but also to show that man, that he could not do this to me, or anyone else again! As a result, I decided to return to my job at the golf course, despite the nauseous and uneasy feelings that I had when I returned. I guess it is also important to mention that the man was arrested the next day on the golf course (yes, in front of all his friends). Part of his bail release stated that he was not allowed to be around young children alone and was not to be anywhere near me.

Almost immediately after returning to the golf course it began. At first I wasn't sure if what I thought I heard was correct, but it soon became apparent that many members, particularly those who were friends with the man who had violated me, were saying horrible things about me and my family. On a daily basis at work I saw members whispering about me and often heard things such as, "she is a little whore", "she is a slut", "she really brought it on herself", and many other awful things. Through it all I tried to hold my head up high, not showing these adults how much what they were saying was hurting me inside. What made the comments even more hurtful to me was that these adults, many of whom were women, had children close in age to myself. I always wondered how they would react if it were their child who this happened to; what would they say then?

Over the next several months of the golf season I endured these comments from course members. Although I know my parents were aware of some of the things that members were saying, to this day I have never told them all of the horrible things that were said about my family or myself. Funny isn't it, during this painful time of my life, I was still trying to protect those closest to me.

The next year or so of my life leading up to the court date I dealt with a lack of trust towards others and avoided close relationships. As a result of the stress from the incident I gained some weight, another difficult thing to deal with at such a vulnerable age. Thankfully, I continued to have the support of my family, a very friendly police officer that took my statement, and the social worker that the court had appointed to my case. She really helped me to deal with a lot of the depressed and uneasy feelings that I was having, and helped me to find my inner strength that ultimately got me past that day.

When the court date finally arrived I didn't really know what to expect, even though the police, my social worker, and my parents tried to prepare me. I was the first person to take the stand, an experience that makes me feel sick to this day. It was the absolute worst few hours of my life. His lawyer tried EVERYTHING to discredit me as a person; blaming me for the incident, and in slightly nicer words, calling me all the things that the members of the course had during the summer months before. The lawyer had me wailing my eyes out throughout most of my testimony, probably making me seem even less credible. Once my testimony was finished, which wasn't until after a lunch break, I left the courthouse without hearing any other testimonies, while my parents stayed behind. I never asked my parents for all of the details of the rest of the day, but do know that a male employee from the golf course, and a friend of the man who assaulted me, lied on the stand to make me seem even less credible. He told the judge that I had talked about sex to him! What a load of crap! I was an innocent, nice, polite, 15 year old, who NEVER would have done such a thing, especially with a 30 something year old guy who weighed about 350 pounds. AS IF!

When the judge rendered his decision to the court shortly after, it was decided that there was not enough evidence either way to prove guilt or innocence. Big surprise, no closure for me!

The next golf season I decided to remain strong and apply for a job back at the golf course again. When I didn't hear from the club immediately, I phoned to find out why I had not heard, when they were advertising that they were hiring. Apparently a paying member was more important than a now 16-year-old employee who had been sexually assaulted by that paying member. This came as another surprise to me as a teenager, what kind of a cruel and unfair world do we live in?

Over the next several years I ran into the man many times. Always in public places; once at my new place of employment (when I was 18), the LCBO. The second he walked into the store with his common-law spouse and saw me, he went pale and turned around and walked out. The entire time that his spouse was in the store I stood at the window, arms folded, glaring at him - now looking rather small in his car.

After a few encounters like this over the years, my final closure came. One day, I happened to be flipping through the local newspaper when I encountered an obituary for the man who had sexually assaulted me almost 6 years before. Although what I am about to say might sound rather sick and disturbing, I will tell you nonetheless. That day, reading his obituary in the paper, was one of the happiest days of my life. It meant that after all those years of living without trust for others, especially the opposite sex, I could finally fully move on, knowing that this man could NEVER hurt me, or anyone else again.

It is hard to believe that almost 14 years have passed since that day on the golf course. Looking back on that day I often think, did that day change me? The answer is yes, but not as you may expect. It made me stronger. It made me more aware of myself and empowered me to stand up for myself and for others. Today, I am happily married to a man who I love and trust with my life. I am also a teacher; one whose greatest strength perhaps is encouraging students to believe in themselves and, no matter what the circumstances, to never give up. We all face obstacles in our life—the question becomes how will you face them? Will you give up, or will you find the strength within to fight; to fight for yourself and for what you believe is right.

Chapter 24: She Is Really Me

She didn't know... she didn't see the signs, until it was too late. Throwing a cat across the street because it was on his car's new paint job wasn't enough to trigger flags. The controlling nature was taken as love for her, as his new wife. The obsessions with financial issues were just a concern for their financial well-being. She didn't notice... or she didn't care.

They were expecting a child early on in the marriage; to be born just two years after their wedding. It wasn't planned. She was young and this was her lifelong dream; to be a mother. It may have clouded her judgment.

The first few years weren't too bad. They had 2 more children, all girls. Then things started to change. He was insistent that the house be spotless, the laundry be done immediately, dinner be on the table when he got home from work and that she not gain weight or "let herself go". He constantly told her she still needed to lose that 'baby weight' she'd gained. She finally put on an old dress she'd kept from their dating years, and met him at the door one evening to prove she was the same size she was when they first married. He wasn't satisfied.

After a few years, money got tight from his mismanagement. They had to move out of the nice, expensive house and in with her parents. Things went downhill from there. He got angry more often, he was cruel and shouted. Things weren't ever perfect anymore. Her mother was concerned, but she wasn't convinced. It was just a hard time on him right now. She loved him and "he loved her too".

Then he lost his job. Things just got worse. He was getting violent. He'd throw things, like dishes, when they weren't clean. He'd started getting violent with his kids when their rooms weren't perfectly cleaned when he said. They had no money and couldn't afford to pay bills. Eventually they had to move out of her mother's home and into a home they'd rented.

The oldest child was nine years old now. The youngest was three. The father couldn't find a job. The mother couldn't keep a job for medical reasons. The father started to do these "get rich quick" type programs, wasting what little money they had. The utilities were cut off often. It was not unusual to pick up the phone to have no sound or to turn on the lights to find no electricity. It was worse in the winter when there was no oil for heat. The children learned to sleep under many blankets and wear large, warm sweaters. He was getting more and more frustrated because life for him wasn't turning out as planned. He had no money and his marriage wasn't doing well. They were having problems now, twelve years after the wedding. The oldest girl was now ten. It became a pivotal year for her. It was in this year that everything changed.

It started with her mother, who, having no one else to talk to, became a very close friend and confidante of the daughter. The pair talked about many different things together, like marriage, relationships and, of course, money. The daughter became the support system her mother so desperately needed. She counseled her mom to stay with her father and to make things work. He wasn't that bad of a guy, right? Besides, she didn't want to be without a father. Who listens to a ten year old anyway?

At the same time, her father took a particular interest in the daughter as well. He started to play fight with her at night; especially on nights when her mom wasn't around. The games escalated into him sending her to bed, and when she refused he'd tear off her clothes making playful comments and coercions, leaving the young girl to think this was a game. It must have been appropriate because her father would never do anything to harm her. When the girl would try to pull a blanket over herself, he'd rip that off too. She could do nothing to cover herself, so he started to antagonize her into retaliating – take his clothes off too. This became a game they played night after night, when the mother was absent.

Eventually he started to have her chase him into the bedroom, only partially dressed, or not at all. He'd pin her to the bed, or force her head towards the ground, where his private parts were. One day he claimed "We'd better stop before something happens that shouldn't". The poor girl was left wondering what that could possibly have been. Would she be pregnant? (knowing very little of the process), would there be other problems? What could she have possibly done that was so "bad"? He continued to play this game for a few years, but eventually the girl got smarter, and realized that if he said 'go to bed' and she went straight away, she'd avoid the whole "game thing". This must have frustrated her father because he became more creative in his approach.

In this family, giving each other shoulder massages was a usual occurrence. Even to pull one's shirt over their head to expose their neck was normal. Usually their chest areas were covered by the shirt; however everyone but the father was female, so it wasn't that big of a deal. On nights that the mother wasn't home, the father began offering back rubs. They'd start on the floor, with her unclothed from the waist up, lying on a towel. Then he'd have her roll over to massage the front where "the muscles were very tight" and "any professional knows that". He claimed that he'd been to professional masseuses where they did all over body massages, and he would do one for her if she'd like. Again, all seemed legitimate; he wouldn't do anything wrong, especially if a professional had done the same thing to him. The towel would be placed over top of her chest to start, but as he moved quickly down towards her breasts, he'd move it out of the way "to get full access to the muscles" claiming that "he wasn't looking, don't worry".

These massages continued at the request/persistence of her father. They eventually became the full body massage as well, starting with her naked on the towel, with another towel temporarily covering her buttocks. It was quickly moved as well for the "full massage experience". Then she'd flip over to have him massage her front muscles as well. This consisted of massaging the whole body (and I mean the whole body) completely uncovered. All the while he'd always claim that he "wasn't looking" despite her catching his eyes on several occasions. He continued to assure her it was normal, and there was nothing wrong with it. This continued for a few years, until she was about thirteen years old. Once when he stopped for a while, without apparent reason, she became really concerned that he wasn't interested in her, or happy that she was his daughter.

Soon though the play fighting returned, complete with the constant grabbing of breasts and genitals during the 'fight'. He always brushed it off as a mistake, and often apologized. One time it escalated as far as the clothes being ripped off again, in his bedroom. She was pinned to the bed, in a very open position. He rubbed his hands all over her and made comments about how she had grown since he'd last seen her like this. She developed fairly early, and quickly. Her breast size was that of a late teenager, or even adult by the age of thirteen. This seemed to entice him, since his marriage had died in that area. Maybe he saw this as the next best thing?

Her mother never knew, as she never told a soul. Everyone had their own problems. While this was happening, her dad was still openly violent and abusive to the family. When he came home from wherever he was all day (as he didn't have a steady job), he'd complain about the dishes not being done, or the clutter in the living room, or kitchen. He'd throw the pots and pans across the kitchen to "get them out of his way". When he insisted on the children helping him to clean the house (which only happened when he went on a cleaning rampage and he suddenly turned into "Mr. Clean"), they had no choice, and were often harassed the entire time. When helping with the dishes, he'd throw things into the dish tray, especially the sharp knives. It was his goal to teach them to have quick reflexes, and it was their fault if he hit them, because they didn't get their hands out of the way fast enough. He'd throw away everything that was in his sight, and didn't belong there. This often included valuables, important bills and papers, school forms, and anything else that "shouldn't be there".

If the children did something wrong to each other, or at school, they were slammed into the wall and held up by their necks while he yelled at them about appropriate behaviour, and how stupid they were for not thinking about their actions. When report cards came home and the girl had a 96% in math class, he asked where the other 4% was. One time the girl was not where she was supposed to be when he came to pick her up, so when he got to her, he almost ran her over with the car. She jumped out of the way to avoid being hit. This was in front of other adults who didn't recognize the signs, and did absolutely nothing to help.

While all of this was escalating at home, the young girl had changed schools and now took the high school bus. Soon she met a group of high school students who wanted to be her friend. They were nice to her, and sat with her, and a few even seemed to like her. In fact, one boy, about 17 years old, used to sit with her a lot. He started to hold her hand. She was only 11 or 12 at the time, and hadn't ever experienced this before. She thought it was nice. He must really like her. Then he started to touch her leg. It sent shivers up her spine, but she thought it was how she should feel. Then he started to slip his hand further up her leg, touching areas he had no right to touch. He liked to touch her in the back of the bus on the way home from school. She still didn't think anything was really wrong, after all her father did the same thing during the massages and 'play fighting'. Soon the boy started to take her hand, and put it on places he shouldn't have. She hadn't done this before, but thought it must have something to do with liking a boy, so she went ahead and did it. These actions continued each day on the way home from school. Not knowing any better, she continued to sit with this boy, and allow the touching to continue. Soon the boy also began coming by the house and meeting her family, telling her family that he was a close friend who liked to "protect her on the school bus". They seemed to like him, and allowed him to come by whenever he wanted.

That winter, they were all having a snow fight outside together. As everyone headed inside, the boy pulled her aside and kissed her. It was her first 'real' kiss. She thought it was ok, but something in her felt weird. She was starting to know that something wasn't right. Each day on the bus after that, he'd either sit with her, or sit across the aisle from her. He'd sit with his zipper undone, with his private part fully exposed. Eventually she decided she didn't want to be part of this process anymore, and began ignoring him, but it was too late – there was no turning back now. Even when she started to work part-time, the boy would follow her from job to job. On one particular job, he would always continually try to catch her alone in the back room and touch her, while in another job that he followed her to he'd continually try and grab her and rub himself against her. As a result, she became very vigilant in never again letting herself be alone with this particular boy.

Because of all of these abusive relationships early in life, there is no question that the young girl's impression of the opposite sex became profoundly distorted. As result, she thought that when it came to boys, this type of behaviour was somewhat normal and, as a direct result, she got easily dragged into situations that were either abusive or far beyond her years. For example, early in high school, she established an ongoing many-year relationship with a boy who treated her absolutely abysmally! She allowed him to abuse her all through high school, only severing the relationship when she finally moved away for school.

Throughout her high school years in its entirety, her father continued to be a very destructive influence in her life. He even tried to kill her once, after picking her up one night after work. He was late and she was upset, and the whole thing just escalated from there. Basically, after a fast and furious car ride home with her father becoming more and more agitated all along the way, she knew in her heart she was fast approaching the point of no return. After all, over the years she'd come to recognize all of the troubling signs. As a result, as soon as the vehicle stopped, she immediately rushed from the car and made her way toward the back door of their house. Unfortunately, her father got there first. Just before she reached the door, her father grabbed her and started choking her, screaming that if she didn't finish cleaning the dishes and kitchen before he returned, he would kill her. He then pushed her forcefully away and ran back to the car, spinning out of the driveway and pulling away in an absolute frenzy.

Needless to say, the girl, now 14 years old, was extremely upset. She entered the house and instantaneously burst into tears. She picked up the phone, but really didn't know whom to call. Not thinking very rationally she grabbed the first knife in the drawer, sitting down to seriously contemplate what it would be like not having to live like this anymore. However, eventually she put down the knife, and again picked up the phone, unsure whether to call the police or her best friend. Ultimately, she decided against both, choosing instead to sob. In the end, she decided she couldn't leave her mom and sisters because they needed her and her protection. Instead she decided to do something about her life, and the way it was spinning out of control.

In the few years following this particular incident, the girl climbed the ranks within a well-established community organization, reaching the top in record time. She also joined some sports teams, which not only made her stronger, but also taught her some very good moves in being able to better defend herself. Most importantly, she also began avoiding her father as much as possible. Within the community organization she also developed some very solid friendships, one in whom she felt reasonably comfortable in confiding. Also at this time, she began attending Church quite regularly, committing herself to Christ in her early teen years. In understatement, she truly feels that without these things happening in her life at this particular time, the story might have had a much more unpleasant ending! It was also at around this time that the 'play fights' with her father became fewer and fewer, as she was no longer willing to tolerate that type of unacceptable behaviour anymore.

At the end of high school, she applied to several universities, however none closer than at least three hours from her family home. She definitely needed some distance! It was extremely hard leaving her younger sisters behind, as at least until up to this time she'd always managed to protect them. Nonetheless, before finally leaving for university, sisters talked to sisters, and daughters talked to mother, and although none of the specific ugly details were ever revealed, she left the family home for school that year reasonably convinced that everything was completely understood where her father was concerned.

Although there have been several setbacks throughout her life in the intervening years, (eating disorders and relationship troubles for example) the constant battle between trying to end her own life or trying to save the lives of others has finally been resolved. She has chosen to influence the lives of others as a teacher. Of course, there is no hiding the fact that the 'she' of this story, is really 'me'. I'm currently 23 years old and determined not to make the same mistakes as my mother. I will recognize the young 'me' in the lives of others, particularly my students, and I will try to help to make things a whole lot better! I've finally come to realize that I can't change the past, but I certainly can do something about the future

Chapter 25: Summers from Hell

I am not your classic case of someone who experienced sexual abuse and consequently went on to suffer academically, get into hard-core drugs, rebel as a teenager or withdraw from family and friends. If anything, I did the exact opposite. Aside from one telephone call I had with my brother almost five years ago, I have yet to record in writing what happened to me over sixteen years ago. I have grappled with whether or not to tell my story, but the time seems to be now right. I have tried, unsuccessfully, to start writing this paper on at least four different occasions. Three years ago, I decided that I couldn't continue dwelling on certain things that have happened in my life and I made a vow to move on. It wasn't until I walked into a university lecture on risk and resiliency where it was stressed that people, in general, have a tremendous capacity in overcoming profound challenges in their lives, that I realized that I had a powerful story to tell, and that it should definitely be shared.

As I mentioned previously, a few years ago I phoned my brother to ask him if "it" really happened. Over the years, I had convinced myself that I had made "it" up in my head. I remember him responding clearly by saying "Yes Mary, it did happen but we are beyond it now. This doesn't mean that we forget, but we are stronger now." Since then, I have rarely thought, and never talked about it... until I walked into that lecture. My story begins when I was seven years old.

In my early years, many of my summers were spent at a close family friend's cottage located in northern New York State. My parents were busy back home in the city running a family auto shop business and, in retrospect, probably enjoyed having several weeks without us around. For the most part, we (myself, my brother Brian, and our two family friends, Jerry and Don whose parents owned the cottage) spent our days basking in the sun, swimming and playing soccer. Sometimes Brian, myself, Jerry and Don would go and spend afternoons and nights at another friend's (Ryan's) cottage in the neighbouring valley. While we were there, we would be supervised by Ryan's mom Debbie, a naturally beautiful woman who always had a drink in one hand and a cigarette in the other. At the time, I wasn't old enough to realize that Debbie and her husband were having serious marital problems as a result of both Debbie's alcoholism and their inability to compromise on the right way to raise their children. What I did know was that their family dynamic was drastically different than my own.

I could never pinpoint exactly what was different about my family when compared to Ryan's, but I can remember Debbie always yelling at Ryan. Actually, to be honest, she had an extremely gruff way of interacting with any of us. I vividly remember her lips often being pursed in a certain way; a result of chain smoking and constantly being angry and frustrated with her life. I realize now that their home was a toxic and abusive one, which consequently resulted in Ryan seeking control and power by hurting other living things and acting out in clearly unacceptable ways. For example, killing animals by ripping off their legs, setting fires, smoking in the bush, swearing, and displaying sexually inappropriate behaviour, were the types of things Ryan consistently engaged in. And all of this, when combined with his absolute disregard for consequence, somehow made him very intriguing for me and my brother who had led, at least up to this time, pretty sheltered lives. Looking back, however, I can clearly see that these behaviours of Ryan's were probably symptomatic of an internal rage that was yearning to get out.

Being the only girl, and the youngest of the entire group, I was always trying to keep up, trying to impress them and show them that I could do everything – just like them. I was always striving to be accepted by the boys, especially Ryan, so that they would include me in their shenanigans. It was this feeling of wanting to be accepted by them, mostly because they were older and cooler than my brother and myself which kept me silent about what was happening to me for far too long.

I remember when Ryan was about twelve years old he started talking a lot about this word "sex" (which I didn't understand as I was only seven), and he would show us his stash of pornographic magazines and videos hidden away in his room, which we would all peek at when Debbie was nowhere to be found. Because I was so young, I didn't think much about it and figured it was just a part of being a boy. After all, I had seen lots of pictures of scantily clad pin-ups in my dad's auto shop. However, Ryan's fixation with his porn collection seemed to peak his curiosity beyond just wanting to look, and it didn't take long before the talk and pictures turned to physical touching. It started with him merely grabbing and squeezing me, but not in a manner that was necessarily sexual.... at least not at first!

When Jerry, Don, my brother and I would sleep over at Ryan's cottage, I always stayed in one bedroom while the boys would always sleep out in a small bunkhouse located toward the back of the property. On the night when Ryan decided to test the boundaries, I remember he had managed to linger behind in my bedroom, trying desperately to remain undetected by his mother. First he gave me this really cool flashlight, which I still remember in great detail, and then told me to go under the covers. I'm still unable to write exactly what happened, but he touched me and made me do things which, at the time, I didn't realize were totally wrong. I do remember feeling like I had to do what he said because, after all, it was Ryan. He was older and very commanding. I felt like I had no option. Behavior like this went on for the rest of the summer and beyond.

I remember another time when the boys asked Debbie if we could all sleep out in a tent rather than in the cottage. Debbie wasn't keen on the idea and I couldn't understand why it was such a big deal to Ryan that we all stay outside together. He nagged Debbie all day for permission. She relented and we all camped outside in the same tent. That night, I distinctly remember Ryan behaving in the same inappropriate manner, however this time it was not just with me, it was with Brian as well. As I got a bit older, I started realizing that this wasn't normal. Not seeing Ryan throughout the winter gave me the chance to think more about what had happened, and when I was nine, just after the summer had started, I finally decided that enough was enough. I was sleeping inside at Ryan's cottage and the boys were outside. Ryan had sent Jerry inside to try and lure me outside to the boys' sleeping quarters, but this time I said "NO"! It was now clear to me that Ryan knew that what he was doing was wrong and, from that moment forward, I refused to go anywhere with him. I started resenting and hating him with a passion.

I must say that I didn't think much about what had happened for many years after. However, I grew to absolutely demonize Ryan in my head. My parents couldn't understand why I no longer wanted to hang out with any of the boys anymore (besides my brother of course), while it had been a major preoccupation in my life in the years before. In the end, they deduced that I was merely disappointed and angry with Ryan for starting to drink heavily and doing hard drugs, especially after his parents finally divorced. However, because I was so obvious in my disdain for Ryan, my parents started to suspect something more serious "was up".

During the summer when I was fifteen, I came home after working late one night and went outside to sit with my brother on the deck of our house. I distinctly remember this night, because the conversation I had with Brian changed my life forever. I remember sitting in silence with him, saying absolutely nothing for a long while, just looking at the full moon. At one point I looked at him real intently and I could tell, based on the look on his face, that he knew exactly what I was about ask. "Brian, did it really happen and did it happen to both of us because I remember this one night when...." "Yes" he interrupted. "Mary, it really happened." We both sat there in silence and tears started coming down my face. I could no longer deny it, as hard as I tried. We decided that night that we had had such a good life and that this was not going to taint anything because our parents had worked so hard to make us happy. My relationship with my brother had changed forever. He became my best friend, my teacher; a person who now knew absolutely everything there was to know about me. He confirmed in my heart what I knew to be true; that my abuse just wasn't a figment of my imagination. At the time, I felt somewhat liberated.

After that summer, and specifically that conversation with Brian, I thought I had dealt with everything sufficiently, but clearly I hadn't. I remember being up late one night, with my dad busy doing paper work at the kitchen table (while my mom slept), when all of a sudden I was absolutely overcome with anxiety and emotion. I just couldn't take it any longer; I had to tell a parent. Sobbing, I called my dad into my room and told him of Ryan's inappropriate behaviour toward me. Although my dad wanted details, I couldn't give them to him. I felt so confused and conflicted. I remember the look of utter shock on my dad's face, and then him leading me in to their bedroom so I could to tell my mom. I remember mom's reaction being nothing short of complete outrage, of course, completely directed at Ryan, and likely Debbie, his mother. She too wanted details and I was able to give them to her, only on her prompting. "Did he do this?" she said and I would respond.

At this particular time many responses to my reveal were discussed, with some of them being completely irrational. However, after talking about retribution, offering excuses, and even considering some possible diagnoses, it was finally decided that to deal proactively with all of the "ugly" details emanating from seven summers previous, there would be the calling of a general family meeting on the weekend, coinciding with my brother's return from a sporting trip. At this weekend family meeting, it was decided we would discuss how we could collectively move forward (as a family) in direct response to the recently revealed (dark) secrets. However, the weekend came and passed without mention of a single thing related to my disclosure. In fact, to this very day, we have yet to speak of it again as a family.

To be fair here though, my parents have always been able to fix everything and this was one thing that they really couldn't fix. They had no idea where to start or what to do given the situation and it is for this reason that I believe they decided to remain silent. No question, this angered me for a long time, but I now understand (although it isn't the approach I would take) where they were coming from. To this day I remain extremely close to both of my parents however, anytime there is discussion of molestation or abuse on TV or the radio, I am unable to make eye contact with either of them. As I mentioned at the start of this story, I didn't turn to negative outlets to deal with my anger, frustration, and sadness. I continued to excel in school and extra curricular activities due to my stubbornness and drive to not let my early experiences negatively impact my life. Of course, it wouldn't be completely honest to say that I've been completely unaffected either. For example, in my teenage years, I would often find myself alone in my thoughts, trying to rationalize everything that had gone on. I also think my early experiences have somewhat affected my abilities in trying to establish solid relationships with the opposite sex. Sometimes it seems like it takes too much effort to connect.

Through it all, my brother has guided and supported me unconditionally. He has always been there for me, and has helped me work through my anger - teaching me how to channel it in a more positive direction. It would be very easy to get bogged down and only deal with the negative, but when everything is said and done I have had, and continue to have, an absolutely wonderful life. I have a great family that has provided me with nothing but the best they have to offer, including the strength required to transcend the abuse of my youth.

I can honestly say I now feel at peace with my life. I know I have dealt with certain things in an unconventional manner, but it has certainly worked for me. Through meditation and confiding in certain trusted people all along the way, I have always managed to move forward. Now as a certified teacher, I understand completely how events outside of school can profoundly influence things that go on inside my classroom. How things happening early in a life can have tremendous influence on human development. Most importantly, I've learned that bad things happen to good people, (sometimes very young people), but these bad things don't have to destroy your life or impede your hopes and dreams. You can get back up, dust yourself off, and move on. This is the one lesson that I vow to consistently teach my students.

Chapter 26: I Am More than a Statistic

At the end of the week I will walk across the stage and graduate, having received my second degree, a Bachelor of Education. This day has special significance to me as it proves that my socioeconomic and family status did not predetermine my fate, as is sometimes the stereotypical view. As I receive my degree, I will be among those that have defied the predictions with respect to children from working class, single parent, female-headed families, forced to live, for a large part of their early (developing) years, well below the poverty line.

From the moment I was born to a single, teenage mother I have consistently defied the odds. Because of my mom's strong beliefs against abortion, she left the man who impregnated her and said goodbye to her youth to raise her (unplanned for) child. However, just hours before she was about to deliver me, she discovered to her surprise not only would she be responsible for dual parental responsibilities for one newborn, but rather two, as she was indeed having twins. Over the next few years my mother made every sacrifice possible; her efforts exclusively put into raising us to the very best of her ability. In hindsight, with reference to these substantial efforts, I must say she did a truly remarkable job under sometimes very difficult circumstances.

Unlike a typical teenager, my mother spent the majority of her evenings and weekends singing lullabies and changing diapers. That is, when she wasn't working as a waitress at a local pub trying to provide us with the basic necessities of life, and stay ahead of all the household bills. Without exaggeration, my mother rarely had time to eat or sleep, let alone have any type of a social life. But at every possible opportunity, she was constantly prodded by her family to try and find us a good father; someone that could support the family and provide us with a decent future. Young and naïve, and under a certain amount of pressure from her family, mom became involved in a relationship with a lazy, chauvinistic and, in the end, very abusive man. She soon married him, which laid the foundation for a tremendous amount of dysfunction in our family from that moment forward.

In short, our new father was verbally, emotionally, and physically abusive to my mother on almost a daily basis. Although he never physically struck either of us girls, the verbal and emotional abuse he inflicted upon us has left invisible scars that have yet to heal, right to this very day. Nevertheless, within two years our family of four grew to five, as a new baby sister was added into the mix. Unfortunately, this new addition to the family changed little, as the abuse from our father actually escalated, and his addiction to alcohol and drugs made him an increasingly volatile man to be around.

Amidst the everyday traumas families face when living with an abuser and addict, we stuck together - my mother and her three girls. But as I look back, it was the financial struggles on top of everything else which made our lives particularly difficult. As might be expected, our father found it difficult to keep a job, and the money he or mom made was overwhelmingly used to secure his weekly supply of alcohol and drugs. In fact, on several occasions, we faced absolute homelessness because of his irresponsible behaviour. But worse than that, was the way he consistently tried to isolate us and control every aspect of our daily lives. Basically, our father controlled who we were and whom we were allowed to see; he controlled what we were allowed to do, and where we were allowed to go – he controlled every aspect of our lives!

I can certainly remember a few happy times throughout this period, however, the feeling that I'm most reminded of, in looking back, is one of constant fear. More specifically, fear of my father! My father used to always say, "Children are meant to be seen and not heard" so when we were at home, we spent a lot of time outside in the back yard so he wouldn't see or hear us, and, sadly, so we wouldn't see or hear him fighting with our mom. It was like we were constantly walking on eggshells around our house, so as not to upset him. As kids, you were constantly kept off balance because you never knew when he would fly into a total rage.

Every night, without fail, mom and us girls would serve him his dinner in the living room, and then we would retreat quietly back into another room to eat our own meals. It honestly felt like we were only there to serve him, to be his slaves, to answer to his every whim. On a good night, when he would fall asleep on the couch after eating, we would sneak back into the living room and tiptoe around him so we could watch a television show ourselves. This was bonus time for us! I suspect, that in looking in from the outside, our family appeared to be as normal as every other one in our neighbourhood (perhaps minus the cannabis plants that were constantly growing out in the back yard). However, no one really knew what was going on behind the closed doors of our house. Or if they did, they certainly stayed well away because they sure didn't want to get involved.

Growing up, I'm not sure I really knew myself that anything was terribly wrong with our family. If you have nothing to compare it to, you just assume that this is how everybody else must live. But I must have known, deep down in my heart, that something wasn't quite right because some nights, while watching television, I would see commercials for the Kids Help Line, and every time the commercial would play I would get a really weird feeling in my stomach. I think something was telling me that I should write the number down and call them. But I never did.

When the nightly fighting would begin, I would immediately retreat to the bedroom I shared with my sister. I would sit behind our door quietly crying, but also listening. Everything I would hear, breaking glass, foul language, threats, I would faithfully copy down into a notebook I kept. I would often fall asleep behind the door, with my notebook in my hand, waiting to run out and jump in front of our father to protect our mom. On a number of these occasions, I can remember becoming upset with myself for not copying down the telephone number for the Kids Help Line as advertised on the commercials, so I could call someone and let them know what was going on in our house. But eventually I would convince myself not to worry, as this was how all families behaved, and there was absolutely nothing really wrong with my family. So I would go through the nightly routine of ripping up the notes, and hiding them in the wastebasket in my bedroom so I would not get caught. Then, the next night, the note taking ritual would begin all over again.

Growing up my mom instilled the importance of community involvement and education in us girls. She was very passionate about us getting a good education and becoming involved in the community, and so she let nothing stand in our way of this. Mom would always say that she wanted us to do better and go further than she did, and by having a good education we would have the opportunity to do so. And because our father had allowed us to spend time engaged in structured educational pursuits, or in specific community groups that he personally sanctioned, (such as the church and girl scouts), I was able to discover many ways in which I could, for at least a little bit of time, escape everything that was going on at home. School in particular became a retreat for me; an excuse to stay away from home for long periods of time.

In my elementary years, I joined as many school teams, clubs, and organizations as I could. I stuck around school as late as possible, always volunteering to help out my teachers in any way that I could. I became actively involved in the local girl scouting club, soccer team, and the church. Also taking advantage of every opportunity to stay away from home, at the age of eleven my sister and I began to babysit in the neighbourhood, and started a small house cleaning business.

When I turned thirteen, life was again dramatically altered, but in an extremely positive way, as a sixth member was added to our family when my mom gave birth to my baby brother. Looking back, I think that our father must have thought that the arrival of my brother might somehow magically repair what was so incredibly broken in our family. Unfortunately, after my brother was born, not much improved, especially between our parents. In fact, the fighting increased, while the money decreased. At this same time I was entering high school, thus started to spend more and more time out of the house. I tried desperately to isolate myself from the "goings on" at home, basically living two separate lives. I definitely focused on my academics, maintaining honour roll status each and every year. I joined many sport teams, and fully participated in the students' council. I gave up all of my lunchtimes to tutor other students, and in my non-school time, I attached myself in a volunteering capacity to many organizations within our community.

Things went on like this until about midway through my high school years, when my mother finally hit a wall and said, "Enough is enough"! She finally found the courage and strength within herself to leave our father, and this time it was for good. One morning before school she told my sisters and me to go to our aunt's house immediately after school, and not to rush home as we usually did. Although no formal explanation was given, I think my sister and I realized what was truly happening, and from that day forward, I can tell you that a tremendous weight was lifted off our shoulders. It was like caged birds finally being set free! Although we still lived in fear of our father, never knowing when he would show up drunk and/or stoned to pick a fight, the constant abuse had finally stopped.

From this specific moment on, our mother and the four of us kids decided that we would stick together and try and make it on our own.

Now with no child support and four children to take care of, mom soon realized that it would be extremely difficult to make "ends meat". So on top of her full time factory job, she now took on two additional part time jobs. In essence, from 6 am until midnight, each and every day, my mom was at some type of job. This meant it was primarily my responsibility to run the house, freeing up my sister to take on a part time job at a local store to help out. I would take my brother to the babysitters each morning and pick him up after school. My nightly ritual turned into: diapers, heating up dinner, dishes, more diapers, laundry, bathing my brother, then reading him a story before bed. I would then move on to my little sister, where I would help with her homework before putting her to bed. When everyone was finally asleep, I would then turn to my own schoolwork.

Even with mom working herself into the ground, it seemed as though we just couldn't stay ahead of the bills and, as a result, throughout this period we plunged further and further into debt. I can remember having credit companies calling our house almost daily, trying to desperately collect some of the money we owed them. The phone never stopped ringing! They constantly made threats about taking away our services; the cable, the telephone, the gas, the hydro, and one by one, their threats became our realities. One winter afternoon I arrived home from school to find mom sitting at the kitchen table crying. I asked what was wrong and soon found out that our gas had run out and we no longer had heat or hot water. For the rest of the month, I remember mom faithfully spending her nights in front of our fireplace, ensuring that the embers didn't die out so the house would stay somewhat warm. To bathe, we were forced to boil our water in a single kettle, repeating the process over and over until we finally had enough to do the job properly. Nonetheless, over the next year or so, the stress associated with poverty, the arguments, and the legal court battles surrounding the separation of our parents, finally took its toll on the family.

During this period my mom's nerves finally got so bad, that at one point she was forced to take a short leave of absence from her main job. It was also around this time when my sisters started to "hang out" with negative peers, and start to experiment with alcohol and drugs, which made things far worse as far as the stress levels in the home were concerned. Me, with my mom's constant support and encouragement, went completely in the other direction, delving further into my education and volunteerism in the wider community. In looking back, I can clearly see that it was my specific way in trying to cope; strategically distancing myself from what was really going on in my home life. Again, even through the most difficult of times, I always loved being at school. No matter what was occurring at home, I felt safe and important at school; like I made some type of a difference there. For example, one year at Christmas time, I co-organized and ran a very successful food, clothing, and toy drive within the school. I was extremely ecstatic at the success of the fundraiser, knowing how many local families we were able to help out that year. And though the results were completely superb, I was also a little embarrassed, as although no one really knew it at the time, some of the very food I was helping to collect was significantly helping my own family out as well. But we got through it, as a family, and I finally made it through high school.

Two profoundly inspirational teachers made a huge impact during my secondary education. These two teachers were extremely proud of my accomplishments. They recognized my full potential, and they always encouraged me to reach for the sky. They always talked about university with me, a concept that was completely foreign to me. At every opportunity they talked of the endless possibilities that lay ahead of me in the future, and this always made me try a little bit harder. My teachers made it possible for me to attend school trips and conferences. With a lot of hard work and constant and unconditional love and support from my mom, I was ultimately accepted into university, my first year completely paid for by scholarships.

University was an eye opening experience for me, as it was the first time that I could truly see just how far my family and I were able to travel, overcoming many obstacles along the way. Sometimes during lectures, I would get very upset when I was exposed to biased statistics about single parent families and many unjustified, stereotypical statements about the working poor. But it also served to motivate me because although I could always see my own life amongst the numbers, I became absolutely driven to prove some of the predetermined conclusions wrong. I'm not going to suggest that it was easy, but throughout university I always managed to maintain an honours standing thereby keeping my scholarships, all the while working at part time jobs and volunteering within the community.

Today, without exception, I look to the future with much anticipation and delight. I am certain there are some major challenges and hardships my family and I will continue to endure in the future, but more importantly, I now have the confidence and belief that everything will eventually work out for us. I know that together, as a family, providing each other with love and support, we will be able to pull through whatever the future holds. I have learned much and grown considerably from my past experiences. I know that as a teacher I will be able to provide consistent support and encouragement for my students, the way my teachers did for me. Remembering what a retreat school was for me, I will make sure that my students always feel safe and cared for while they are in my classroom. Most importantly, I will recognize my students' potential, and help it flourish, regardless of their socioeconomic or family status. In my classroom I will maintain high expectations for everyone and help each student see that they can defy the statistics. As I have personally proven, statistics do not determine how high one can fly!

Chapter 27: Life at the End of a Bungee Cord

Resilience or transcendence theory dictates that some children demonstrate the incredible capacity to overcome horrendous childhoods, and, yet, go on to develop completely healthy "normal" relationships and live very positive, productive lives as decent law-abiding adults/citizens. I wouldn't consider my individual circumstances to be exceptionally severe or even particularly unusual but I do know that they proved enough of a struggle that there were times when I thought that I wouldn't make it at all. It was while flying high above the clouds on a return flight from the far reaches of the province, courtesy of a school board that wanted me badly enough to fly me to meet them, that I finally realized the very great distance that I'd travelled to get to this very point in my life. Not just in a geographic sense, but in a physical and spiritual sense as well.

The years leading up to my adolescence were normal enough, although an accident when I was three left my dad barely able to walk and unable to continue working at a job that he absolutely loved. Despite this, we went camping every summer, one year to the West coast, the next to the East. My sister and I were both happy enough and until high school, my grades were fine. Then, without warning, a dark shadow descended on the family, and everything changed dramatically for us from this point forward.

While away on a trip to the United States with the high school I was attending at the time, things for my family went horribly wrong, as I was to discover immediately upon my return from my American adventure. In short, while I was away, my dad experienced the severe onset of depression and, in a clinically depressed state had seriously considered bringing his life to an abrupt end. We know this for sure because my mom walked into their bedroom while my dad was busy loading a single shell into one of his guns. After this, the details become a little fuzzy. All I know is that my dad was hospitalized for several weeks, and we weren't allowed to visit him - at all. What I do know for certain about this time, is that my sister and I took over all of the responsibilities of the house, including the care for our mother who had come down with what she called at the time a bout of allergies, although it now seems more likely that her illness was related to the profound levels of stress that she was under.

When dad came home, things seem to return to normal, or about as close to normal as they had been before his hospitalization. But this all changed dramatically a few weeks later when he called me into his room to help him sort out his medications. This job was not new to me so I thought nothing of it as I dragged myself away from an important school essay that I was working on at the time. As I sat at the foot of his bed, helping to arrange the medications he was required to take, my father turned to me and clearly said, "It's all your fault, you know". I remember this conversation as if it only happened yesterday. Needless to say, I was stunned! As I turned to face him, no doubt with a questioning look plastered across my face, he proceeded to explain to me that my grades weren't as good as they had been in elementary school, that I was putting too much pressure on the family, and that I wasn't taking enough responsibility for the running of the house. He then looked me straight in the eye and said as clearly and evenly as I had ever heard him before, "If it wasn't for you, I would never have put that shell in the gun." No tears, no expression at all!

Although initially shocked at this series of events, I tried to convince myself that this was not my dad talking; it was merely someone else in my dad's body. I remember calmly handing him his medications, going for a glass of cold water, and then returning to work on my essay. However, shortly thereafter, my brain finally caught up to the words uttered by my dad, and they suddenly hit me like a ton of bricks. I immediately broke down sobbing. When my mom came in to check up on my progress, and discovered my state, it was decided that I should see a doctor myself, and immediately.

Less than a week later I was an outpatient at our local hospital, seeing a social worker named Amy, on a three-times-a-week schedule, and placed on a waiting list to see a psychiatrist. It took quite awhile for me to get an appointment to see the psychiatrist at the hospital, so in the meantime our family physician prescribed the SSRI antidepressant Paxil. Over the course of the next few months, the doctor played around with my dosage, trying to find the combination that worked best for me.

I remember this particular period in my life being an extremely rough one. Sometimes I was one person, all hyper, gregarious, and cheerful, the next, a totally different personality; lethargic, quiet, reticent, and withdrawn. In trying to describe it best, it was like living on the end of a bungee cord. I would dip down into an unimaginable low, and then rise to an incredible high, only to drop down to the low again. But with every plunge, I would sink deeper and deeper into a depression; never quite rising to the highs first experienced on those initial jumps. It was as if the bungee cord was becoming longer, related directly to a corresponding reduction in its overall elasticity. All in all, a few months into treatment, (actually just after first seeing the psychiatrist), things started to really unravel on me - especially in school.

On top of the extreme ups and downs I was experiencing in moods, many of my school courses were going very badly, and, to be quite honest, at this particular time in my life I was no longer interested in putting in the effort that might more positively influence my grades. I was failing many of my tests, and I was incredibly behind in submitting many of my assignments. One evening, feeling completely overwhelmed, I remember thinking what's the point in going on? In not being able to satisfactorily answer this question, I ended up just sitting on the floor of my bedroom, with a tall glass of juice, my CD player playing, and a full bottle of my antidepressant medication. Without getting into too much specific detail, after knocking back more than a month's worth of medication, I eventually lost complete consciousness.

I don't remember much until I was back at home and off all of the medication that the hospital had pumped me full of to stay "normal" while recovering. I wasn't sure exactly what had happened after I fell asleep that night, but considering I was still breathing, I didn't really want to know. Amy immediately recommended I talk to my doctor about changing my medication. Soon thereafter, the news about the side effects of Paxil hit the news. My doctor and I decided to try Celexa. The process of getting the Paxil out of my system, and the Celexa into it was another incredibly painful experience. I spent many days sick, and often couldn't muster the energy to go to school at all. Thankfully, when I was going through the roughest of stages on the road to recovery, school was almost out for the summer so I spent the worst part of the withdrawal period within my house.

The next few years were about as uneventful as I can remember. The Celexa seemed to be working and my lows almost disappeared entirely. My friends noticed the change and I started to become the social butterfly I had once been. At the very end of my Grade 12 year, I remember one poignant moment when a friend and I were teasing the boy she liked by telling him that she thought he was cute, in a foreign language. Being the teenagers that we were, we giggled about his reaction for days. When school started again in September, she was still interested in this boy, Henry, and finally had the nerve to tell him in English. He admitted he thought she was sweet and they started dating. It was all very romantic and he even brought a daisy for me one day when the three of us went to a movie together. This was also the same September that the terrorist attacks hit New York. As if the shock of what had just happened wasn't bad enough, one of my teachers said that we were still going to write our test that day because after all "we are not Americans". I was absolutely furious. I wrote the test and then phoned home to check up on my parents. They asked me to stay at school and we would talk at the end of the day. By 3:30, the winds had carried the black smoke from the twin towers across Lake Ontario, and we could see the sky over Toronto turn a murky black. It was, and still remains, the scariest thing I have ever seen in real life.

Something about the 9/11 tragedy served as a trigger for my dad, and he once again suffered a psychotic episode. He was hospitalized for his own safety and released days later when things seemed to be under control. Thankfully, they were, and October began as smoothly as possible given the situation. But October would bring more tragedy for my friends and me. During one of the beautiful days just before Thanksgiving, my friends and I were lounging in the cafeteria at school when one of our teachers joined us. We immediately knew something was wrong, just by judging the look on his face. First he asked us all to sit down, and then proceeded to tell us that during his short drive home that afternoon, our friend Henry had been involved in a very bad accident. Apparently, going around one of the last corners before his house, he had lost control of his car and swerved into oncoming traffic. Henry was pronounced dead at the scene.

Henry's parents held a funeral in the largest church they could find and more than 300 of his friends and school colleagues faithfully attended. I can tell you, there were many tears shed on that afternoon. Of course, I did what I could to console my friend, but she was absolutely inconsolable. Just a few weeks later she dropped out of school for the remainder of the year. The following year she decided to attend a different school, making it virtually impossible for me to reach her. Sadly, we quickly lost touch. Without question, the impact of Henry's death, and the loss of such a close personal friend to another school and another life, hit me like a lightning bolt. As a result, given my fragile state, I ended up quickly spiraling downward again. I ended up hospitalized, the specific details of which I can't even remember. Although, I do remember being given my medications by IV, and being fed by a nurse so they could ensure that I was eating, but nothing more than that. Slowly, I once again improved, and once my stability was firmly established, I was released.

No question, after this episode, things started to definitely look up. I was accepted at a major university, and into their teacher-training program. Life during my first year at university was pretty standard, nothing really out of the ordinary, at least until late into the school year. Then one day I receive a panicked phone call from my cousin. Being only 8 months older than me, this cousin and I have spent most of our lives sharing the same friends and more or less growing up together. When I asked her what was wrong, she immediately broke into sobs, but also choking out the words, "Matthew is dead". In effect, as I was to discover, three more of our friends had just been killed in another traffic accident. Although this tragic event did indeed start to initiate another episode, this time I was prepared. Because I had been completely upfront with my university roommate, about my medical history and how I could cycle down to incredible lows, particularly if triggered, she watched me very closely for the next few days and ensured that I got some immediate help from counselor's within the university itself. This time, recognizing the signs, and with the help of a very good friend, I was able to get well out in front of the descent, and completely evade any period of hospitalization this time. It was a very good lesson to learn!

After a very short period of recovery this time, I quickly bounced back to becoming the "me" that everyone recognized, especially my friends. I became heavily involved in university life and kept myself as busy as possible. However, halfway through my third year, I was tested again. It was my cousin on the phone again, and again she was hysterical. This time a really good friend of both of ours had committed an act so unexpected, so out of the blue, that the whole community was in absolute shock. Apparently, after a rather uneventful day out with friends, he had returned to his house, and hung himself from one of the beams in his garage. His parents returned home to find him there the next morning. This time I battled really hard to fend off the shadow, however, in my extreme efforts to keep my emotions and feelings in check, another very negative coping mechanism started to manifest itself. To get some relief, I found that cutting myself somewhat helped. However, before very long I came to realize that this type of behaviour was certainly not the answer to my problems either. I knew that once again I would need some medical intervention to get a handle on the way things were evolving.

Eventually I stumbled onto a doctor who very proactively started to manipulate different medications, eventually settling on the drug Effexor. I have been taking this particular medication for quite some time now, and have found it works very well for me. Every day that I take my medication, I take the time to remember all my friends who were taken away far too early, not getting the opportunity to be where I am today. I'm finally coming out the other side. I finished high school, survived university, and have now become a certified teacher. No matter what may happen in the future, no one can take that from me. I'm on the road to recovery, haven't had suicidal tendencies in almost two years, and have even started to live a much healthier life. My parents are both on the way to recovering, despite several relapses themselves. Most recently, I realized that had it not been for the many people around me, I might not be where I am today. My friends, for seeing a change in my personality, my parents for helping me first seek help, my doctors for helping to find the right medications, and most importantly my social worker Amy, for giving me the tools to succeed when she wasn't able to be there. Because of her courage to listen and provide me with the beliefs that I am stronger than my depression, I have survived. I am now well placed to recognize the symptoms in others, and offer guidance in getting the requisite help. I now know better than most that you don't have to live your life attached to the end of a bungee cord.

Chapter 28: Functioning with the Dysfunctional

Growing up, I often thought of my family life as perfect; one older brother, a stay at home mother, and a father that ran his own very successful business. We would retreat to our cottage in another part of the Province on weekends, spending the entire two months there in the summer. If we didn't head to the cottage, we went hiking as a family. We went on two trips a year; west over Christmas, and south over the March Break. However, this happy life started to unravel in the mid 80's when my father had an affair. My mother knew that my dad was having an affair, but she presumed it was likely a person that my father met on some of his business trips. Instead it turned out to be my mother's best friend, whom she helped get a job within my dad's company. I was 10, my brother 13, and although we didn't know at the time, we were about to embark on a very turbulent journey.

When it became apparent that my father was going to divorce my mother, in understatement, her life was shattered. I didn't know what all of this really meant, as all of my friends had both of their parents at home so I had nothing to compare it to. However, I can still see to this day, in my head, a friend of the family who was assigned to explain to us that because our parents were going through a very difficult time, that we should not expect, at least for a time, their support. Basically, that we would need to rely on each other in that regard. His words could not have been truer.

My parents went through an 'ugly' divorce, battling over everything; the house, the summer property, and custody of us. Ultimately, we remained in my mother's custody, and for the first two years after their initial separation, my mother cried constantly. I remember coming home from school and seeing my mom on the couch crying. My mother ended up going into a deep depression, seeing a psychiatrist, and being prescribed heavy doses of medication to both help her sleep and cope with her profound sadness.

During these initial two years, I clearly remember four traumatic events – ranging from fights, police involvement, attempted suicide, and break and enter. As can be expected, I witnessed numerous fights between my parents. In one instance, my father came over just before I was to head off to a sporting event. As their fight intensified, my father ran out of the house and into the ravine behind our house. My mother chased after him. The chase ended up in the front of the house, with my mother clinging to the hood of my dad's car as he was trying to leave, just like in the movies. It truly was a sad sight! There was me, in my track suit crying, just wanting to go to my game and escape all the turmoil.

On another occasion, when my father came to pick both my brother and I up for our usual weekend visit, my mother would not let me go this particular time, only willing to let my dad take my brother. Of course, my dad wanted both of us, but my mother wouldn't let me go to see "the bitch", as we referred to my dad's "other woman" at the time. Even after my dad left with my brother, my mom forced me into her car and drove to my dad's new house where she continued the fight for the whole world to see. There I was separated from my brother, alone and scared in the car, while my parents went totally at each other. The whole episode finally ended when my mother, in a rage, took me back home. Only this time, my dad called the police.

I remember, I was sitting in the driveway in my mother's car when a police cruiser pulled in behind us. The policeman approached my mother, who was completely hysterical by this time. On this occasion, the police took me away from my mother and delivered me back to my dad. My emotions were so mixed up, what do I do? I felt horrible for my mom who was inconsolable, but I also wanted to see my dad and brother too. At the time, I remember feeling terribly confused!

A third vivid memory includes my mother's attempted suicide. She threatened to take all of her prescribed anti-depressants in front of my brother and me. As I wrestled with my mother to get the pills away from her, my brother just sat there and watched. I was able to get to the phone and call my dad at work; I didn't know who else to call. He came right over, as did one of my other relatives, and they somehow reasoned with her. To this day, my brother and I haven't talked about this incident, but I wonder why he just sat there and didn't try to stop her. I can only speculate that it was because my mother favoured me and treated me better than she did my brother. To this day, I still worry about my mother's past attempt, and wonder if she will ever try again.

My last prominent memory is when my mother drove us to our cottage, which she was not allowed to do, as the courts had formally awarded my mother the house, while my dad retained ownership of the summer property. When we arrived at the cottage, my mother forced my brother to open a window, and me to slide through so I could unlock the doors. I knew deep down in my heart it was wrong. I kept saying to mom that we shouldn't be here, but my mother kept saying that she helped build it, and my dad had no right to take it away from her. It was all really odd! While we were in the cottage, my mother started to re-arrange all the furniture, so that it appeared just the way it was before the divorce. I know that my dad found out (how couldn't he with all the furniture rearranged) but I don't know if he ever did anything about it.

I must say though, during these times, my brother and I became closer and closer. We actually went from the bickering siblings to working as a team. We had no other choice, as the advice from our family friend was so accurate – (for long period of times, we really only had each other to rely on). Although, to be fair, we were also fortunate to have extended family that helped to create, by times, a real sense of normalcy for my brother and me. Luckily, we were still able to spend our summers with our cousins at their cottage – completely free from all the crying, sadness, and fighting. As the years passed, my parent's squabbles became fewer and fewer, and things eventually got a whole lot better (and somewhat back to normal).

As I now pause to reflect on my adolescence, I can safely say that we had several caring adults in our lives, which definitely helped us get through this very chaotic time. For me, it was the sense of belonging and importance that I felt when I began to play organized sports. The clubs were generally run by coaches, all of whom were also high school teachers. I excelled at sports and received lots of praise, which certainly served to boost my confidence and self-esteem, and at a time when I was extremely vulnerable in that particular regard. In many ways, the coaches at our school somewhat served as surrogate parents for us for a while, even driving us home after our late practice sessions. During this pivotal time, although my mother and father didn't show much interest in me, and come to watch me play and see me excel, my brother faithfully did and that seemed to be good enough for me. It seemed to get me through!

I have always wanted to be a teacher, and although it's ten years later than I wanted it to be, it's better late than never! I know from experience that when it comes to working with kids, things are not always as they appear. I have many accomplishments that I am very proud of; my athletic career, my marriage, and my wonderful kids. I truly believe that without my involvement in sports, but particularly having the powerful influence of my brother always to fall back on, there could be a completely different ending to my story.

Chapter 29: Here's to Exploring New Horizons

I was always a quiet child. My parents said I was a stark contrast to my sister who was very vocal and demanded lots of attention. My neighbourhood was pretty quiet and it did not have any children around my age. I had no local friends, so often, having an imagination came in handy. This was not to say I didn't have any friends. I grew up having my cousin, Freddy, as my best friend. He was a year younger than me and when I was old enough, I rode my bike over to his place to play or vice versa. I would mostly see my cousin on weekends and the odd evening after school, and we spent most of the summers together.

My parents were (and still are) very loving parents. With my dad often working 3-11pm shifts and my mom working till 5, my sister and I often were home before them and would make our own food. My aunt would often be there watching TV, to babysit until my mom got home. Sometimes, my dad's shifts would change, allowing him to be home by 3, though he would often be tired from work and would be sleeping on the couch. If he wasn't sleeping, he was watching sports. In many ways my dad was great, but he wasn't a patient man. I knew not to bug him while he was watching sports, because he didn't have the patience to answer my questions about the game and would send me out of the room for distracting him. Don't get me wrong, he was fun to be around in many situations, but it was on his terms. He wasn't the type to play catch with me, teach me how to skate, or ride a bike. I don't think he knew how to deal with kids and it wasn't until I got older that he could relate to me better.

My mom was always busy cleaning, doing laundry, cooking or chasing after my sister or arguing (yelling) with her. My sister rebelled against everything it seemed, and my mom really enjoyed that I played quietly on my own in my room and rarely ever made a fuss. My parents never were abusive or excessive in their discipline. There was no alcohol or smoking ever in our house. My mother came from a family of heavy drinkers and an abusive father. My mom was the only sibling of 5 who didn't drink or become involved in drugs.

My dad came from a very poor family, with 7 siblings. His parents were old fashioned and believed in being swift with discipline and short on love (they had separate bedrooms). My dad told me once that my grandmother told him (when he was 8) that he was not to say, "I love you mom", because that sort of talk was for babies. In my life I can count on one hand the amount of times my dad said, "I love you" to me, but I never doubted he meant it in many of the other things he did for us. My mother, on the other hand, was always saying she loved us, and hugs and kisses were her strong suit. It may not have been the most functional of upbringings, but I felt very loved.

School, for me, started off very pleasant in the early years. I have many fond memories of my fellow students and of singing songs in kindergarten, field trips to see maple syrup being processed in grade 1, sitting in a circle with my fellow classmates petting bunnies in grade 2, etc. I didn't have a lot of friends at this time, but I didn't really seek out a lot of friends. A few people made fun of me for being the smallest kid in our class, but it was mostly just teasing. I had one main friend at school named Dustin. I was still friendly with the other students and we got along, but Dustin and I spent most of our time together, both in class and at recess. We loved making everything into a game. There were some kids that never let me play with them and, to some extent, I felt hurt by this, but as long as I had Dustin to play with, things were just fine.

My 3rd grade teacher is someone I will always remember. She dressed as a witch each Halloween and I can't think of a costume that was more fitting for her. She was very strict and very scary. If you were caught not listening, she would tell you to stand while she picked up your desk and shook the contents out on the floor. Then, she would yell at you to pick up all the mess and to hurry up about it, while the whole class watched. If you were goofing off, often she would tell you to hold out your hands and she would whack your knuckles with the thin side of a meter stick. If you were especially bad, you had to spend 5 minutes in the trunk, which was a large old-fashioned storage trunk, which sat at the back of the room, where we had to sit in darkness and think about what we had done. I really hated that teacher, and being in that class.

One day, while playing Terminator with Dustin at recess, Dustin accidentally stepped on my thumb - and bent it backwards. I had badly sprained it and my hand started to swell instantly. I was crying pretty loudly and Dustin brought me over to the recess monitor, who ignored my pleas to call my mom. She didn't seem like she could be bothered by my sobs and told me to "stop crying and go off and play." In repeating through my tears that I really hurt my hand and needed to call my mom, she only scolded me for not listening and said I shouldn't have been playing so rough. So I sat holding my hand and crying until the bell rang and I went to my classroom. By this time, my crying had become sniffling and I approached my teacher to ask her if I could call my mom. She swatted me on the back of the head for being out of my seat and yelled at me to "sit", ignoring everything I had just said. She handed out a quiz, but my hand was so swollen, that I could not grip my pencil. As she walked around the room, she came to me and saw that I was not working. She threatened to put me in the trunk if I didn't start working. I told her I couldn't write, because my thumb and my hand really hurt. She then told me to hold out my hand and so I did, hoping she would see the swelling. Instead, to my surprise, she wacked my hand with her ruler saying she didn't tolerate lies in her classroom. I immediately fell to the floor in pain and began wailing. I think this really took her by surprise, because she sent me to the school nurse to have my hand checked.

It wasn't long after this incident that my parents decided to put me in a new school. I found out, years later, that my 3rd grade teacher was fired along with other teachers at that school for excessive abuse of students and the principal was fired for being drunk many times on the job. My parents decided that I might enjoy being at the same school as my younger cousin, and I agreed that this would be great. Little did I know the pain this change would ultimately cause me.

In starting grade 4 at a new school, I felt pretty scared. I was shy and I didn't know anyone at this school except my cousin, who was in a grade below me. I was by far the smallest kid in the class and I looked like I should have been in kindergarten. The kids at this school didn't seem interested in playing Transformers or GI Joe at recess, but were more interested in talking about girls, kissing, fighting, sex, drinking, smoking, and other more adult topics. I still wanted to play games and thought girls had "cooties". I was having trouble fitting in and didn't know the topics the kids talked about such as orgasms, marijuana, and sex positions. The first friend I made was a guy by the name of Stevie. He kept asking me to do things for him and he would give me candy. It was easy things, like pass someone a letter for him, or grab someone's backpack and bring it to him, or fetch things for him at lunchtime. Doing these chores for him quickly started to get me into trouble with fellow classmates and through this, I began to understand that he was just using me. Eventually, I stopped being his friend and sought to find a better friend in the class, however, because of my previous actions on behalf of Stevie, I was not viewed very highly by the rest of the class. Making new friends became a real problem!

Luckily, a new kid started at the school that week, by the name of Liam, who had moved in next door to my cousin. He quickly became friends with my cousin and through him, became friends with me. He was into a lot of sports, and it seemed like a lot of kids at this school already knew him. He was instantly the most popular kid in class and I was his friend. The next month, I was a friend to most kids in the class, even though I didn't understand the meanings of many of the things they talked about. It was hard for me to understand why they wanted to look at naked pictures of ladies behind the school or why they didn't want to play with toys. I think the class saw me as different, but as long as I was Liam's friend, they didn't dare make a big deal about it.

Things changed one day during lunch. There were no teachers or monitors watching over our class and Stevie got the attention of the class with an announcement of something he thought everyone should know. Stevie decided to write a fake letter and read it to the class, which described Liam and I as being gay lovers. I don't know why he did this, except to say that he was always looking to put people down and make fun of them. The whole class laughed at us. Liam, being the most popular kid in class, must have felt he had a lot to lose and quickly turned the joke around on me. He yelled at the class to shut up and grabbed the letter away from Stevie. He denied ever seeing the letter and then pointed at me and said that I was "the faggot who wrote the letter!" I tried to defend myself by saying I didn't write the letter, but no one wanted to listen because they were all laughing at me. Liam proceeded to push me away from him saying, "get away from me faggot," while the rest of the class was chanting, "faggot, faggot, faggot" at me. I didn't even know what that word meant or what being gay meant, but from what Stevie read, and its reaction, I understood enough. I was so angry at the class, and especially Liam for turning on me. I ran out of the class crying. A lunch monitor caught me in the hall and yelled at me to get back to class or else he would send me to the principal. He walked me back to my classroom to make sure I stayed in class. Upon entering, the kids were all quiet while he was there. I went to my desk and put my head down, but almost immediately I could hear the kids making fun of me again about being gay (and how they didn't want to be any where near me). My mind was racing and I was so angry and frustrated. I tried to concentrate on the sound of my breath, between the desk and my arms, which were around my head. Oh, how I wanted to shut everything out, and be somewhere else!

Without question, this new turn of events started a downward spiral for me. With Liam now making fun of me and wanting nothing to do with me, all the other kids quickly followed suit. Within the week, the bullying started in earnest. First, it began with being teased constantly throughout the day (each and every single day). I was forever being called faggot, loser, douche bag, nerd, gay, idiot, etc. No one wanted to play with me at recess, even my cousin. It spread to the other grades as well, with even kindergarten kids starting to make fun of me. I felt like the whole school hated me, and figured the rest of the world did too. I felt so ashamed and embarrassed. I probably should have told my parents at this time what was going on, but I was extremely embarrassed and I didn't want them to know about how much of a loser I was. It was easy to hide this from my parents at this point, because they were used to me being quiet in my room, and they were both busy with work or issues around the house. My sister was already in high school at this time and was in the popular crowd. She didn't like having me around and she constantly fought with me at home. She loved putting me down and making fun of me, so I didn't want her to find out anything about what I was going through. It was enough I was being teased at school, I didn't want it at home too.

Soon the bullying at school turned to abuse. Being so small, compared to the rest of the class, I was an easy target. There were many things that happened to me over the remaining years in elementary school, but needless to say, things went from bad to worse. I was physically beaten up almost every day, with some days being worse than others. I had kids from many grades bullying me, with the boys mostly participating in the physical abuse, while the girls were busy creating new rumours, gossip, and saying hateful things about me. At times, some girls found it fun to beat on me as well. There was one recess monitor, who didn't seem to care about what any of the kids were doing, so it was easy for the kids to pick on me. If they ever got caught, it was seen as boys are being boys, or they would just say they were playing a game and they weren't hurting anyone. This seemed to be sufficient for the recess monitor. There were woods surrounding the grounds, a large wooden jungle gym, an annex, and other places kids could hide or drag me to if they wanted to avoid being spotted.

The abuse at times was pretty severe. In class and in the playground, kids would hit me with hockey sticks or bats, often leaving bruises and cuts all across my body. They would gang up on me and pelt me with rocks. Many times before school, after school, or at recess, kids would "jump me" and try to hurt me. They would do various things, from holding me down and beating me, to kicking me in the groin. If it wasn't a beating, it was public humiliation. I often was met in the bathroom by a group of boys who would shove my head in the toilet, or who would try to pee on me, or douse me with water. They would tell the teachers I was trying to look at their privates, and it would always end with the whole class laughing at me. Often, kids would gang up on me, hold me down and remove my pants. The kids would gather around and laugh as I tried to take them back, as they played "keep away". I was embarrassed and ashamed, and when they were tired of this, they would throw them into a tree, or a thorn bush, always giggling as they watched me struggle to get them back. Another pleasure of theirs was to throw me into the trash bin (outside the school) and hold the lid down while I tried to get out. This would leave me dirty and smelly, which then lead to being called smelly, stinky, or trash bin.

Sometimes the abuse and beatings were more severe. Kids often deliberately took turns sharpening their pencils, and jabbing me as they walked by me on their way back to their seats. Another game they played was to throw small paper airplanes, with needles taped to the front of them, into my back. As always, these types of activities came with warnings that if I told on them or made any type of noise, they would beat me even worse after school. I knew this to be a real possibility, because on more than one occasion, I had received a severe pummeling after the final bell. Several of these beatings involved one particular boy, who one day brought out a knife. I remember him very clearly waving the knife in my face as I lay pinned to the ground and him saying, "I am going to gut you like a fish if you tell anyone about this." He then gave me a deep cut on my wrist and, on another occasion, he gave me a gash on my chest (both of which I still have the scars to this day).

What bothered me most about the beatings was the feeling of helplessness. I was so small and weak. I would try with all my might to fight back, but I couldn't do anything. I could only lie there and take it. Soon I stopped fighting at all, giving in totally to the pain. In fact, I often welcomed the pain. Psychologically though, it was torture to know you can't do anything to stop someone from hurting you or embarrassing you. There was no other option but to always lose. I would sometimes provoke getting hurt, or not even try to defend myself. Instead of raising my arms to block a rock from hitting me, or running from getting hit from a bat, I would stand there and take it. I no longer cried when I got hurt. Much later in life, I learned this was something called "learned helplessness," which, ironically enough, I evoked in mice (in research labs) many years later. While I felt bad for the mice and didn't enjoy hurting them, I also felt distant from it, thinking I wasn't much different than a mouse in a cage…. Sometimes, you are just the mouse born into a bad situation.

You may be wondering where my parents were in all of this. I was extremely embarrassed and did all I could to prevent my parents from finding out. I always had a story to tell my parents, if they inquired about a cut or bruise they happen to notice. I would tell them I got hurt playing with the other kids, or that I fell out of a tree making a fort. I would tell them that I got cut by a hockey skate, or slipped on the ice and banged my head. I always played the "I am so much smaller than everyone else so I get hurt" card. And it usually worked. My parents knew I wasn't popular, but they didn't know I was extremely depressed about it. They tried to get me involved in things like piano, soccer, karate, art programs, etc., but I wanted nothing to do with any of it. I resisted any social event. I didn't want to meet new people, or have more situations where people could make fun of me. I didn't want to be known as "the loser" in even more situations.

One of my lowest points during this time was when I was at my cousin's place, on a weekend, playing with him in his house. He didn't hang out with me nearly as much as before, but we still seemed to get along just fine. This particular day, there was a knock at the door and he went to see who it was. It was friends from school. They wanted him to come out to play, but he told them that he couldn't because I was over. I was in the other room, and he didn't know I could hear him. His friends scoffed at him and asked him point blank, "why do you hang out with that loser and faggot?" He told them that he had to because his mom makes him; that he hates having to spend time with me, but he is forced to. Of course, I overheard this and it broke my heart. I didn't say anything to him about what I had heard, but after his friends left, I told him I had to go home for supper. I never called him again, or went over to his place anymore. He never even inquired as to why. It was like he just forgot about me. To this day, I rarely see him or talk to him.

I hid out in my room a lot and started to draw "dark" pictures, which I often ripped up and threw away once I was done. I wrote poems and stories with very "dark" themes. I often looked in the mirror, always hating what I saw. I would hit myself in anger, telling myself that I was no good, ugly, and ask why I was so stupid. I often banged my head against the wall or the bedpost. I hated myself for being such a loser, and wanted to constantly beat myself up. I started to believe what all the other kids said about me. Often, I would angrily repeat those same hateful words to myself in the mirror. I hated everything about myself. I wanted him to go away, to hurt him, to lash out at him, and to blame him for everything that had made my life so miserable. I couldn't stand seeing myself in photos, or to even look at myself while I brushed my teeth. I would often jab needles and pins into my arms, just to feel the pain.

Pain to me was real, it was tangible! The rest of the world seemed like a dream or fairy tale to me. All the regular thoughts and actions you would expect kids to have meant nothing to me anymore. Playing and fun were concepts that were distant to me now. I went from being a normal kid, wanting toys for Christmas, wanting to go to birthday parties or to Disneyland, to being a kid who wanted nothing more than for kids to stop picking on and teasing him. I desperately wanted a friend, and someone (anyone) to notice me and take some pity on me. I longed for people to stop hurting me. It was also around this time that I started to wish for far more sinister things. I started to wish for my life to end. My needs became so simplistic. I started trying to sleep as much as I could to try to forget. My dreams seemed more real to me than reality and, often, I wasn't sure which was which. Time even seemed to be distorted to me. I would be sitting in my room for what felt like hours, but only 20min would have gone by. Then, other times, when I was hurting myself, I thought I was doing so for only a few minutes but, in actuality, sometimes hours had passed.

I didn't like to leave marks on myself because I didn't want my parents to start to question. I didn't want them to feel disappointed; to find out their son was such a loser. My mom would say things like, "you're so handsome," and I remember feeling that this is just something moms say to their kids, but it isn't true. I felt like that phrase was mocking me, and it embarrassed me, because I didn't believe it. In hindsight, I know my mother was being loving, but at the time, to hear someone say you are handsome and/or special, felt like lies, taunting, teasing, and just empty words. Sometimes, I felt my parents knew I was different and they were just trying to make me feel better, or to trick me into thinking I was just like everyone else. I became very withdrawn and didn't want to talk to anyone. I avoided people and any situations where I could possibly be teased or beaten up.

I know my parents were concerned, because they kept prodding me to tell them how I was feeling or what was up with me; but I generally refused to talk about it. Though one time I did tell them about being beat up at school, whereby they promptly called and made a complaint, even though I told them not to. That next day, the teacher made an announcement about me, noting that some of the boys in the class had apparently beaten me up and that he wanted me to point out who in the class did this to me. Of course, I refused to tell him and he just said, "If you won't tell me, then I can't help you." I already knew he couldn't help me, and felt like I was a nuisance to him. I knew if I pointed out the boys, this was a death sentence to me. None of the boys spoke up or confessed, so he kept the whole class in during recess. Of course, the class hated me for this. After school that day, I got one of the worst beatings I had ever had. This is when I received the gash on my chest from the boy with the knife. I learned not to tell my parents or ever attempt to talk to the teachers anymore. To me, there was nothing they could do to save me. When I got home that day, I cleaned myself up before my parents got home. My mom noticed the scrapes on my face and some cuts on my arms and asked if the boys did this at school? I said no, that I had avoided them by climbing a tree, and that it was the branches of the tree that had caused all the visible damage. I learned how to really sell my stories!

Moving on to high school was not much of a change for me. The same kids that bullied me in elementary school came to the same high school. What happened was, those who didn't know me at high school were told lies and stories about me. Stories that quite predictably made me sound bizarre, gay, stupid; a real loser. It seemed like within the first day, each one of my classes had heard rumours about me, and already people I didn't know were picking on me. That first week, I was shoved into lockers, had my head dunked in the toilets, had my arm twisted behind my back until I pushed a penny down the hall with my tongue, was picked up and thrown against the lockers (adding several new scars), was held down and had part of my head shaved, had my clothes taken from the gym locker room and thrown out into the middle of the gym, and, finally, several times throughout the week, I was put into a head lock and choked until I passed out.

On one occasion, I distinctly remember trying to reach back and poke the eyes out of the guy that was choking me. I wanted to press my thumbs through his eye sockets until I felt nothing but his brains. I didn't care about the consequences if I did this, but my arms were too short and I was far too weak. There were times when all I thought about was the ways in which I could pay people back for what they had done to me. Could I get a bat and sneak up on them and beat them until they didn't move? Or could I sneak a pencil in my sock and the next time they went to beat me up, jab the pencil into their neck? It was morbid; it was wrong; but I felt true hatred for some of them. Instead, I always did the right thing. I was the good boy. I still believed what goes around comes around, and that being good would eventually pay off. Why not? All the movies,

TV, fairy tales, etc. tell us about happy endings, or how the good guy eventually wins out. The bad guys always get it in the end, right? Wrong! Reality doesn't work this way. I remember for many years, I kept asking myself, "Why me? Why me?" But I quickly came to this conclusion... "Why not?" Life is random and sometimes things just happen. I was unlucky. There was no greater power, no fate, and no destiny that lead me to this. It just was the way it was! I just had to accept who I was, my situation, and, ultimately, surrender!

What I did to survive was to avoid people. I had to become invisible and blend in with the background. Years ago, I started writing letters to myself as if I was talking to a close friend or someone who cared. I would write explaining all my feelings, what had happened that day, what I wished for, and whatever dark thoughts I had. It was my way to vent and cope with what I was going through. I continued this all through high school.

Luckily, my fellow students eventually got caught up in being popular, going to parties, dating, and/or playing sports. I still got picked on from time to time, but for the most part, I generally became a nobody. I went home for lunch, and home right after school. I talked to no one. Anyone who tried to talk to me, I ignored them. I had accepted the fact that I was a loser and completely worthless. All I cared about was breathing and eating. I figured my purpose was to make others happy by getting teased and beaten up. At least I had a purpose. I did my homework, and did the best to appease my parents, I took up watching people and trying to figure out why people are the way they are, and why they do the things they do. I enjoyed biology and science, because they gave meaningful explanations to life, and they seemed concrete. I liked logic, because it was devoid of emotion. Emotion seemed to ruin everything. Why couldn't people just be logical?

Something started happening to me by my senior year. I had not had any friends since grade 4, so I was accustomed to being alone and lonely. It wasn't unfamiliar anymore, and while I didn't like being lonely, I didn't really care if no one wanted to be my friend. When people tried to tease me, I would challenge them by saying, "is that the best you can come up with?" Then I would insult myself in a more vulgar and hateful way. There was nothing someone could say to me that I had not already said to myself. I didn't back down from people or take offense anymore. I learned to use humour, directed at myself, to challenge those who tried to hurt me. I found this particular tactic to be especially effective. When they didn't get the response from me that they expected, or when onlookers would sometimes laugh at my humour, it seemed to completely disarm some of my abusers. It wasn't until years later that I found out some these younger onlookers actually thought I was a really cool guy in high school, because I appeared to be completely unafraid, or easily intimidated. Little did they know what I was really thinking at the time.

It was at this time, late in my high school life, that I made my first real friend. It was a guy named Theo. He was a big, tall guy, the type most people didn't want to mess with. The girls thought he was good looking, but he was different, like me. He wasn't in the popular group. We liked video games and comic books, Star Trek, and all things geeky. We got along. He treated me like a sidekick, or "tag along" during school, but after school we appeared as equals. It was that first summer after grade 11 that I went to work for his dad in a highway construction company. The company was made up mostly of family members, thus they didn't really like that I was hired, because I was merely a friend. Theo didn't have a very good family life and his dad treated him like one of his workers rather than a son. He had his own issues, just like I had mine. At work, I was asked to do many things I shouldn't have done, and was tested time and again. They wanted me to quit, but I had something to prove and I met all their challenges, no matter how exhausted and sore I got.

What I didn't realize over the summer was that with all the physical labour - (for 10 or more hours a day) - it had whipped me into pretty good shape. At the start of grade 12, people thought I had gone on steroids over the summer, but all I saw in the mirror was the same skinny, scrawny, loser. I remember that first week, one of the guys that was always out to hurt me, went to push me and I grabbed his arm and easily twisted it. He went right down on his knees in pain and begged me to let him go. I did so, more out of surprise than pity. I didn't know my own strength and, for a while, I asserted this new strength unnecessarily.

Half way through that year, Theo dropped out of school to work full time for his dad. I had joined wrestling (at my gym teacher's request) and excelled in it. I was 126lbs, but very strong for my size. I was liked by my teammates, but I kept them at a distance because I didn't want them to find out how much of a loser I was. I avoided parties and outings for fear of ridicule. I even had girls like me, but I avoided them too. It was a mixture of not truly believing they liked me, and a fear of a girl finding out I had never even held a girl's hand before.

In many respects, at this point, I was no longer being bullied, but now I was the one creating my problems. I pushed people away. I refused to have fun socially. I avoided dances, hanging out, going to the beach, etc. I still saw myself as a loser, even though everyone else didn't see me this way. This continued into university. It was half way through my first year that I really started to come out of my shell. There wasn't anyone I knew from high school there; it was a brand new setting, with new people... a fresh start. People seemed to like me. I was funny and people seemed to want me around. I was still very hesitant to let people get too close to me, but I was starting to not see myself as a loser anymore.

Slowly, through university, I started piecing my life together and putting some of my past behind me. I worked as a custodian at school, to pay for my tuition each year. I was getting the highest grades ever and was on the Dean's list each semester of my undergraduate years. I tutored in the school's learning center, and it helped me gain a whole lot of confidence. Out of university, I applied for a summer job with a large government agency. They looked at my grades and offered to send me to graduate school, to work on a project they needed someone for. I didn't have much free time in graduate school to go out. However, it introduced me to the world of teaching; something I began to see, I just might have a calling for!

I know my past experiences have shaped who I am. What I still struggle with is making friends. The logical side of me knows, because I have moved around so much, been spending my time studying or working, and having little time for socializing, that these situations have led to my difficulties making close friends over the last few years. Though, I must admit, there is a side of me, sometimes, that wonders if perhaps there is something about me that puts people off and puts me in a bad light. I seem to be able to make acquaintances just fine, but can't seem to really make long-term connections with people. I see others, with the same workload (s) as me, with these great friendships. Perhaps they have lived here longer, have mutual friends, or have other situations that brought them together. I keep telling myself to not lose hope; that things will eventually get better. Sometimes, you feel lonelier when you are out with a bunch of people, yet isolated in a crowd. You are on the periphery of conversations and sometimes you aren't invited in unless you invite yourself. I suspect, these are the residuals from my past.

I go through periods of feeling great and having fun, but I can, at times, feel down and out of place. In the end, life is what you make it. You can drive yourself crazy trying to predict events in life and try to avoid negative circumstances, but really, it's the struggles in life that allow you to grow. Hopefully, you gain knowledge from these struggles and with knowledge gain some wisdom. I think for every negative situation, there is an equal amount of good situations that are just as likely. I think, throughout my life, I have managed to hold onto hope. It isn't hope for any specific thing; it is just hope! Life is random, and there can be excitement in randomness. Predictability can be boring. So here's to exploring new horizons.

Chapter 30: A Sign of Something Else

A lot of things have been going through my mind both during and after our class today, and I felt I needed to write some of them down. I hope your okay with me sharing some of this with you. I know, you're probably thinking, heck here we go again, another one of your students telling some sad old story, and you having to listen and/or read it. However, I've noticed students coming to you all the time, talking about their various personal experiences, and you really seem to listen to them. So, as you've already probably guessed, this is another one of those stories, so let's just say you've been sufficiently warned! I know you do this type of a thing in the summer when you have your students do an essay on risk and resiliency; however, I would like to discuss it now, as I don't want wait.

Today in class you talked about the case involving Jeremy, and the descriptions of self-mutilation brought back some interesting memories of my own high school years. I grew up in a rural community with two very supportive parents and a loving family. However, from the time I was seven years old, just around the time that my father's mother died, my father has been suffering from clinical depression and some type of anxiety disorder. As a result, he has been on and off some form of medication ever since that time.

I can tell you there's nothing more horrifying then watching your father have an emotional meltdown because when you're that little, if your parents don't have full control, then who does? Certainly not a seven year old, who barely understands why Dad is constantly sad, sometimes becomes completely enraged over seemingly small matters, or becomes really ill from all of the medications he is forced to take. In fact, when we were camping one year, he had an adverse reaction to one of the many medications he took at the time, and he ended up in the hospital. All I remember is him lying on the ground, red-faced, and my mom trying to keep it all together, while my sister and I were sobbing, wondering what was going on, and whether or not he was going to die. Unfortunately depression, anxiety disorder, and schizophrenia are all things which have occurred on both sides of my family...so I suppose it was not terribly surprising that things ended up for me the way they ultimately did. But one thing I know for sure is that everything started to go horribly wrong for me once I started being consistently picked on in school.

In short, I was constantly bullied as a child, from kindergarten, right through until my last year of high school. I was teased about my weight, my glasses, my freckles, or anything else that the kids could think of. I spent most of the time completely miserable at school; absolutely dreading it. Although I was a very talkative child at home, the minute I stepped onto the bus in the morning, I clammed up completely. I was painfully shy all through school and generally kept to myself, except for a couple of very close friends who I somewhat confided in. I think this was my way of avoiding potential confrontation with some of my peers, who made my life a living hell at school on a daily basis. For the most part, I basically coped by bottling up how I was really feeling and, as a result, I kept things pretty much under control all the way through elementary school. However, when I reached high school, things definitely took a dramatic turn for the worse.

In high school, a particular group of girls decided to make it their business to harass and tease me relentlessly- anytime they got the chance. And while it had been the boys in elementary school who made my life absolutely miserable, it was the girls in high school who were by far the worst. Sure, there were the older boys who always made fun of me as I passed them in the halls, but that wasn't so bad because I didn't have to deal with them in class. However, where the girls were specifically concerned, I generally had to put up with them in both the halls and class. Of course, there were places in the school that I would avoid entirely, because it meant dealing with abuse from both the girls and boys. Sometimes I'd go miles out of my way just to avoid the harassment. No doubt, after several years of this, any self-esteem that I'd managed to acquire as a child had pretty much vanished. The old adage that if you're told something for long enough, you'll eventually start to believe it, was particularly true in my case.

All through high school, I felt I was ugly, useless, and generally not worth very much as a human being at all! Eventually, when combined with the constant fighting at home, and my Dad's unpredictable mood swings and general volatility, I became more withdrawn and unhappy. Ultimately it was during this period (for about five years) that I fell into the first of three major depressive states. I also started 'cutting' myself at this time, with various sharp inconspicuous objects. At school I would use compasses, pins, needles, etc., while at home I'd actually use knives. All through this high school period, I wore long sleeve shirts to hide any marks, and I'd always make the cuts high enough on my arms so that if my sleeve were to slide up, no one would notice.

Thinking back on it now, none of my teachers suspected a thing, as they probably thought I was just a very shy kid who always chose to sit at the back of the classroom. Believe it or not, my parents never caught on either. In trying to rationalize the behaviour, I think I was trying to numb all the pain I was feeling on the inside, by hurting myself on the outside. It at least seemed to distract me for a bit. Anyway, everything came to a head one night when I lay in my bed, pondering which knife in the kitchen I could use to slash my wrists and finally be done with it all! I remember just sitting in my room, just staring blankly at the ceiling and holding onto the knife, trying to work up the courage to do it. I had even written a note to my mother, saying how sorry I was, and how much I loved her, my Dad, and my sister. However, at some point in my descent, something seemed to just click. I seemed to just "come to". Realizing how very sad I was, and how very close I had come to doing something extremely foolish, I sensed that something was very wrong with me (inside my head), and that I was going to end up just like my Dad if I didn't do something about it -- and fast!

The very next day, I told my mother that I desperately needed some help, but I stressed that I didn't want to go the route of doctors and medication as I saw what it had done to my Dad, and I was scared of taking something that could ultimately make me feel far worse than I was already feeling. I began seeing a therapist, and this lasted for about a year or so. She helped me come to terms with my depression, and helped my Mom and I work out our relationship, which was rapidly eroding by this point. I learned a lot about asserting myself and changing my thinking patterns and habits, and how to deal with confrontational situations in a much more effective manner. I never told my Mom or my therapist about that night, and I tore up the note and threw it out...I have been back to see the same therapist twice since then, (both times because of a depression), but for the last year and a half, things seem to be getting better. I am more in control of my moods and emotions (most of the time) and through my sessions with the therapist, I have succeeded in building up some of my previously eroded self-esteem.

Though I went through most of elementary and high school with very little self-esteem or positive self-concept, I am now at a point in my life where I feel I'm starting to build a bit of a reservoir, which seems to serve me well, especially on the bad days! It was very encouraging to hear you say that it is our job as teachers to offer care and support for our students even if the things that are having a direct negative influence on them have absolutely nothing to do with what's going on within the four walls of our classrooms. As you so correctly say, "If it's getting in the way of my teaching and your learning, then it's definitely my business". I agree with your position completely, "That if it's not me as teacher who takes up the challenge than it may be no one, and someone is always better than no one"! As a teacher, I hope to be someone who gives a damn about my students, beyond just the academic considerations. That was certainly the type of teacher I needed!

Self-mutilation is a delicate issue, and is almost always a sign of something else. From experience, it's usually a sign that there is something far darker going on in the child's life which is causing them to cry out for help. Many people don't even understand what exactly it is, and why someone would even consider it. The stigma attached to it has meant that only a couple people actually know that I ever did that to myself. It is something I would never ignore if I suspected a student was doing it to themselves, and would not hesitate to deal with it and even probe deeper, to ensure that they got some help.

In closing, I'm afraid that I haven't explained myself very articulately, but this is the best that I can do. Talking about my personal life has never been something that I've been very good at, and it's only in the last couple of years that I can even speak about it at all. In the end, I suppose my experiences will only serve to make me more aware of how students are feeling and what I can do to bolster and build their self-esteem. At minimum, as a teacher I will constantly encourage my students, and demand of them that they treat one another with kindness and respect.

Anyhow, I just wanted to say thanks for being one of those teachers who cares so much for their students, and for being one of those who will go to bat for a troubled child, even when others are not willing to 'go there,' whatever their individual reasons might be. That's the kind of teacher that I hope I'll be in the future!

> We are spirits passing through the doors of time,
> with an invitation heard before we find,
> shadows on the mountainside.
> Eagles find the souls they hide.

Chapter 31: Elie Wiesel and Me

Arguably the most powerful of all the books written by Elie Wiesel is the trilogy Night, Dawn, and Day, which, despite the author's insistence that they are not necessarily autobiographical, contain many of the major events of his own life. In completely digesting the books, I feel reasonably confident in saying that Elie Wiesel, in describing his innermost thoughts, feelings, and actions, is the poster child for Post Traumatic Stress Disorder. However, what I did not realize is that Wiesel would show me, through his writing, how this disorder was truly applicable to my own life. In examining some of the diagnostic criteria from within the mental health domain, Wiesel through his writing would appear to exhibit all of the major symptoms or characteristics of PTSD. He suffers from insomnia, nightmares, and other sleep disorders. He suffers from bouts of severe aggression and often transfers this aggression onto someone he loves or feels safe with. He suffers from detachment issues and often forces himself away from meaningful relationships or social situations. This often leads to feelings of complete alienation or acute loneliness.

When I first met my fiancé back in the late nineties, he was an angry young man completely dressed in black and standing alone at the back of a crowded room. When I laid eyes on him I knew I would not be able to walk away. Unfortunately, my immature fourteen-year-old mind could not build up the courage to speak to him. I just stood there, staring, and wondering what would make him stand so all alone, and so very quiet. A young man as good looking as him could easily have integrated himself into the crowd without any second looks from all those around him, and it seemed odd to me at the time that he would choose to isolate himself in such a manner. Three weeks later, he returned to my life, bent on one knee and begging for gum. This time we were locked together for good. He chose to speak to me, which must have meant he was allowing me entrance into his inner sanctum. Little did I know that it would be almost 5 years later before he would truly allow me to see him for who he really was.

When my husband was a young boy he was repeatedly sexually abused by a male friend of the family. I do not wish to impart to you the horrendous circumstances of his abuse. However, I would like you to picture a boy, not unlike Wiesel portrays in his books, tortured relentlessly in his mind, and unable to feel safe enough to tell anyone of his innermost demons. As a result, he carried this baggage (shame) with him throughout his entire young life.

When I look back on our now ten-year relationship, particularly early on, there were countless indicators that he was indeed suffering. There were countless signs that he desperately needed someone more educated and worldly than a naïve fourteen-year-old girl to help him. In hindsight, he displayed all of the symptoms of PTSD. For example, his nightmares would leave him curled into an almost inhuman ball and having fingernail marks on his skin from trying to literally hold himself together. He was oppositional to almost any authority figure that tried to get close to him. He lacked any tangible social connections, and you could count the number of valued relationships he had on one hand.

As we grew older and our love grew more intense, my husband began to push boundaries. He never once became violent with me, but the constant emotional rollercoaster ride that I was continually on, and the psychological abuses that I was forced to endure, certainly chipped away at my overall self worth and self-esteem. As a more educated woman, I now understand that this was his attempt at testing me. This was his concerted effort, as Wiesel so effectively illustrates in his writing, particularly concerning the people who really matter, to push loved ones away so you can end it all in not just physical but also psychological isolation. Lucky for my husband that he married me because I am not one who is lightly pushed away, and I'm certainly not one who gives up easily. Thus, despite all of the tears and many sleepless nights, I hung in!

Just around his 21st birthday my husband finally told me of the horrors of his youth, and the fact that he had been abused. Without anyone else to turn to, as he had disowned his family by this time, we turned to each other and to a Male Crisis Centre to get the much needed help that he so desperately deserved. They spoke to him about the possibility of his susceptibility toward drug abuse, violence, and suicide if he did not receive psychotherapy to once and for all exorcise his innermost demons. As he progressed in treatment, our relationship grew stronger and stronger. Since he no longer believed that he was at fault and not worth loving, he finally allowed me to fully love him.

I know now that my husband suffered from PTSD. Of this there is absolutely no doubt in my mind. The writing of Elie Wiesel helped me see that. I always understood that my husband's abuse had affected our relationship, but I never considered it to have a clinical foundation that definitely needed to be aggressively dealt with. I never once have blamed him for his behaviour.

In looking back now through analytical lenses, one question that seems to still trouble me a great deal, where both my husband and Wiesel are/ were concerned, is why did nobody ever notice that something was incredibly wrong? Why was there never any attempt to help, even if it had been dismissed, that could have simply eased some of the quite obvious burden? I know that I have confidently written around 100 papers on why I want to be a teacher. However, I now can say with all honesty that I wish to be a special educator to help kids like my husband. No one will walk out of my classroom without having been asked some specific questions – perhaps in a quiet isolated moment. For every 99 responses of "I'm fine" or "Mind your own damn business" there might be one that will thank me for even questioning them at all, because deep down in their troubled hearts they will know that I truly care about them. In my classroom my students will always know that they have an adult who is willing to talk to them; an adult who will try to make things better for them irrespective of the challenge.

"There exist some evils so terrible and some misfortunes so horrible that we dare not think of them, whilst their very aspect makes us shudder; but if they happen to fall on us, we find ourselves stronger than we imagined, we grapple with our ill luck, and behave better than we expected we should". (Jean de La Bruyere

Chapter 32: It's Just an Appendage

One ordinary day in November, a life-changing event happened to my daughter. It was like lightning striking when there didn't appear to be a storm visible on the horizon. Out of the blue, my daughter's course of life was forever diverted to a direction that both terrified and mystified all who knew her. This event had a powerful affect on our entire family, and all of her friends as well. The accident was about more than the resulting physical disability. It was really about the mental disabilities that surfaced and developed in places where they were least expected.

To begin, my daughter is a vivacious, strawberry blond who was an active and impulsive sixteen-year-old when she was working in her part-time job at a local store. She was working with a meat grinder during hunting season, but didn't know enough about the meat grinder to know that she had not been shown all the safety features and procedures when using the grinder. As she was handling the refrigerated meat, her hands grew colder and numb, stealing the sense of touch and the knowledge of where her hands were in comparison to the working mechanisms of the grinder. Her hand was caught as she dropped in the meat and was drawn into the machine along with the meat. As the pain struck, it was displaced from the hand to her chest. She thought she was having a heart attack. Fortunately, there was a nurse shopping in the store at the time of her accident, who was able to calmly take control of the situation, call for an ambulance and calm down a very hysterical girl. My daughter was immediately rushed to the local hospital, but later flown to Toronto where it was determined that her hand was just too mangled to save.

After the surgeries, my daughter was eventually sent to a rehabilitation centre where she was taught how to use her prosthesis and tie up her shoelaces with one hand. While she was there, she met many other people who had also lost limbs, many of whom thought that losing a hand was the worst thing that could possibly happen to a person. Meanwhile, my daughter always thought that losing a leg would have been a far worse thing to have happen. The point being that everyone in 'rehab' generally thought their own injury was far more manageable than someone else's. At the time, this was a clear illustration to me of how some people are able to endure their own personal crises by projecting a more dire set of circumstances onto someone else, thereby better enabling them to cope and move effectively forward in an altered physical way.

Before the accident, my daughter served as an instructor for a ski team at a local ski hill on the weekends. After her accident, to her credit, she continued coaching the children as if the accident had never happened. I think the children actually served as a very powerful outlet for her. Of course being children, they had absolutely no inhibitions in asking about her missing hand, even wanting to know the goriest of details. My daughter was able to talk openly with the children about her accident and this seemed to really help. Adults on the other hand, were generally a different story. For my daughter, adults appeared to be the ones who had the most difficult time in dealing with her physical difference, and this, early on, generated some uncomfortable times for her. As my daughter tells it, the children's openness always provided a welcome release for her and gave her ample opportunities to vent her own true feelings, fears and frustrations. In fact, in relation to her accident, it was in learning to manage the openness of the children that better equipped my daughter to deal more effectively with the reluctance and reticence of the adults.

When the children first encountered my daughter after her accident they didn't know that she had lost her hand. They just thought she was hiding her hand up her sleeve for some unknown reason. So, she tended to play games with them. She would tell the kids that her hand had fallen off in the snow and they had to look for it, which they always did with a great deal enthusiasm. Then the questions would start. "Did it hurt when your hand was in the meat grinder? Was there lots of blood?" The children were always openly curious. Conversely, many adults would try and disguise their curiosity for a variety of reasons. My daughter would always describe these moments, with sly glances directed at her partial limb, as being rather awkward ones for her.

In looking back in an analytical way, there is no question that guardedness interferes with the natural exchange of empathetic feelings that exist for the welfare and well-being of others. My daughter encountered this when she went back to school ten days after her accident. She had a gym teacher who was intent on creating an environment of equality for her. This effort, though genuinely well-intentioned, made my daughter feel that she was forcing her difference on everyone else around her. For example, when playing volleyball all the students were only allowed to use one hand. The other had to be kept out of play. My daughter vehemently objected to this because she felt she was imposing her physical difference onto others and she didn't want others to be penalized because of her. In essence, she was made to stand out when all she wanted to do was blend in and be treated as normal. She wanted to adapt, not the other way around. She believed then, and still does, that it is her personal challenge to overcome...and overcome she has!

The Canadian National Paralympic Ski Team was a godsend for my daughter. As a natural born skier with innate abilities she was able to focus her energy on her skiing, first at the provincial level, and later at the national level, to win a position on the Canadian National Disabled Ski Team. Her teammates were amazing in their support and encouragement of each other. The team members had become impervious to fear because all had personally stared illness and/or death in the face. They had all encountered tremendous inequality in their private lives, some of which challenged their dignity as self-sufficient human beings. But, on the ski hill and among themselves, they were individuals with unique talents and abilities that consistently generated a response of admiration from all those that watched. They encouraged each other to be the best they could be. The only weakness they allowed was at the end of a race as you collapsed over a finish line. With this group, self-pity was not an option.

In the end, my daughter chose to overcome adversity when she could have chosen to sink deep into depression. She never once said "why me?" and wouldn't entertain the notion of giving in to weaknesses that were self- defeating. She was and still is determined to be self-sufficient and positive about doing anything she puts her mind to. She has made the conscious decision that if she wants to do something, there is no reason for her not to try. It has been my experience to find that she usually finds a way to do anything she wants – with absolutely no limitations! She is truly a resilient person!

Chapter 33: Nobody Ever Told Me I Was a Good Boy Before

I began my career as a Child and Youth Worker at a highly specialized school in a psychiatric facility in Ontario. On my second day, an emergency staff meeting was called. We were briefed on a student we were getting. We were told to read through his file. My jaw dropped when I saw the three-inch binder jam-packed with reports. I wondered to myself how a child could amass such a thick dossier in under eight years. As I scanned the documents, words such as "SEXUAL PREDATOR", "MONSTER", "SUSPECTED ATTEMPTED MURDER", "VOLATILE", and "FIRE STARTER" leapt off the pages. I sat there stunned. I could not figure out how people could say such things about an innocent little boy. How could a little boy do such things? I was certain there must be some sort of mistake. The director went on to say the newest "intake" had severe behavioural problems, was very violent, unpredictable and aggressive. Apparently he would attack people for no apparent reason. We were informed he would be a day patient, and not a permanent resident – at least not yet!

I sat there thinking and wondering what I had gotten myself into. I really didn't think I was prepared to deal with such a child. I questioned my career choice and my ability to do my job. I had basically no experience. This was my first job out of college and I certainly didn't have a clue as to how to handle an eight-year-old "MONSTER" who could, quite possibly attack me.

The next morning, I stood at the door with my three colleagues, (there were two teachers and two child and youth workers in the class with nine to twelve students), expecting "Jack the Ripper" to get out of the taxi. To my amazement, the cutest little boy I had ever seen emerged. He had little round glasses, a red baseball cap, and blue jeans on. I remember, he carried a red backpack and was smiling from ear to ear. I thought for sure the reports must be mixed up. I was certain they had sent over someone else's file. In my mind, there was no way this little boy was capable of all the atrocities I read about the previous day. As he entered the room, I smiled at him and welcomed him to our school. He looked directly at me and said, "Go fuck yourself bitch." He then proceeded to spit and kick at my colleagues and I.

The first two weeks that Georgie was with us was sheer hell. On many occasions, we had to clear the room and get all of the other students away from him. He was so out of control, it would have been impossible to physically restrain him. The safety of his classmates was always of huge concern to us. Georgie would attack peers or staff without warning or provocation. In fact, biting seemed to be one of his favourite past times. On two separate occasions, we had to call for "back up", where they had to eventually tranquilize him in order to protect him – from himself. I could not understand how someone so young could be so violent and angry.

As the year progressed, I began to understand Georgie better. We began to build some rapport. Each morning that I met him, I greeted him with a big smile and a warm welcome. On the rare occasions when he smiled back, my heart would just melt. We had several team conferences, which included parents, but Georgie's mom never attended. She always claimed that she was far too busy, as she had five other children to worry about. Of course, the Children's Aid Society were involved with the family, with the agency noting, among other things, that Georgie had tried to burn down his house on at least two different occasions. With respect to his family, we were to learn that Georgie's mom was extremely obese, suffered from severe asthma attacks, and was a chain smoker. We also learned that Georgie and each of the siblings had a different father. The children called these various men in their lives "uncle", as they couldn't appear to keep their names straight. The first time I met his mom, she was eight months pregnant, but I couldn't tell. She had a very hard time walking the one hundred feet from the parking lot to the school. She had to stop several times to catch her breath. I couldn't help wonder how she looked after all those kids, as they ranged in age from a year and a half to eleven.

After Georgie was with us for about four months, he was removed from his home and he became an inpatient/resident. As it turns out, Georgie was molesting his younger siblings. The authorities had suspected this was going on earlier, hence, the "sexual predator" label. However, up until he was eventually removed from his home, nothing could be factually proven. I could not figure out why he was the only child removed from the home, and, with reference to this, a few thoughts kept running through my mind. Where did he learn this type of behaviour? What was happening to this child? Is this how he was taught to show love and affection? I was sickened by these thoughts and continually discussed them with my colleagues. However, nobody seemed to have any answers, just lots of questions. During the CAS and police investigations, it came out that Georgie had been sexually abused by several of his "uncles", starting from the first day he was brought home from the hospital. It absolutely broke my heart, and sickened me, to know that Georgie actually thought you showed love and affection through the performing of sexual acts.

After learning this about Georgie, I was very disillusioned. I actually thought about quitting at this time. I thought, I don't want to go through life knowing about such horrors and witnessing their terrible effects. The worst part was that I felt completely helpless to do anything about it.

Once the CAS and police investigations were complete, Georgie became a crown ward. Mom was told to make a choice, either Georgie or the "uncle"? Not surprisingly, she chose the uncle. However, at least to me, that was the best thing that could have happened to him. In my mind, he was finally free! But for Georgie, at this particular time, this meant he was completely "cut off" from family. As bad as it was, it was all he had. As might be expected, his behaviour at this time was so volatile and unpredictable that he was deemed too high a risk to be considered for foster care. Plus with his past, no one was willing to take a chance on him. For all intents and purposes, he was a lost child.

One day, I had to leave work early for an appointment. Georgie had been having a very good day (no restraints, no violent outbursts) so I grabbed a scrap piece of construction paper out of the recycle bin and wrote him a note. I told him he had a great day and that I hoped tomorrow would be even better. I stuck the note inside his backpack and left. I never gave the note a second thought.

The next morning, Georgie came in and asked me if he would get another certificate if he was good. I had no clue what he was talking about. Then he reached in his pocket and pulled out the scrap of paper I had placed in his backpack the night before. He had carefully folded and stored it in his pocket for safekeeping. I smiled from ear to ear, and assured him he would indeed get another certificate if he was good. The certificates became more and more elaborate and Georgie's outbursts became fewer and further between. The combination of a stable home life (residence at the hospital), being successful in school, and receiving positive recognition for his behaviour seemed to be having a positive effect on Georgie.

Then, one day, the CAS called. They had a childless couple who were interested in getting to know Georgie; interested in spending some serious time with him. The mother used to work for a child protection agency in another province, and was well aware of the situation they might be getting into. Georgie was very tentative at first, and didn't want to waste his time. However, the couple initially peaked his interest by offering to take him out for an ice cream cone. After this, they would consistently come and visit with Georgie for at least one hour a week. Gradually, these visits increased. Soon, Georgie would go and visit them. Eventually, he went for sleepovers. First one night, then weekends, then a couple of nights and so on, until he moved in with them. Over a calculated period of time, Georgie was slowly integrated back into the regular school system. This was a slow process and a lot of teamwork and support was involved.

Eventually, my career advanced, and I was not there to celebrate all of Georgie's successes and accomplishments. However, on the day that Georgie finally moved into his new home for good, one of my colleagues called me, all excitedly. She told me that when Georgie's meagre belongings were being packed up, he was absolutely adamant that he wanted to personally carry his "treasure box" so that it was safe and didn't get lost. She asked him what was in the box that made it so special and he immediately replied, "All my certificates for being a good boy." When I heard this I sat down and I cried. My colleague went on to say that Georgie had told her I was the first person to ever tell him that he was a good boy.

This whole experience has taught me many things. The most important thing is that yes, I am in the right field, and I do have something to offer these sometimes very troubled kids. Previous to this experience, I had often wondered what could I possibly have to offer when I've never even come close to experiencing some of the things that many of these young kids are forced to experience. However, I've learned firsthand that care and compassion, a positive attitude, and genuine belief in what you're doing can go a very long way. Georgie touched my heart and life in ways I cannot explain. Whenever I think my life is tough, I think of Georgie and other kids I have met throughout my career. I look at their resiliency, their heart, their courage and I know I can face whatever comes my way. These kids are my heroes.

Chapter 34: Claudette's Tale

December was when I first met her. The exact year and day doesn't matter, though if forced to recall, I could list them both. At this point in time, she was on her second marriage and just gave birth to her fifth child. She was, and still is, a woman of immense strength, filled with love and caring, with a spirit more generous than any single person I have ever met.

She was born to a French-Canadian family in 1944 living on a farm in Northern Ontario. She had seven siblings, with only one other being a girl. Her father was a domineering, demanding, controlling, mean spirited man. Punishment was always doled out in generous portions and was almost always physical in nature. Needless to say, life was very difficult for this young girl who witnessed and experienced first-hand the devastating effects of having a strong disciplinarian father. For example, she was forced to watch as her father casually killed the family dog, only because the dog had grown too attached to her mother. Basically, he hated the dog, not because the dog was aggressive or unruly, but because the young girl's mother loved it so dearly.

She would soon grow up and leave home at a very young age just to get away from the abusive, restrictive, and controlling environment of her father. Her siblings all did likewise, either leaving before her, or shortly thereafter. Soon after, she met a man whom she married, having three children within this union, all of them boys. But in marrying so young, she soon learned that her husband certainly wasn't 'Mr. Right', at least not for her. Hence, in summoning a courage she didn't know she had, she did a very brave thing, (especially for the time and place), and divorced her husband. However, as might be expected, a woman of this quality wouldn't stay single forever, and eventually a new man entered her life; a man who would stand by her for the next 35 years, and continues to stand beside her right to this very day. With this new 'soul mate', she would give birth to a daughter, and then two more sons.

The daughter was a fireball as a youth and barely controllable, giving birth herself at a tender age. The youngest son was diagnosed with cancer soon after birth. Several years would follow that would see her family spend long periods apart as she remained in Toronto to attend to her ailing son at Toronto's Sick Kids Hospital. Her devoted husband remained at home to work and provide a stable home-life for the other two children. After eight years of battling the illness, the young child eventually succumbed to the deadly disease long before anybody should rightly leave this world. It was a terrible blow to the family - and to this mom especially, who took the loss of her child with tremendous difficulty, as anyone might expect. Two years later tragedy would strike again, as her only sister would pass after a prolonged fight with the same disease that took her young son. How did she react? She did what she had shown a history of doing, she dug deep within herself and drew from her reservoir of strength, which she seemed to have in great supply.

As the years passed, her two oldest sons, from her first marriage, grew openly critical of their mother and absolutely hostile towards their stepfather. They were never accepting of their mother leaving their father, particularly to marry an Anglophone miner. The two boys anger and resentment toward their mother eventually resulted in them cutting off all contact with her for many years. The youngest son of her first marriage remained the only one of three who, from the outset, was complexly accepting of his mother and the new life she had chosen. In fact, he ultimately decided to live with his mom and stepfather, becoming an integral part of a very tight familial arrangement.

More time passed and she was faced with yet another crisis. Her mother would have a stroke rendering her slightly paralyzed on the right side of her face and making her prone to bouts of confusion. Her generous spirit welcomed her mother into her home where she was able to offer the personal care that only a daughter can muster. One morning, she woke up to check on her mother only to discover that she'd had another stroke. This second stroke left her mother all but bedridden forcing her into 24-hour homecare, which involved bathing, feeding and changing diapers. Two years later, on her birthday, she would discover her mother dead in her bed at the age of 86.

At this point, she had suffered through a failed marriage, the slow and painful death of a young child, a similar fate for her only beloved sister, finding her mother dead in bed, and the complete shunning by two of her older sons from her first marriage. Yet, as per usual, she trudged on; she persevered!

Sadly though, this hard luck tale doesn't end here. Just three years ago she was awakened by a phone call that informed her that her youngest son from her first marriage had been killed by a passing transport truck, striking him as he stood on the side of the highway. This son left behind a wife and three children. However, it must be noted, that his death was felt not only through her family, but through the whole Ottawa region as well. He was a true hero in every sense of the word in the larger community due to his heavy involvement with autistic children. In many respects, it has since been said that this son truly reflected her values, her strength, and her determination.

Though her spirit was dealt yet another heavy blow, somehow she once again found the strength to continue, to fight on. One pleasant aside emanating from this tragic series of events was that her oldest son, who had previously been completely estranged from her, approached her at the funeral, wanting to make amends and bridge the chasm that existed between them. Thus, on this darkest of days, she found a degree of hope. As well, four months ago, she finally tackled a lifetime monster of her own. She quit smoking after nearly 45 years; a monumental victory for a monumental woman. She looks better and healthier than ever. She smiles often and laughs easily.

In conclusion, I know this woman's tale well. You see, I suffered through much of this turmoil with her and I am constantly amazed at her resiliency. I am the other son from her second husband. I am truly blessed to have been a part of this woman's life. She has made me strong. A farm girl with a grade eight education has taught me more than anything I have learned earning two degrees and a diploma. In her own way, she taught me the impenetrable strength of the unbroken spirit. Her name is Claudette, and I am proud to say she is my mother!

*Addendum – In early 2009, my mother was diagnosed with stage III lung cancer. The same disease that claimed both her son and sister now threatened to claim her. The cancer wasn't detected nearly early enough, and she was informed early on that there was only a 20% chance that she would see herself clear of the disease. Round after round of chemotherapy and radiation would sap all of her strength. The pain she was in was immeasurable. At one point, a doctor, one of the many who worked to save her, told her that should she continue seeking treatment, the pain would increase directly in the face of her odds decreasing. With death staring her down, she didn't blink - she continued to fight.

On February 20th, 2011, my mother lost the most important battle of her life and finally succumbed to her most deadly foe. Cancer destroyed her physically, made her weak, robbed her of her ability to breathe, and ultimately stole her life. However, it never managed to break her indomitable spirit. She now lives only in the memories of those who knew her and we are all stronger because of her. The Irish have a saying that to live in a heart is to live forever. My mother lives in a great many hearts!

Chapter 35: Christine Carol Taillefer (1975–2006)

I have heard the saying over and over again that having a handicapped child in the home directly affects the other members of the family, but that was never our case as we always said that people with disabilities are given to special families like ours.

On October 29, 1975 Christine Carol Taillefer was born with Down syndrome. She spent the first 7 months of her life in the hospital due to severe health issues. She took her first step at the age of three, and had several major surgeries throughout her three decades of life. Christine was on "deaths door" more then 5 times throughout her short life, and went through many trials and tribulations all along the way. Sadly, my sister's long battle finally ended on June 20, 2006 at 5:20 a.m. at Laurentian Hospital in Sudbury, Ontario, Canada. The day before she died, she told the family "her heart was tired and that she was going to die like a true hero". We all sat by her bedside, as we always did. She was able to personally thank everyone who cared for her over the past 30 years before she slipped into a morphine coma, never to awaken. Christine was my life, my joy, my gift from God because having a sibling with Down syndrome has taught me the most important lesson in life; that it should be lived to its fullest!

Growing up, my mom always taught me that silence is golden, that you don't judge a book by its cover, and you should always keep your ears and eyes open and your mouth shut. She warned me that there will be times when people will make comments about Christine, or say things that may upset you, but all you need to remember (my mom constantly cautioned) is that "Christine is as normal as you or I, it's just at certain times she may need a little extra help". In other words, (my mom was insinuating), just tell everybody the truth! Related directly to this, both my parents consistently told me that I would be a better person for having had a sibling like Christine in my life, which proved to be very true. For example, because of Christine's direct impact on my life, I have grown up to be a passionate, service-minded adult who wants desperately to make a difference in the lives of others, particularly those who are less fortunate than me.

In growing up with a sibling with Down syndrome, you learn very early in life to have a tremendous amount of love and compassion for others with disabilities. But, to be honest, living with a big sister with "special" needs wasn't always clear, unobstructed sailing. Although Christine was a very positive member of our family, always lighting up a room with her positive attitude and inherent good nature, she also needed some extra help with many of the things that we may take for granted in life. Like when she would get dressed, or put her shoes on, it sometimes would take a very long time, and lots of individual guidance. Sometimes she would need a little extra help in doing her hair or brushing her teeth, but we learned to be patient with her, always encouraging her to try a little harder and always celebrating the occasions when improvement was noted. Among the many things that I admired most about my big sister was the fact that she never stopped trying to get better at things, even if the challenge was an incredibly daunting one. She truly inspired me in this manner!

The fact that Christine didn't learn to do things as easily as the rest of the family made it so much more of an achievement, so much more fulfilling when she would finally get it. I know that some people think of Down's syndrome as an affliction, a very negative thing, but that's not the way my family ever viewed it, and certainly not the way Christine herself viewed it. The fact that Christine had Down's syndrome didn't change the essence of who she was; she was still Christine, still my BIG sister. Even if my sister couldn't walk properly, or talk properly, or even feed herself properly, she never lost sight of whom she really was, nor did we – her family. My sister had such a love for music. She was forever dancing, singing and playing her guitar. In fact, when it came to memorizing the lyrics to a song, Christine was far better at it than I was. If that, in and of itself doesn't tell you something, then I don't know what does. So, although Christine struggled with some things - there were also some things that she was indeed very good at.

In looking back, without question growing up with a sister with Down syndrome has influenced my life in many positive ways. I have a great deal of empathy and deep-rooted respect, especially for those who have physical and intellectual "differences". It's without doubt why I've chosen teaching as a career and, more specifically, "special" education as my primary focus within that teaching career. I so much admire my parents for always taking the time to be open and honest with me, explaining the intricacies of Down syndrome to me at an early age, and guiding me in such a way that I was better prepared to support my big sister with some of her many challenges. My parents and I never had one big conversation, but a continuing dialogue as new questions and concerns emerged, particularly as Christine aged. Mom and dad were always there to answer any questions, providing information that prevented unnecessary confusion and worrying. No doubt, there were the odd occasions when I would experience frustrations and negative emotions, but then I would just spend a little quality time with my big sister and these negative feelings would quickly dissipate. That was Christine's special talent, despite the uphill battles she faced everyday of her life, within seconds of being around her she always made you feel better about your own life.

My mom had very high expectations of my care giving responsibilities for my sister when I was growing up. For example, I never knew what it was like to ride a yellow school bus until high school because I always took the handi-transit van with my sister, which at times led to feelings of resentment, pressure and guilt. But I'd quickly get over it because I knew deep in my heart that if the roles were reversed, Christine would have absolutely sacrificed anything for me. Although my sister required a great deal of attention from my parents, I can honestly say that I never, even for the briefest moment, felt neglected, which, in retrospect, is quite an accomplishment where my parents efforts are specifically concerned. They always recognized my uniqueness and faithfully acknowledged all of my accomplishments, all the while going miles out of their way to ensure that Christine thrived; that within a certain set of limitations she became everything that she was capable of becoming.

In conclusion, not a day goes by where I do not think about my sister Christine. She will forever be my guardian angel and it is because of her that I now live each day to its fullest. I try to learn something new everyday. I take risks that I never would have taken before, and ultimately I truly believe I wouldn't be the person I am today if it weren't for my big sister (but also not excluding the contributions of my big brother, Claude Jr. as well). My parents, Claude and Candace Taillefer, did their best to give us a great childhood and the security of knowing we were in a family that loved us, no matter what mistakes we made or what "problems" we may have had. It never mattered how bad my day may have been, I could always look at Christine and know that I could make it through whatever bad things that may come my way. She faced every fear, every obstacle, and every challenge with the courage and strength that many of us can only dream of. Even today, as an adult, I reflect on her love of life, her passion for life, and her generally happy demeanor to help make even the worst of my days seem just a little bit brighter.

Finally, on top of everything else, as a newly certified teacher about to embark on a long career in education, the gift of my sisters life has left me better prepared to be a truly "special" educator, particularly in the way I perceive and effectively deal with intellectual and physical difference in my classroom, and in the wider school. Thank you Christine!

The Innocent

She thinks no evil does no harm, her disposition is always calm.
So full of love and kindness to, she only sees the good in you.
Anger, lust they're not real, such normal impulses she doesn't feel.
She is innocent this is true, of hate and fear and things we do.
Such perfect trust, so hard to find, exemplifies her piece of mind.
With us upturned and heart sincere, her thoughts may seem quite far from here.
A deeper knowledge, yet not expressed, perhaps she's wiser then the rest.
She's sweet and gentle, meek and mild; she's our lovely Down syndrome child.

This poem was written by Reef Wilson for my sister Christine when she was born. Reef was a close family friend.

Chapter 36: In the Dark Room

Imagine for a moment being in a room with no windows, and no light except for a glow emanating from beneath a locked door. You can see very little other than the darkened shapes of the larger pieces of furniture. There are other people in the room, but they don't seem to have any trouble navigating the area. One person tells you to pick up the pen on a desk across the room, to write down something for them. You begin making your way across the room, stumbling over smaller objects and slamming your shins into the larger ones. Eventually, you find the desk and pick up a writing utensil and start writing. Suddenly, the person chides you, telling you that you've picked up a pencil, not a pen. The other people in the room laugh! You have to start again.

This scenario illustrates what it's like to be very hard of hearing, and having to get through a class without hearing aids - relying almost entirely on lip reading. I would often hear questions asked of me by the teacher inaccurately, and so would answer incorrectly - much to the amusement of my fellow classmates. Sometimes the teacher would join in, but thankfully teachers like that were few and far between, as I hope to show in my story.

When I was born, everyone thought I was a perfectly healthy baby girl. However, two weeks later, my mother noticed something strange about my mouth and called my older brother over to make a comparison. It turned out that I had a cleft soft palate. I also had a small hole in my heart, which would eventually correct itself, but leave my heart a touch too weak. The bigger problem was my hearing. Shortly after I had my palate repaired at the Hospital for Sick Children, my mother again noticed something peculiar. Whenever someone would speak to me, I'd put my hands on their face and turn their head toward me - I was trying to lip read.

What the doctors discovered was that because my palate was too short (not hitting the back of my throat like a normal person's), it could not create the correct "popping" of the ears to clear the fluid from my inner ears down the Eustachian tubes. That, in turn, created conductive hearing loss. Since then, I have had a total of nine surgeries on my ears - one of which was totally botched - to put in tubes for drainage purposes, the last of which was just before my 18th birthday. It worked, at least for a while. Unfortunately, the number of surgeries has left both of my ear drums profoundly damaged. Today, on the hearing loss scale, one ear is moderate-severe, while the other is severe. My greatest fear is that someday I won't be able to listen to music. Hearing loss, amongst other things, has had a major impact on my life.

I started pre-school and speech therapy when I was 3 years old. Thankfully, my impairment wasn't so severe at that point as to hinder my acquisition of language, though I did have a lot of trouble with my Ss and Zs. Most people had difficulty understanding me, except my closest of friends, who would always try and "translate" for me, if necessary. I also took an intelligence test before I entered school, to ensure that I had no cognitive disabilities. I didn't, but that hasn't always stopped people from thinking that I do. Perhaps that's why I've always needed to "prove" myself scholastically.

I started and went to the same school up to Grade 3, and the only time I was treated any differently was when I would leave class once a week for speech therapy (located in the same building). Since I grew up with the same kids, they never teased me. They were used to me, I suppose! The only negative event I can remember in relation to my hearing/speech impediment during these early years is when a French teacher kept me in at recess, trying to force me to roll my Rs, which I'm physically incapable of doing. I remember I was initially driven to tears, but still managed a small feat of self-advocacy when I told the teacher that I couldn't do it, and if she kept me in again I'd go to the principal and complain. From this point forward, I always tried to build up good relationships with teachers, at least when I could.

Speaking of self-advocacy, I have to make a small digression, in order that you may understand how and why it was necessary for me to self-advocate. My parents did advocate on my behalf when I was very young, but I learned very quickly to take care of myself. Neither of my parents thought that I had problems large enough for my education to be truly affected. They thought, of course I would ultimately succeed because "it really wasn't all that bad." No excuses here! Not even when my hearing got so bad that I had to resort to lip-reading on a full-time basis. Basically, I had learned to compensate so well, they didn't know how bad my hearing actually was. I even went to the audiologists by myself half the time. Something else happened during those early years as well - suffice it to say that I'm a survivor of abuse from outside the home. But in my family, "it didn't happen." So I learned more and more to rely on myself.

Relying on myself became even more necessary when we moved between my Grade 3 and Grade 4 years. I was in a new city and a new school and, to top it off, my old school either misplaced or forgot to transfer my "official" records to the new school. In effect, it was like I had no school history prior to my start in this brand new location. Needless to say, this generated some very challenging scenarios for me, starting on the first day in my new school when I received a major jolt. Basically, this is how it went. When I asked where my teacher's room was, with my speech impediment raging in my nervousness, I was brought immediately to the segregated Special Ed. room. Of course, I refused to go in, self-advocating once again, totally adamant that I was supposed to be in Mrs. Appleby's regular Grade 4 class and not in a Special Ed. class. Eventually, I was able to convince them of this fact, and they eventually escorted me to Mrs. Appleby's classroom, which turned out to be a very fortunate thing because Mrs. Appleby ended being an absolutely wonderful teacher. This started right away with Mrs. Appleby letting me choose my own seat; right at the front of the class (which, I must add, became a mainstay of my educational existence). My new classmates on the other hand, were another story, as I wasn't used to being teased.

In Grade 5 I was fitted for hearing aids, which, to me, was like having a desk lamp turned on in a dark room, and I absolutely hated them. They made everything sound electronic. And to make matters worse, the other kids would purposely put their hands up to my ears, making my hearing aids emit a high-pitched squeal, leaving me on most occasions with a perpetual migraine. Hence, before the year was out, I tossed the hearing aids in a box swearing to never wear them again. In response to this, my Grade 5 teacher offered to explain my challenges to the class as a whole, but I would not agree to this as I didn't want to provide my classmates with any more fodder for their jokes related to my hearing and speech differences.

Because I lived in a reasonably remote location, and the lists are longer than the services offered, unfortunately I was unable to continue my speech therapy. Probably the worst moment related to my speech impediment came in Grade 6, when our class collectively put on an Operetta (a musical play). Anyone who wasn't on stage got stuck in the chorus, which was fine with me because I enjoyed singing my heart out without being the center of attention. On the last day of rehearsals though, the teacher in charge of the chorus took me aside and told me that I was to stand in the back row and lip-sync. I was completely crushed by this! In fact, I haven't sung to this day—not even in Church........... But I found another way!

Three events happened in middle school which have stayed with me to this day. One was the realization that I may never be able to speak properly, which led to the decision to write. If people weren't going to take me seriously when I spoke, then they damn well were going to take me seriously when I wrote. Since then, I've been professionally published on several occasions. Writing has been very therapeutic for me.

The second thing that happened was in discovering my love for Instrumental Music. Luckily, I came across an amazing teacher who introduced me to all kinds of music, and another way of expressing myself within that specific art form. After meeting her I went on to learn the French Horn, and just now I'm learning to master the Celtic fiddle.

The final thing that happened to me was a miracle, but wrapped initially in a disaster. In Grade 8, tragically, one of my friends committed suicide. However, it was through this horrible event that I was first introduced to teaching as somewhat a serious "calling". My teacher that particular year, in trying to get us through the chaos of that tragic event, went above and beyond the call of duty. He spent the rest of the year nurturing us, helping us heal and making it his business to ensure that each of us knew exactly how special we were. It was also the first time I had ever seen a teacher cry (that they were indeed human, and needed support and friendship as much as anyone else).

By late high school, by self-advocating, I had developed a very positive relationship with most of my teachers. For the most part, they all recognized my hearing impairment for what it was, and let me do whatever I needed to make sure I got the most from their lessons. In addition to always being at the front of the classroom, I always positioned myself next to someone from whom I could copy notes. I borrowed books and videos when I had to, and talked endlessly to my teachers after class if I didn't get a concept previously taught. However, general classroom discussions, particularly those involving my classmates, became more and more of a problem for me, as my capacity for hearing got progressively worse. Initially, I would ask people to speak up, but after a minute or two, their volume would always go down again, which became incredibly frustrating for me. Eventually, I learned just to tune out, always returning to my own little world inside my head.

Again, by late high school, although the persistent teasing had pretty much stopped, my speech was still a major problem, so I just decided to proactively do something about it. Basically, I decided that I was going to force myself to learn to speak properly, which, quite surprisingly, led to some absolutely wonderful experiences. I joined the Drama Club, became Chief Photographer, then Chief Editor of my high school newspaper, registered for the Yearbook class, and was eventually elected onto the Student Council. I decided to 'take on' anything that would demand that I talk to small or large groups of people.... Now most people don't even notice that I have an accent at all. But, by no means, was everything perfect!

In late high school, in my quest (zeal) to meet my own high standards, and in trying to establish an uneasy truce with my past, (all on my own I must add), I started to develop coping problems directly related to stress. Consequently, I battled depression for years. Despite that, I kept my focus on school and was finally, in the second half of my Grade 12 year, "officially" identified as a 'Special Needs' student. (Although, I have to laugh at that, as I was almost done high school before being "officially" recognized). At the time, my counselor said that she didn't suspect that I had a hearing problem, or any problem at all for that matter, because my grades were always so good. (I would suggest that there is a valuable lesson embedded in this for all aspiring teachers to learn).

Finally, in my final year of high school, I received another set of hearing aids, only this time I wanted them. Unfortunately, though, they were complete "lemons", and I was only able to use them for a total of about 5 weeks throughout the entire school year. I didn't have them for graduation, but what I did have was this: entry into a first-rate university and, more importantly in my eyes, a scholarship offer based on my academic excellence (awarded by the teachers of my very own high school).

It wasn't until I was well into my first year of university that I finally realized just what I had managed to accomplish, and just how far I had come! It was driven home by one specific event attached to one specific class; a history class. By this time, I had a new set of hearing aids that were working really well, but on this one occasion I went to class without them. Well, by the end of class I was exhausted, completely drained, and thought, "I can't believe I got through high school like this." But I did! And that's the point. My luck with teachers cannot be ignored - whether I let them help me or not. I can name on one hand all the bad teachers I have had from JK all the way through to my graduation from Teacher's College. Thankfully, there are too many good ones to count.

Someone once asked me if I wished I could have perfect hearing? Let's go back to the dark room for a moment. Imagine being in a virtually black room all your life. You might be able to handle a desk lamp - heck, maybe even two. But what if someone opened the locked door and let the full brilliancy of the sun shine through? Not only would it be painful to eyes that have never seen that sort of light, but you'd lose so much. Sure, everything would be clearer, but you'd miss the intricate details you've learned to pick up with your sense of touch and other senses. Details unique to your perspective - to who you are! A friend of mine once said that it's probably because of my hearing impairment that I have such a "rich inner life and imagination." I would never want to lose that part of myself. Therefore, my answer to the question asked at the beginning of this paragraph is NO!

Chapter 37: The Fear of No!

Where do I begin? I come from a happy family in a small farming community. I grew up with both my parents and my brother, both of my surviving grand parents next door. I had good grades and all my teachers used to say I was a pleasure to teach. I did what my parents asked with little hassle or resentment. I completed high school near the top of my class and went on to complete two university degrees. From everyone else's perspective, I had a happy life many would envy. How could I possibly be writing this about myself when others who have done so, have written about such terrible events, which I have thankfully been spared? When compiling a list of factors, which would describe someone who is at risk, I would seem to be exempt from any great threat.

So how can I possibly be writing this about myself? The most important fact few people ever knew or even know to this day is I detested the majority of my time in school. Why did so few people know this? I regularly achieved grades, which were among the highest in the class and was even in a gifted program for a couple of years, so why would anyone ever think I could possibly dislike school? In truth, I felt isolated from my classmates and was always uneasy around all but my two best friends. I have always been a large person and was hassled and bullied by some of my classmates throughout my early years in school. In fact, when I think back on it objectively, I suppose I wasn't picked on any more than my fellow students. But objectivity is not something I possessed in any great measure in grade school. The majority of my memories of grade school involve me doing everything in my power to avoid embarrassment and to lessen the opportunity for anyone to tease me. I devoted myself to my schoolwork so no one could call me stupid or razz me for getting into trouble with the teacher for not doing my homework. I took the opportunity to do any extra assignment that would exempt me from having to do presentations in front of the class, in order to avoid any situation that could lead to embarrassment. During recess, I avoided sports and games, because I was not a great athlete and did not want to be embarrassed. In fact, the only sport I played in grade school was intramural floor hockey. Having a father who loved hockey, I had a net and stick to practice with in my basement at home and was better than many of my fellow students. After two years, we stopped having floor hockey and I went back to avoiding physical activity at school. During track and field days, I would usually avoid doing any of the events and instead offer to help with time keeping or running the play day games for the younger students. My teachers always appreciated my offers of assistance and would let me do this; after all I was a good student and was just being helpful. My fear kept me from playing games which I loved and which I would play all weekend and during vacation with my brother and cousins at home. Instead, I would spend most of my recesses alone or maybe talking with one of my friends if they weren't busy playing some sport or doing another activity. During gym class, I was always terrified I would make a mistake or screw up in some way. Anytime I would let someone score a goal or do something that let him or her score against my team, I would be distraught. Despite the fact it was only gym class, I would feel like I let down the other students on my team, and was terrified that someone would comment on my error. I was always relieved when I went back to the regular classroom, where I could sit and work on my latest assignment, preferably alone.

All of these attempts to avoid embarrassment led me to be more and more isolated from my classmates. Except for my two good friends, I only worked with my fellow classmates grudgingly. I'd always hear of other students' birthday parties and celebrations but would not be invited. The most important reason for this was that I would never express any interests in these events or feign indifference, as I never wanted to be told I couldn't come to an event. I also viewed them as just another situation where I could be embarrassed and therefore, worked to avoid them. Despite this, I was usually upset I was not having fun like the rest of my class.

By grade 6, I had reached the point where the emotional toll and the effort of avoiding social situations was becoming too much for me. I began missing more days of school with claims that I did not feel well. During this time, neither my parents nor teachers were very concerned, I continued to complete my homework and catch up on anything that I missed, so my grades remained at the same level they had been. In fact, being so isolated from my peers, I was determined to keep my teachers and parents happy because of a fear that I might alienate them if I let my grades slip. I saw my family doctor a few times, but when he found nothing wrong with me he just suggested that my claims of being sick were just a case of being tired. I seized upon this excuse and used it several times throughout the year, often when social activities or events were planned at the school.

Finally, around March or April, one bad day at school resulted in me completely breaking down. Our teacher had just asked us to form groups for a project and my two good friends were in other groups. This left me the task of asking to join another group. Being a good student most other students would probably be happy to have me in their group, but I did not see it this way. The fear that someone might say no, if I asked to join his or her group, caused me to start crying. My teacher took me out of the class to the resource room next door and talked to me for a few minutes. After asking me if I would like to talk to someone else, he got my friend to come and sit with me until recess came. The whole time I was sitting there with my friend, I continued crying. During recess, the teacher came back to the room and I let rip with everything that had been bottled up inside of me for so long. The teacher just sat with me throughout the recess, encouraging me to let it all out. He left for a few minutes to ask another teacher to cover his class after recess and came back, so I could vent some more. Over the next couple of days, he encouraged me to let my fellow students know how I felt. In small groups I talked to everyone in my class. Despite being embarrassed by the attention, I was relieved my fellow students did not think less of me and were actually very supportive. One of the students, I had always tried to avoid, because he was always making jokes or playing practical jokes on others. He was very upset that his actions could have had such a terrible impact on me. From that day forward, he never did anything in the least bit mean to me and was in fact very supportive and often tried to get me to join him in group activities in class or during recess. Eventually, I also shared what had happened with my parents. They were rather shocked as I had always been positive when describing school but they were also extremely supportive.

The remainder of my grade 6 year as well as grade 7 and 8 were much more positive. I still didn't participate in a lot of activities, but I felt more like a part of the class. I still felt nervous in groups or when in front of others, but it was nowhere near as bad as it had once been. When the time came to move on to high school, many of my old fears came back to the surface though. Thankfully, most of my fellow students and my good friends moved on to the same school as me. Throughout high school, I remained focused on my grades, but enjoyed spending time with my old and new friends during lunch and spares and did not fear group projects and presentations as I once did. I still didn't participate in many social activities outside of school, but I was happy and by the end of OAC was enjoying school more than I ever had previously.

When I moved on to university, my greatest fear was that my best friend was attending a different institution. Luckily, many other friends I made in high school were attending the same university as me and were in my program. Despite my best efforts, I could not maintain grades in university at the same level I had in high school. This was probably the best thing for me. For once in my life, I was forced to define myself as something other than the best student in the class. By my third year of university, I was very close with a group of friends that included the students I had known from high school. Following graduation, I remained close with my friends and continue to be to this day. However, I was not particularly successful in finding a job and had also begun to question whether or not this was a career I really wanted to pursue. I had always thought of teaching as an option but I was unsure if this was something I could really do. I returned to my old grade school to visit with my former grade 6 teacher who was now the principal. He was extremely encouraging and genuinely excited when I told him I was thinking of becoming a teacher. He helped set me up with several teachers, some of who had once taught me, in whose classrooms I could volunteer. My experiences in these classrooms made me certain that my decision to become a teacher was the right one.

So what does all of this have to do with resilience? Some people thrive in spite of their environment or situation and are considered resilient. At the other end of the spectrum, I nearly self-destructed in spite of my environment and situation. I honestly do not know how I would have succeeded without the support and love of my family and friends. It was because of them I continued to work as hard as I could when my feelings of isolation were at their worst. I have nothing but the greatest respect, for those who have overcome great obstacles with so much less. I can also say my former grade 6 teacher had an enormous impact on my life and I owe him a great deal of gratitude. When I was at my most vulnerable and feeling ashamed and weak, he forced me to see the impact I had on others and just how much my classmates cared for me, despite my best efforts to remain aloof from them over the years. He is also one of the driving forces that led me into teaching; something for which I can never thank him enough.

Chapter 38: She Makes Me Want To Be a Good Teacher

When it comes to illness, abuse, or special education, I think we all have a personal story to share. That's why special education is so important. It affects us all. That's why I chose to be a teacher.

Typing this now, I am somewhat reluctant to continue, for fear of cheapening my sister's story. I attempted to ask my sister for some of the details that she remembers, but a lot of what happened she can barely recall, and much of what she told me was very generalized. For this reason, I can only tell you what my parents, sister, and I recall.

Last summer, I was helping my mom clean out our garage. This consisted of us going through and sorting some large storage containers. The job took a lot longer than we anticipated and this was largely due to the fact that whenever we opened a box, we uncovered some past memory. During this chore, I uncovered a box labelled "Anita's schooling." My mom noticed and asked me to leave it; she wanted to sort through it herself. I handed it to her and started on a different container. Turns out the new box contained photo albums. I got lost in the old pictures. I laughed at our funny hairdo's, our clothes... and that's when I heard my mom crying. I looked up. She was looking through my sisters report cards, and she was actually sobbing.

When my sister was born, a year and a half before me, she was born five weeks premature and weighed only 5lbs. My mom claims that she had the smallest hands she had ever seen. As a baby, Anita had many allergies. My mom had to make sure that everything was made of cotton, and wash Anita's clothes in a very specific type of laundry detergent. If she didn't faithfully do this, she would break out into a major skin rash, which would then be very hard to clear up.

When I came into this world, I was greeted by a very loving older sister. I was born a fat baby and my sister thought I was a big teddy bear. As my dad describes it, Anita was always very attached to me. If my dad, mom, or grandparents bought my sister a gift, she would ask "Where's Sammy's gift?" Anita taught me how to ride a bike; to tie my shoes; and to blow bubbles with gum. When I think of our childhood together, I think of sunshine, sprinklers, popsicles, Nintendo and swimming at the beach. We were happy kids, with happy parents.

However, my sister was a completely different kid at school. Her fine motor skills were delayed and making circles and shapes proved to be quite a challenge for her. Apparently her perception was off a little bit. But still, she enjoyed coloring and had an excellent memory. Another thing that made Anita's early school life difficult was that she was by far the smallest kid in her grade. This seemed to make her very timid of other kids, and it was also at this time that she began biting her fingers and blinking her eyes excessively. Another odd thing with Anita's early schooling is that her teachers never heard her speak. One teacher phoned my mom about this, and my mom could not believe it. Anita had always been very happy and sociable at home.

Quite naturally, the onset of these types of behaviours worried my parents greatly and, as direct result, they decided to consult with a doctor. However, much to my parents delight, the doctor reassured them that Anita was a very bright young girl, and that the problems she was having were nothing to worry about; claiming that Anita was just shy, and that eventually she would outgrow everything.

In grade 1, Anita abruptly informed the family that she did not want to go to school anymore. My parents took her for more tests, and the doctors found a new list of allergies. However, they assured my parents that my sister's shyness and difficulty with school was something she would soon out-grow. My sister still refused to talk in class, so the teacher gave my sister a tape recorder to talk into. Mid-way through the school year, Anita showed great social improvements. She was now one of the most popular students in the class. She also had a few boys that liked her. My parents were thrilled. I remember her birthday party that year. At least 20 kids came, and I was very happy for her.

Although there were definite improvements socially at school for Anita, the academic side of things was not improving very much at all, particularly when it came to writing. She would consistently confuse b's with d's, and p's with q's. To counter this, my sister would write a capital B, Q and a small d, and p. This was not acceptable for her teacher. My sister also had considerable difficulties with mathematics. As a result, she was forced to repeat a grade. The most upsetting part of this, was that all of her new friends continued onto the next grade.

As a child I remember this period as being a rather tense time in my household. One day I remember coming inside after playing road-hockey. My dad and sister were sitting at the kitchen table. My sister was crying. There were number flash cards lying all over the table. I remember my day saying, "No! Let's do it again. When you add this number card to this number card, what is the total?" When she wasn't able to quickly respond (or respond at all), I remember my dad becoming incredibly frustrated. He desperately wanted her to learn, and couldn't at all understand why she couldn't!

I couldn't believe it. This was the first, and only time I saw my dad kind of fly "off the handle". I remember being somewhat startled. I walked right past the table and went to my room. This very tense situation went on for well over an hour. "When you add this card to this card, what do you get; what is the total"? Then, there would be absolute silence! Then, "Unbelievable. I don't understand.

It's so bloody simple. How is it you don't understand? LISTEN TO ME!!!! TWO PLUS ONE IS WHAT?"

I think my dad gave up on helping my sister after that night in the kitchen. It took him years to come to terms with the fact that his daughter learned in a very different, nontraditional way. Don't get me wrong; my dad always had the best of intentions. But I think from that night on, my sister was always afraid of letting my dad help her. From that day on, she was always afraid of school too... of numbers... of learning. She began to think that she was stupid. I don't think she ever had a chance. My sister shuts down when she is nervous. For instance, my sister was terrified of her first grade teacher. My sister got so worked up in her presence, that she couldn't write her name. This was odd, considering she could easily write her name at home. My sister got worked up easily, and when she was stressed, she couldn't think. I think we are all like that to a degree!

Shortly after, my sister was moved to a new school with a Special Education program and this is when life got really tough for my sister. Anita did not like her new school at all. She was very shy and nervous, and had a hard time concentrating. When I ask Anita about this time in her life, she informs me that she was severely bullied by older kids while there. Where were the teachers? Who was protecting her? How can you learn when you are scared? What chance did my sister have? These are questions that I now ask because all of this happened within very important developmental years for her. Who could learn in conditions like these? I remember when I was in grade 8, I was the small kid, and I was the one that was bullied. That was a miserable year for me, both emotionally and academically. How can you focus on academics when your emotional life is in disarray? It is for this reason I can really sympathize with my sister. Needless to say, my sister's academics did not improve. The few friends she made during this period, turned out not to be friends at all. In essence, they would pretend to be her friends only to take advantage of her and embarrass her. As she recalls, it was also at this time when people began referring to her as retarded.

In grade 7/8 my mom and dad noticed that my sister began acting even more strangely. She would make odd noises, and say things that didn't make a lot of sense. Again, they went to the doctor, but this time, the doctor had nothing to say or offer. My mom was determined. She knew something was odd. My sister had a favourite TV program and my mom knew this, so she set up a hidden video camera in front of the television set. She then pressed record, and left the room before my sister noticed. Later, when my mom and dad watched the video, they knew something was definitely not right. The video captured all of my sisters' ticks, jerks, and twitches. My mother brought the tape back to the doctor's office, and shortly after my sister was diagnosed with Tourette syndrome. Immediately after the diagnosis, my sister was given pills. Anita remembers that the pills had a number of side effects "The pills made me throw up, made me fall asleep in class, and gave me terrible nightmares." My sister began getting dangerously thin, and so she was taken off the medication.

In grade 7/8, my sister was still small and very quiet. Her Tourette's was at its worst through this period, and she was bullied incessantly at school. I remember at one point my dad just couldn't handle it anymore so he went to the school and "tore a strip" off the Principal. But things didn't really improve for her. In fact, the bullying got so bad that my mom eventually quit her job, so she could give Anita as much support as possible. I remember this being a very tough time for the whole family.

When Anita was in Grade 8, I was in Grade 7. This was the first time I had been in the same school as my sister. It was at this time that I got a first-hand account of Anita being bullied. I remember one day, I was heading out for recess, when I noticed five or six grade 8 boys surrounding my sister. I heard them teasing her, and I noticed she was crying. I remember one of them saying, "There's a time when you become too fucked up, and you just have to kill yourself." I was so angry I blacked out. My sister tells me that I kicked one boy in the groin, and punched another boy in the face. Kids left her alone after that.

When my sister went to high school, life became even more difficult for her. At lunch, she would hide in the bathroom stall. After school, she would hide underneath the stairs. She had a few "friends", but they wouldn't be seen with her in public. Needless to say, school was not a happy place for her. It was at this time that Anita began taking an SSRI, but just for a year. She says "it felt like she had the devil in her." She became very aggressive and didn't feel like herself at all. When, on top this, she began to experience major panic attacks, she was diagnosed with Bi-Polar Disorder. Finally, after it was further discovered that Anita had a profound variant of dyslexia, she decided she just couldn't take any more and dropped out of school completely.

After about a year, Anita began to slowly recover, particularly from the depression. There are a great number of positive things that I can take from my sister's story. If she had been a weaker person, she could have gotten involved in crime and illegal drugs. Also, she was never abusive with herself or anyone else. Today, my sister is a much happier person. She is a productive member of society; she has a steady job, volunteers faithfully at a large community organization, and has some very good friends. Most noticeably, my mom and sister have a bond that goes beyond anything I have ever seen. They are fun to be around. Over the past five years, the biggest difference I notice about my sister is that she smiles again. She is one of the most genuine people I know.

When I look back at Anita's school experience, I have mixed emotions. My sister had a hard life, and she didn't deserve a lot of the things that came her way. When I see a picture of her as a little kid, I see so much potential. I remember her being smart as a kid, and even now, she seems so innately intelligent. I don't think her potential has ever been fully realized. I'm left to wonder if she had been diagnosed with a profound learning disability and appropriately accommodated at an early age, would her life have turned out completely different? Also, what if my father had interacted with her in those early years with compassion instead of frustration, how might this have changed things for her? And maybe, if her peers had of been more supportive of her differences, instead of constantly belittling and making fun of her for having them, she would be a completely different person today. Who really knows for sure!

Nonetheless, one thing I can definitely say with a great deal of confidence is that my sister Anita is a big source of motivation for me. She makes me want to be a good teacher. Because of her, I will fight for the kids that need help. I have always felt guilty for not being able to help her more when I was growing up and

I think I owe it to my profession, to help the next generation of children who are very much like her. They have so much to offer!

Chapter 39: The Past Is Where It Belongs

August 23rd, 1981 a baby boy named Christian was born into a family of recent western European immigrants. His parents were only teenagers at the time of his birth, and because they were so young when he was born and had both just immigrated to Canada, they had very little support both financially and emotionally. This caused much stress on the parents of the new baby and caused things to go very wrong right from the beginning. As baby Christian grew into his toddler years his parents continued to be impoverished. They got all of their food from the food bank and were consistently worried about paying bills and putting food on the table. Eventually Leo, Christian's father, said he had had enough with living so far below the poverty line, so he wrote the provincial high school equivalency test and passed it with flying colours. He then decided he should go to university in hopes of one day finding a job that would be able to support his family. While Leo was gone to university in another city, Martine was left to take care of the toddler on her own.

From the outset, Martine was a very troubled woman. She was sexually, emotionally and physically abused by her father and brothers as a child, and probably because of the way she was treated as a youngster, Martine had a really hard time coping with life as an adult. Even little situations seemed to overwhelm her. So as you can imagine, leaving this young mother alone with a toddler while her husband went off to University to live in a town faraway, was not a good situation. It wasn't long after Leo left for his first year of university that Martine started to change quite dramatically. She always had general coping problems, but with Leo now gone for the greatest part of each and every week, it seemed as though the floodgates had been blown completely open. For the most part, from this time forward, she was no longer able to care for herself, let alone her small growing child.

Leo would come home from university on the weekends to visit with his family and almost immediately he began to see the trouble that his wife was in. She no longer cleaned the house, did the dishes or laundry, or consistently fed her young son. Leo did not want to give up on his dream of graduating university, so even though his family was in real trouble, he still left to go back to school each and every Sunday night. However, when Leo was home on the weekends he methodically spent the greatest amount of his time cleaning up and taking care of

Christian, basically all of the things that had been neglected in his absence during the week.

As the school year went on Martine's condition continued to get worse. She became increasingly angrier, would stay in bed for days on end, and became progressively more paranoid and delusional. After letting this situation escalate for several months, Leo finally brought Martine to a doctor. The doctor ran several tests, but almost immediately sought out the expertise of a specialist, who decided to institutionalize her for a time. Martine was indeed profoundly mentally ill. She was ultimately diagnosed with Manic Depression and Paranoid Schizophrenia. The doctor prescribed specific medication to treat her illness, but Martine consistently refused to take it. She did not seem to want to help herself.

By the time Christian was six, the battle lines between Leo and Martine had been clearly drawn. By this time his mother was paying absolutely no attention to him, which meant that if his father wasn't around then he was, for the most part, completely neglected. Although his father tried to ensure that he got the necessities of life, including food and a little parental attention, he was just too busy to do it all very well. He was still struggling trying to see to his university obligations, all the while working at two part time jobs. Eventually Martine became absolutely impossible to deal with and Leo could no longer take the constant yelling, fighting, and accusations that he was out to ruin her life. Thus, when Christian was only six years old Leo formally left the family.

With this sudden turn of events, Martine had no choice but to move into a government-subsidized housing project. It was located in a rough part of the city and, without exception, was a very challenging place for any child to grow up. Nevertheless, even more challenging for Christian was the fact that even at the young age of six, without his father, he had to take on all of the major responsibilities of the house. He cooked, did laundry, took care of their property, went to school, and did anything he could to stay out of his mother's way and not upset her. He describes this stage of his life as the "stepping on eggshells period", as his major preoccupation became doing everything in his power not to set his mother off. If he said the wrong thing, or if he laughed or smiled, his mother would yell and scream telling him that he was not allowed being happy because she was so miserable. It was as if she wanted her own little boy to be as angry and depressed as she was.

Christian was determined not be like his mother. He went to school and acted like a normal little boy. Little did everyone know he had all the responsibility of a full-fledged adult. Christian was very secretive about his life. He never wanted his friends or his teachers to know about his family problems. He would go to school smiling, and he would have a healthy lunch with him (that he shopped for and made himself). As far as everyone knew, Christian had a wonderful life. Christian went on like this for years. Eventually though his mothers condition worsened and she became suicidal. One day when Christian was eight he came home from school to find his mother unconscious in the bathroom with every pill bottle in the house emptied and lying beside her. Christian called 911, and his mother was institutionalized once again. This happened several times during Christian's elementary years, in fact on eight other occasions during these years he was required to call 911 due to his mother's suicide attempts.

When Martine was institutionalized, Christian's dad Leo would come and stay with him. This was a treat for Christian, because he was actually able to be a kid and have someone take care of him. Eventually though, Martine would get out of the hospital and Christian would go back to his life of pretending that every thing was okay. Because Christian was so determined not to be like his parents, he developed excellent social skills and became an outstanding student and athlete, which made him very popular amongst his peers and teachers. Although it seemed to everyone else that Christian had the perfect life, it was so far from that. He would come home every night to his sick mother. He would do his chores, which included cleaning, making dinner, doing the dishes, and making their lunches for the next day. Christian would try and get his chores finished so that he could do his homework, but sometimes his mother would just stand there and yell at him. Christian was a smart kid who seemed to be quite well adjusted. He learned to internalize everything. Since he was all on his own, being an only child whose father seemingly abandoned him, he would lie in his room at night and deal with his own anger and anxiety by thinking and internalizing his feelings. Christian's life went on the same way all through his public educational years, including both elementary and high school.

With every year that passed, Martine's condition worsened and she became harder and harder to deal with. Christian was still keeping up as the intelligent, athletic, and social guy that everyone had come to expect. Eventually though, it became harder and harder for him to keep up the façade, to keep all his familial secrets hidden. His friends began to wonder why they were never invited to Christian's house or why they didn't even know where he lived. This was a struggle for Christian and he began to lie to his friends. To keep up, especially on the economic side of the equation, to keep the illusion of normalcy alive, at thirteen Christian got a part-time job working at a large national retail store. This enabled him to buy the clothes and shoes that allowed him, at least on the surface, to look just like all those around him. He went to school during the day, worked every evening and then went home and did chores all night. All through school, Christian had nice clothes just like his friends, went on field trips just like his friends, but all because he worked so hard to earn the money to do these things.

Instead of being very proud of her son, Christian's mother became increasingly agitated because he seemed to be so happy, well adjusted, and able to independently provide for himself, and here she was incredibly unhappy and forced to live on the little disability money she received from the government. As a result, no sooner had Christian acquired the part-time job at thirteen years of age when his mom started forcing him to pay rent. She thought it was unfair that he had all these nice things and thought that if he was working she should get some of his money as well. Ultimately, Christian trudged on this way all the way through high school, finishing at the top of his class. At prom he was crowned Prom King and was awarded athlete of the year. After living eighteen years of what seemed to Christian as hell, he still was able to accomplish so much and overcome his completely dysfunctional childhood. Basically, within the unit that is described as family, for all intents and purposes Christian raised himself.

As I now reflect and try and figure out how a boy who came from such poor immigrant teenage parents, who lived in subsidized housing, who had his father abandon him when he was only six, leaving him to be cared for by an extremely mentally ill mother, was able to transcend all the negative forces that were working so powerfully against him, I am truly baffled. When directly challenged with this question, this is how Christian himself answers. "First, I was fortunate enough to have really great elementary school teachers. They saw my potential and encouraged me to be the absolute best I could be. Second, throughout everything, my religion has always been an important part of my life. On the occasions when my father was around he would always take me to church, every Sunday. My father taught me the importance of faith and praying. When things got really rough for me at home, I would always go to my room and pray. When I did this I didn't feel so all alone because God was always there with me. Finally, it's this simple; I didn't want to be like my parents. I became so driven to be different from my parents. I wanted to be happy, to have friends, to have a good job, and to be able to one day fully support my own family".

After high school Christian enrolled in university in a professional program, where acceptance rates were exceedingly low, and academic standards incredibly high. He graduated at the top of his class, and he was eventually nominated as class valedictorian. Christian is a success story because he never gave up. He had teachers who believed in him, a faith that kept him strong, and an overriding drive to become something far different than his parents. For Christian the past is where it belongs – in the past! The future now belongs to him.

Chapter 40: Not Too Bad!

My educational experience was an interesting one, to say the least. I was born the second child in a family, where my older brother performed well academically. As most children in this situation, I felt the pressure to perform to the level that he was achieving in school. In general, this should not have been a problem if it were not for two major factors. First, I grew up with ADHD, which impaired my ability to pay attention in class, and often resulted in a scolding from my teacher, and consequently from my parents later. The second factor was that I was gifted. Unfortunately, neither of these two problems was formally identified until I was nearing the end of Grade 7.

There are two experiences that I can remember from my early educational experience that discouraged me from working at my academics. The first of these experiences came in the first grade. My teacher, as most grade one teachers do, divided the class into three groups based on academic ability; the bears, elephants and lions. I, with five other students, was placed in the "lions" group. This group consisted of the six students who were capable of higher than grade level work. Twice a week, the members of the group would attend an enrichment program, in which they would work on topics of personal interest. Except for me. Because I was overactive and had difficulty concentrating in class, I would be held back to do work with the rest of the class. Since the classroom was arranged by these various groups, I was then isolated from the rest of the class. As you might imagine, I began to believe I was not as good as my group at school, and that there was something wrong with me. I slowly began to despise going to school because I did not want to sit alone for half of the day.

The second experience was far more traumatizing. In the second grade, I decided that I would try to impress my teacher once again. I was excelling in both Language Arts and Math, every student's dream. Eventually, I was so far ahead of my class in math (often finishing every question from the chapter in the first day or two) that I brought in a math workbook from grade five, and was completing the math problems from that text with ease. My teacher was not happy that I was moving so far ahead of the class, and told me to take my workbook home. She wanted me to stay with the class and only work on the assignments she was giving each day. I went home in tears. When my parents asked me why I was upset, they set up a conference with my teacher. My teacher, once again, insisted that I should stop doing the math work that I was choosing to do because it was too far ahead of my grade level. My parents decided to go along with her decision. I was now doomed to sit in boredom for days on end during math period because I was no longer permitted to do other math work. I quickly discovered that there was no point in doing the work in the first place when I knew that I would be done so quickly, and without any challenge. This set the stage for the rest of my elementary schooling and even for the first couple of years of my secondary schooling.

As I mentioned, I was finally identified as having ADHD and being gifted when I was in the seventh grade. Unfortunately the damage had already been done. I no longer had a desire to perform well, because I had been told that by doing so, I was not making my teacher happy. When I was identified, a whole new set of problems came into play. My parents and my doctor decided to experiment with medications. For the next few years I suffered through wild mood swings, lack of sleep, and lack of appetite. The medication was presented as a cure for my hyperactivity, as if there was something wrong with my behaviour that needed to be fixed. There is nothing more crushing to a skinny, little, thirteen year old than to be told that he is broken. And what was worse was that it was my own parents telling me this. By the time I was in the tenth grade, I was willing to give up. My parents were getting frustrated that I wouldn't try, and I no longer had any desire to. I finally had a teacher who cared about my potential. She was my science teacher, and she let me do assignments and projects that reflected my abilities, and interests. I was still excessively active in the class, but she made me feel like it was a good thing. I still remember my parents going to the parent-teacher conference, asking how much my behaviour had been disrupting the class. I can still hear her answer in my head, "There is absolutely nothing wrong with Matthews's behaviour. He brings a lot of energy into this class, and it is a pleasure to have him here." It was the first time I ever had someone stick up for me.

That teacher motivated me to start performing in school. Before her, I had been achieving 60s and 70s. After that conference, my grade in her class went from a 63 to an 87 at the final. My overall average eventually soared into the 80s, and I went on to University, and graduated with Honours. I now am a certified teacher, just completing my Bachelor of Education. Not too bad; not too bad at all!

Chapter 41: My Story

My story of resiliency is more a testament to my mother's resiliency than my own. It is also one that I hesitated to write. My life and the circumstances surrounding it are so normal that I do not even recognize it as being that out of the ordinary. When you have nothing to compare it to, it doesn't appear to be all that unique. In juxtaposition to so many other stories, mine has really been a figurative walk in the park. However, in reflecting upon it, I have always recognized that it could have been so much worse and, certainly when examined within a risk/resiliency perspective, I knew almost immediately that there was a whole lot to explore, especially on the "what went right?" side of the risk/resiliency equation.

I am really not sure why my mother married my father. I am sure there was sincerely some love there at some point, but soon after they married, it all went wrong. My father became an alcoholic and abused my mother. He was in love with power and manipulated her in every way possible. From the outset, he controlled her money, her social life, and her ultimate happiness. He would go out with his friends at night without her and, most often, would return drunk. He often drank away much of their monthly budget, leaving little money for food and the necessities of life. He would often come home from his drinking sprees looking to bully my mother (and I mean in every possible way). If she dared refuse his requests, he would just hit her or throw her across the room. I was born into this unhealthy environment and my arrival certainly did not change the overall state of my family's situation.

My mother once described to me the turning point that was a major factor in "what went right" - in both her life and mine. She told me of a thanksgiving meal she was hosting at our home. Family members from my father's side of the family had gathered to celebrate the holiday. My father was watching sports on TV. I was two years old at the time, and in an attempt to get my father's attention, for some reason or another, I was dancing in front of him, blocking his view of the TV. Apparently, he was more interested in sports than giving me any kind of audience, so he just hit me. My mom refers to this specific moment as her "wake up call." In the final analysis, she could put up with him abusing her (and even forgive him for it), but when she witnessed it start to happen to me, she claims she saw everything in a much different light.

From my particular perspective, a child's memories of their early years are pretty much non-existent so in that sense I am somewhat blessed. The few fleeting glimpses I do have into that period of my life are from the period immediately following "the incident" (referred to directly above). However, I do remember coming out of my room late at night to see my parents in the middle of a yelling match in our kitchen. I remember sneaking back to my room hoping that no one had seen me. I remember the people that we stayed with immediately after my mother and I fled our family home. I also remember being on a train travelling to another part of the country. I remember having no real concept of what was really going on, or why, but I know I never questioned it. I only now understand how much pride that it must have taken from my mom to have to admit her marriage had failed and that she had been putting up with spousal abuse for so many years.

Somewhere in the midst of all this chaos, my mom showed a great deal of independence and initiative and went back to school and got a professional degree. This definitely proved an asset in our lives as it very quickly enabled us, as a family, to move forward in a positive way. She, almost immediately, got a job with a flexible schedule and was able to raise me on her own, without having to leave me to the fulltime care of babysitters or daycare. For me, without question, the significant adult in my life, that helped me through all the ups and downs, was my mother! Without fail, with respect to both the good and bad, she was always there for me! She always was able to effectively balance her professional obligations with raising her child and so, despite some significant turbulence in my life, I never, and I mean never, felt alone or unloved!

My father did reappear in my life on several occasions in those early years, however, suffice it to say that none of these experiences were in any way positive. He would always attempt to buy my love with all kinds of gifts, and he would always initially pretend to be "the perfect daddy". And, largely, because this is what I wanted him to be, I would always initially believe him, which only served to hurt me even more when the inevitable would always occur. Unfailingly, on each and every occasion, his true colours would always come through. Threats, verbal and physical fights with my mother in front of me, and always the lack of monetary compensation in ultimately raising me. In the end, none of his actions ever supported the façade. I trusted him so unconditionally, but he broke that trust each and every time. The only thing that went right here was that eventually he stopped trying at all. Finally, to put an end to this very unhealthy cycle, my mom promised to not sue him for child support if he would stop following and/or contacting us. For us, the money was not worth all the turmoil and through some small miracle, the bargain finally stuck. I have not heard from my father since I was seven!

My mom, despite struggling with melancholy off and on, has always been a positive beacon in my life. She puts on a brave face. As a child I bought it, even if it was fake at times. My mother always instilled hope in me. I really believe that is important for a child. It takes a whole lot of effort and energy to worry. Even when things were bad, my mom made sure that her problems were not made to be my problems. I was free to be a child and even though I knew my childhood was not a perfect fairytale, I was pretty accepting of the circumstances because that's just how it was!

At a young age, I also found two different areas where I was very successful. These two pursuits gave me a lot of gratification and gave me something on which to focus my efforts. They gave me hope and provided a sense of belonging. They took my special interests and talents and let me run with them.

Firstly, at the age of seven, I was formally identified in school as being a "gifted" student. Having not had a lot of social success at school previous to this, largely due to the frequent moves in my life in trying to get away from my father, but also because I was an extremely shy child, who generally lacked any degree of confidence, I felt completely unnoticed within my educational life. Suddenly, after being identified as "gifted", I finally had the school system "officially" recognizing me, telling me how smart and what a 'special' person I was. With direct reference to this, I strongly believe that the 'special' education I received as a "gifted" student was just as important in my life as the programs put in place for lower achieving or "at risk" students. In fact, in my opinion, there still is this general belief that is floating around to this day (in many educational realms) that gifted children will always "be okay" - no matter what; that they will get through school, and do so successfully even without any intervention and/or adaptations provided for them. I absolutely refuse to buy into this! While it may hold true in a purely academic sense, I think we really do a disservice to the social and emotional well being of this population when we ignore their needs or make their needs less important than those of other groups. I really don't think I would have been as successful in life without having the school system send a clear message to me that I mattered, and that they had high expectations for me, and cared about my future. The 'special' class I attended one day a week gave me the only friends I ever had that could completely understand me. They never judged me or looked down upon me for being smart, or for putting on full display my intellectual capabilities. It greatly pains me that this kind of support is noticeably absent for a lot of gifted students today, and that this group seems to come last on the list of 'special' education priorities.

Secondly, I began taking gymnastics lessons. Gymnastics did not come as easily to me as school, but this was also a blessing. It gave me a challenge. I never really felt a sense of achievement in school because I did not have to try all that hard to be successful, but this certainly was not the case when it came to gymnastics. It kept me occupied after school and on weekends. It gave me a social situation where I was on the same level as all my peers. It forced me to perform and overcome my intense shyness. It provided structure and boundaries. It taught me a work ethic and how to persevere through incredible challenges, but most of all it provided some life-long friends. My coaches also became additional positive adults in my life, not just where the sport was concerned, but in providing some valuable life lessons as well.

Without question, between stumbling onto gymnastics, being identified reasonably early within the school system as being gifted, but, most importantly, having a truly wonderful mother, have in combination provided me with many of the positive traits that make up who I am today.

In conclusion, my story is certainly one of success, but certainly not remarkable by any measure. Before writing this I would have never called myself resilient, however, in looking more closely at resiliency literature; particularly in trying address "what went right?" with respect to my success, my life fits so many of the characteristics identified in the research. No question, I did indeed have an unfortunate start to my childhood, however, much of this was neutralized very early on in my development. The chain of events that blazed a trail for my success, thankfully, was put in place very quickly so that any "damage" done was of the very minimal variety. For every stroke of bad luck I had, I had equally as many positive things happen to me. High expectations in school, positive life lessons learned in gymnastics, social success through 'special' education and sports, having a passion I could follow, and having caring and supportive adults in my life, particularly my mother, all contributed immeasurably to setting me on a successful life path, which, I must add, I continue to follow!

Chapter 42: Just Like Me

Throughout my life, I have been faced with many challenges and struggles. These struggles first began when my mother was pregnant with me several decades ago. Initially, she was informed by her doctors that she would not be able to conceive any children, so when my parents found out that they were pregnant with me, they were, to say the least, completely overjoyed. While my parents were celebrating the idea of me coming into this world, my mom found out that her father was terminally ill. Needless to say, the next nine months were pretty stressful on my mom, which led to several complications. There were many unscheduled hospital visits, and lots of bed rest. My mom was going through so much that it led to at least three beginning stages of labour, which had to be stopped because it was way too early to deliver. Sadly, three weeks before I was born my grandfather died, completely devastating my family. He never got the opportunity to meet his very first grandchild. When I was born, the doctors gave me a clean bill of health and I was sent home.

During my early childhood, I was physically and mentally developing just like most kids my age. My parents spent a lot of time with me and did everything they could to keep me healthy and happy. I remember my parents spending a good part of their evenings reading to me. However, when I entered elementary school, my teachers and parents started to notice a bit of a difference (from my peers) when it came to my overall language development, especially when it came to word pronounciation. As a direct result, I had to work with a speech and language pathologist for many of my early years in school.

As I got older, with curriculum expectations increasing, it became very obvious that my reading and writing skills were not developing at the same rate as my peers. I distinctly remember being in grade two, a time when most of my friends started to read full-length books. I was so ashamed because I was still only able to read little kid picture books, with approximately one sentence per page. I remember feeling so different; and I certainly didn't want to be different. I remember my mom trying to help me in the evenings with the different components of language, and I would scream and cry with frustration because I was unable to comprehend the information in front of me – (or even easily speak it). I was trying really hard but struggling so much! Finally, when I was in grade three, the resource teacher finally decided, of course, with the permission of my parents, to have some general assessments conducted. Quite naturally, the results noted some general problems, and made some suggestions/recommendations on how I could potentially improve both my reading and writing skills. In short, my parents and teachers continued to do what they could, based on the general recommendations, but I still continued to struggle in school.

As I got older, I started to immerse myself in other areas of school, especially sports, which always left me feeling a bit better about myself. However, when it came to the academic side of things, it became more and more obvious to me that something was wrong, and, in understatement, it frustrated me immensely. Finally in grade six it was decided to segregate me from the rest of my class, several times a week, to more intensively work on my reading and writing skills. Looking back, this decision to remove me from the rest of the class upset me considerably because although I knew it was for my own good, I also knew that my friends might think I'm somehow very different from them. Anyway, I kept trying to move forward.

I remember distinctly, when I finally made it to grade 8, I was so excited because I knew I was likely to graduate thereby embarking on a brand new direction in my educational life. The year started off really well, with my new teacher at one point, even using some of my work as an example for the rest of the class. I was absolutely thrilled because no teacher had ever done that for me, ever. But after the first month and a half of school, I started to notice that we were getting a lot of supply teachers; which ultimately led to our class eventually finding out that our teacher would never be returning. Story goes, that he had been heard making a lot of inappropriate / unprofessional comments about students, which apparently led to his removal. Although I was initially sad, my mom later informed me that one of those (inappropriate) comments (among many) was directed specifically at me. She then went on to tell me, that when she spoke with my former teacher and asked him how I was generally doing in his class, his first response to my mother's inquiry was, "Well, she's not too bright". As might be expected, my mother was absolutely disgusted, and immediately walked away from him. I don't think she was at all sorry with respect to his removal. Although she told me this story several years later, I remember my feelings at this time being somewhat mixed. I remember thinking, "Who does this man think he is?" while another part of me was thinking, "But maybe he's right?" It was hard for me to rationalize all of this stuff at this particular time in my life. I had such a hard time in school, and my grades were always suffering. I knew I was probably trying harder in school than any of my classmates, but no matter how hard I tried, I just couldn't get the results. I was overwhelmed with despair, and started thinking that maybe school was just not for me! But eventually, grade eight was over.

As a "minor niner," I was pretty happy about entering high school, but also terrified. I started having a bit of hope about school again because I would get the opportunity to choose the courses I wanted and I would have teachers who did not know my history as a student. But as per usual, this hope started fading pretty quickly because school became even more difficult with the overall increase in curricular expectations. I wanted so desperately to do well in my classes, and I worked my butt off, but again the initial results were poor. When grade ten came along, the special education teacher concluded that more assessments were most definitely in order. The results of these tests were eventually sent to the school psychologist, where a diagnosis was finally rendered. The special education teacher, my mother, and myself were, at this point, informed that I was identified as having a profound learning disability. Although I had heard of this term before, I never in a million years thought it would apply to me. The reason I say this is because my focus was on the word "disability". I started questioning my intelligence and thinking that now it has been absolutely confirmed, I am not a very smart person. I was really contemplating the idea of dropping out of school altogether, when I turned sixteen. However, not being a quitter, I eventually decided to keep plugging away – and see what happens.

I continued to work really hard in school, but I also decided to perhaps push myself a little too much. I started signing up for classes that were very challenging for me. For example, when grade 11 came, I decided that I would take Biology (what was I thinking)? Since I was getting older, I started thinking about my future after high school and I started recognizing where my particular strengths and weaknesses were. I knew science was an area that provided a significant challenge for me given my particular learning style, but because my friends were taking it, specifically for University purposes, I thought that I should take it as well – because I didn't want to close any doors; (but I struggled so much in that course).

At one point in the semester, the special education teacher and the Biology teacher decided to call an IPRC meeting, with, of course, my mom and I included in the process. As I look back, this was a very stressful, intimidating, and terrifying experience for me, primarily because I felt like I was being judged as a person. As the meeting progressed, and after all the formalities were out of the way, eventually my grade 11 Biology teacher starts talking, and almost immediately I could feel my face getting hotter and hotter. Although I don't remember too much of what she generally said, I do remember her specifically saying, "She is not good enough for this class. She has set herself up for failure." No sooner were the words out of her mouth before I could feel the tears running down my face. I was so upset (as was my mother). I thought, who would have the audacity to say such a hurtful thing, and in front of her mother. I came away from that meeting feeling so low and utterly dejected. Of course, I ultimately dropped my Biology course, as I truly felt I wasn't really given any other choice. I had completely lost trust in my teacher, and I wasn't going to let her affect my self-esteem – any more than she already had. In many ways it was the final straw. I was really starting to get tired of all the negative comments I had heard from my teachers and peers throughout my entire educational life. I was frustrated with how much work I was putting into school and not getting anything back in return. I could not understand how I could spend hours on an assignment, while my friends could spend minutes on theirs, and they would consistently get much better marks than me. Why was I not able to retain anything, or completely comprehend? I just didn't understand why my ability to learn was so different from everyone else's. However, after some serious introspection and time, my anger and frustration started to morph into outright motivation for me. My "aha" moment came when I finally realized that I had to accept the fact that I learned very differently, but that was absolutely okay!

I was lucky in that all of this (internal) acceptance and understanding happened at a time when I had a number of teachers in high school who were incredibly supportive and very encouraging. For example, around this time I found myself doing really well in art classes, and actually started thinking that this may be something that I could possibly pursue in a post-secondary way. (Yes, post-secondary studies). I was actually starting to think about going to university. I also got myself involved in various clubs and sports teams at school. I believe that these things (sports and clubs) are really what kept me hanging around. These clubs and teams taught me to push myself, and take real advantage of my particular areas of strength. They also taught me to take pride in my accomplishments. I was also really lucky to have parents who encouraged the idea of being involved in clubs and sports teams outside of school, because these were areas where I could naturally excel. (For me, for the briefest of moments, through sports and clubs, all the academic stuff could be put on the back-burner). I think, in the end, in late high school, when it mattered most, some of these things started to really contribute, in a positive way, to my self-concept, because eventually I started to feel pretty good about myself! Although, I must confess, when it came to the raw academic side of things, I still had my days where I was completely stressed out, and seriously questioned whether or not I had the will to continue. Even on the good days, I always had a bit of anxiety in the classroom because I never wanted the teacher to ask me any surprise questions or have me read aloud. In short, the feeling of being judged, never ever completely left me.

When my final year of high school finally arrived, the anxiety and stress levels were ratcheted up considerably. I knew that one chapter was closing, and a new one (whatever it was) was about to begin. I knew that I needed to really think about what I wanted for my future, and what was best for me. I was still thinking about post-secondary opportunities, (and the thoughts of potentially going to university never really left me). When I made the honour role in the first semester (which had never happened before), I started thinking that university could indeed become a reality for me. When I started doing my research, my special education teacher immediately tried to discourage me from considering the university option. I remember, like yesterday, her saying to me, "University is not the route for you. You really should be looking into college." However, for the first time I didn't cry about it and/or let it get me down. I actually used it as an incentive, motivating me further to make the university route a reality. Deep in the inner recesses of my head I had the idea of becoming a teacher, and I knew that if this was even to be remotely considered, university was the only alternative.

When it came time to make applications to universities, right away I became absolutely overjoyed as I started receiving acceptances from all across the province. I was so unbelievably delighted, but at the same time worried because, despite all the good news, for what appeared to be the longest of times, I still hadn't received anything from the university that was my number one choice. Finally, one day my mom came home from work with a big smile on her face. She handed me this large envelope, which confirmed all my post secondary wishes. I had been accepted by my university of (first) choice. Needless to say, I continued to work hard for the rest of the year, and before I knew it, high school was finally over!

When I first went to university, I wanted to make sure that they were aware of my learning differences, so they could provide some of the supports I had received in high school. However, because the university didn't recognize some of the assessments relied upon by my old high school, the university ordered that a whole new battery of psychological tests be conducted. I remember distinctly this was a very stressful time for me because I was grilled and examined for hours, which took an awful lot out of me. This all took place the summer before university officially started. When I finally received the results of the tests, the first clinical interpretation we received was a very confusing one in that no specific learning disability was officially diagnosed. Certainly some profound statistical aberrations were brought to our attention, identifying general areas of academic weakness, but no specific identification was offered. This of course meant, in an official way, that the university would not be providing me any support with respect to my learning difference (like my high school had previously done). To say the least, this absolutely terrified me.

Well, my mom was not ready to accept this first diagnosis and, in understatement, was willing to take on a fight, by way of advocating for me once again. Not willing to accept the first clinical interpretation, my mom pushed for a second interpretation of the results, only this time from a psychologist who specializes within the broad field of learning disability. Within a very short period of time this new psychologist looked at my test results and almost immediately he explained everything in intricate detail to my parents and me, that indeed I did have a very profound and very specific learning disability. I must confess, a part of me was somewhat upset because the psychologist so clearly laid out my learning strengths and weaknesses, making very clear to me that I would need to advocate very strongly on behalf of myself if I was to find any success at the postsecondary level.

The next four years of university were very difficult for me. When everything is said and done, university tends to focus on a particular style, the lecture style, that really tends to exploit students with my particular learning difference (weakness). To be successful within a lecture format, you need good auditory, comprehension, and memorization skills; and you also need to know how to write or take notes (and all at the same time). The ability to do all of this, in a multi-task sort of a way, was very difficult for me. But I worked and worked, and was not willing to give up. I had never worked so hard in my life. Over the years, I learned to cope, to gravitate to my strengths, all the while teaching myself new strategies which were geared to making my academic life a far less stressful one. I re-wrote my notes, I tape-recorded the lectures, I used pictures and colours. I developed exemplary organizational skills. However, when it came to essay writing, well, that was another story. It was definitely the worst part of university for me. Over time, I actually started having major anxiety attacks when I had to write because I became so easily frustrated. I always knew what I wanted to say, but I couldn't easily get my words to the ends of my fingers. I can't say that I feel a whole lot more comfortable today writing essays, but I know that I have made considerable improvements even in this area. Like they say, practice does make perfect, especially when there is no anxiety involved. I learned a lot about myself during my four years at university. I learned that I can do whatever I want when motivation and hard work are applied in equal doses. You can indeed reach your goals! I learned the importance in being able to ask for help and/or support when it is most needed. But most importantly, it was also at university where I learned to accept the fact that I do learn in a very different way; that I have a learning disability, and that is absolutely okay!

In my fourth year of university, I got this amazing opportunity. I was chosen by my learning strategist to participate in a Learning Disability mentorship program. There were several students chosen from our particular university and we all had the opportunity to share our stories with other university, high school, and elementary school students. We also were able to share our stories with teachers and parents. I really enjoyed telling others about my experiences and giving others the chance to know that they are not alone. That was a problem that I faced growing up, I really felt alone, like I was the only one who had a "problem". It was such a great program and it had such a positive effect on me. I was able to work with other students who had been identified learning disabled and I tried to pass on my strategies to them. I also got to train them on assistive technology to help them in their studies. It also gave me the chance to really examine my own learning disability – up close and personal. I started making connections as to why things worked and didn't work for me. It was the first time in my life where I started to truly understand my identification, which gave me a great deal of confidence in moving forward.

During those four years of university, I was working towards a goal. This goal was really what kept me going. I realized that my educational pursuits over the years had consisted of both tremendous struggle, but also an awful lot of success. I met some amazing teachers along the way, who truly inspired me. I also met many others who probably should have been involved in another profession. If you happened to learn the way they taught that was fine, but if you didn't, too bad for you! But to be honest, it was the inspirational ones whom I most thought of, especially when it came time to think about my future. I thought maybe I could be like them; maybe I could be a teacher too, and make a difference in the lives of others, just like they did for me.

When I look back at the last twenty three years of my life, I can say that I have experienced many challenges and struggles along the way, but as things became clearer to me with respect my particular and very specific learning style, I never lost sight of my final goal – to become a teacher. I can honestly say that I do not have any regrets because everything that I have experienced in my life has contributed to the type of person I am today, and the type of teacher I will become. I am really proud of that person. I am a hard worker, who is motivated and willing to do what it takes to reach my goals. I believe a part of this came from the struggle and the identification I have. I am also blessed with having wonderful parents who were willing to fight for my hopes and dreams. They encouraged my strengths, supported my weaknesses, and fully celebrated my successes. I am finally in a place in my life where I feel more content and not so confused about my learning disability. Even though I went through a lot as a child and I know I will face more challenges in the future, I know I can carry those things with me as I embark on my journey as an educator and an adult. I will definitely recognize bits of myself in my students, and I will ensure that they get every opportunity to reach their full potential—**just like me!**

Chapter 43: A Conversation between Mother and Daughter on Risk and Resilience

Daughter:

When first given this task, in listening to your lectures and in looking at some of the research, I knew right away that my own situation very much qualified in meeting the most specific requirements of the assignment. I was unquestionably (and statistically) a child and young adolescent who would have been considered very much at-risk, as were my brothers, who've all grown to be incredibly resilient, successful adults. On the risk side, variables like poverty, familial dysfunction, separation and divorce, learning difference and/or "special" educational need, among other things, all are certainly well represented within our family's story, while on the resiliency side of things - one fundamental factor stands out in stark contrast to all others; and that is the incredible effort, and unwavering love and support consistently supplied by our mother.

Mother:

My daughter tells me you are interested in knowing some of the techniques used to help my kids become successful in life, despite some profound challenges early on in their development. I told her I was available for email or phone calls if you wanted more specific information. Many of my coping mechanisms/strategies, particularly in dealing with extremely stressful, challenging situations, were learned from my mother who had been raised in a farm family. But much of it, I suppose, was just plain dumb luck and circumstance. For the sake of my family's survival, I needed to come up with something, as I didn't really have any other choice!

Daughter:

I would disagree with that. Mom gives herself very little credit. She may not have had the formal education that some professional's had/have but she was/is incredibly intuitive. She would come home with a new strategy with respect to making the family more functional, and she would always try new things. Sometimes she brought it from work, sometimes from conversations with others, sometimes, I'm sure, it just occurred to her upon reflection. In the end, it doesn't really matter! What does matter is that she kept trying to make things better. If a strategy seemed sound, she tried it! Sometimes it worked, other times it didn't. So she took elements of the things that did work, and mixed them with other things. She pieced together strategies until she found something that worked for our family as a whole (for our particular challenging situation at the time). As we grew up, of course strategies had to adjusted, so she just kept on trying new things. Not that we really knew that was what she was doing. For example, we just knew that suddenly we could earn stickers for completing a list of tasks each day – like brushing our teeth, making our beds, not fighting with each other before breakfast, not fighting after dinner, doing the dishes, etc.; then, at the end of the week, if we had enough stickers, we could pick out something special (under a certain price limit of course) from the local store. That's just one example of the things she tried with us. At the time, it was structure and routine, which our family very much needed. It was very important to our family at this time. It kept us functioning as a "real" family as odd as that may sound. We had to negotiate our behaviour with one another, with us kids, helping one another attain the required stickers. Remember, at this point, where Mom was seriously trying to inject some order into our family, things were not going all that well for us collectively. My brothers and I were constantly at each other's throat (literally). I distinctly remember at least one occasion where we had to rush to the hospital because one of us had seriously injured the other....My father had been gone from the family for over a year at this point. He had slowly removed himself from our lives, only reappearing on occasion to throw a little disruption and chaos at us. Basically, he would periodically show up in our lives just long enough to scream, fight and yell at/with Mom, and break down the front door when it was locked (always sending the school photos that were hanging in the front hallway crashing to the floor). Funny how I remember that! No doubt at this particular time, there was a great deal of upheaval going on in our lives and none of us were doing all that well. I know letters were flying between lawyers and, court dates through this period, were fairly common.... But Mom shielded us from all of that, at least as much as she could. Dad would always try and pull us in, but Mom would always hold firm stating that kids had no business being in the middle of adult problems and fights. That our role in all of this was just to remain normal kids; - go to school, learn, play, build tree forts with our neighbors, and try to love both parents equally! No question, through all the turmoil, Mom kept trying to stabilize the family and have it focus on its strengths. She constantly reminded us that we weren't just a bunch of people who lived together, but were rather a Mom and kids who all loved one another very much. That we could get through this together!

Mother:

First, with respect to risk/resilience, I think that general attitude is a very important component. For example, for us, as a family, we lacked money but we were **NOT** poor!

Daughter:

That's true. We rarely had money for much of anything. I remember learning certain economic truths at a very young age (since I was the oldest child) For example, a movie rental for one night was equal to the price of a bag of milk for the week. Which one do you think the money went towards? But that doesn't mean that we went without anything really important because, in my view, we didn't! Mom made sure we always had what we needed. Always! Again, I'm not sure how she did it. But she did. Always! I know she was constantly worried about money and would frequently go without eating herself. We would all sit down to dinner and she would get a glass of milk, claiming she wasn't hungry just yet but would eat later. She never did though! And, on many occasions, I would find her in the basement leaning against the washing machine with her head in her hands. She never acted like anything was really wrong. But she also never lied to us. If we asked a question she always gave us a truthful answer, but only in as much detail as our childish minds could handle. We all knew we didn't have money for the things our friends did. Early on, playing on hockey teams was out of the question for my brothers, and I couldn't figure skate like I had before my Dad left, but we all understood why..... I remember, one year she made a deal with my Dad to pay half the money so my brothers could play hockey. When he agreed to this arrangement, she immediately went to work trying to find equipment for the boys to use. She ended up getting a whole bunch of used equipment donated by families who had boys who'd outgrown the equipment. My brothers were finally going to get to play hockey like they'd been yearning to do for years. And then Dad backed out and wouldn't pay the money required......... Anyway, it's not important now, but as kids we just learned to value things quite differently, especially when compared to most of the other kids that we went to school with.

Mother:

We were a family. Each individual member was important to the whole; we needed everybody to pitch in to make it run. Everyone had assigned chores to do and everyone was held accountable in completing these chores. I was the head of the family, no contest; no debate! It was not a democracy, although I would always listen to their opinions and ideas. In the final analysis, I had ultimate veto power over everything (they laughingly called it voodoo power, I think from an old Sting song). I demanded respect for myself and for each member of the family, which included always respecting themselves!

Daughter:

She's actually wrong about Sting; it's really David Bowie from the movie Labyrinth (laughs).... But it's true. We held impromptu family discussions whenever there was something that affected the family. Sometimes it was while driving in the car somewhere, other times it would be a collective gathering in the hallway between our bedrooms. Anywhere! The location didn't really matter. She always listened to us seriously, and always took into consideration any of our ideas and/or opinions. If something didn't seem feasible, she would always faithfully and considerately explain her reasoning to us. She always listened and respected our individual ideas, but within this arrangement she also demanded that we respect the views and opinions of each other as well. If one of us had something to say, we all had to listen quietly and respectfully. If we wanted to disagree, that was absolutely okay and was encouraged, as long as we disagreed in a respectful manner. We were never allowed to put another person down just because we disagreed with them! In Mom's world, and the world she created for us, everyone had the right to their own ideas and opinions, and they were to be valued and always considered seriously. This was a big deal to Mom. She insisted on it! It helped us to learn how to respect others, family or otherwise, but also taught us that what we thought or believed in was important and valued. It didn't matter if others disagreed because our thoughts were just as valid and important as anyone else's, regardless of age.

Mother:

My kids always looked the best they could. They were always clean. They bathed every night. My daughter's hair was always brushed and dressed up. She wore ribbons, barrettes or an appropriate hair closure. It was never worn long, and left looking untidy. My sons always had their hair brushed, and cut when needed. All clothing worn to school was clean, brightly coloured, appropriately matched, correctly fit, never torn, never patched. Track pants were only worn for gym days. Black shirts were not worn to school at all. Patched cloths were saved for play clothing. I realized teachers were as human as the rest of us and made subconscious judgments based on appearance regardless of their intentions. I wanted my kids to be seen as bright, intelligent, normal kids.

Daughter:

It worked. No teacher ever knew that we weren't 'the same' as the other kids from our appearance. They had to get to know us as people **FIRST**. After they knew us it didn't matter that we didn't have money and that we frequently relied on social assistance, subsidies, after school programs, or even food drives that happened around holidays. We were 'normal' kids to them by that point, and it no longer mattered!!!

Mother:

I lived in the most affluent area I could afford. I preferred to be the lower income of a middle-income neighborhood than the highest-income in a lower income area.

Daughter:

She later showed me some of the places that we were almost forced to live in. Being on social assistance sucks for so many reasons, but among them is the fact that you basically lose the ability to decide where you want to live and raise your family. You can be forced to live where they tell you to or you lose the money you need to live on. She fought them on this, though! Mom is one tough woman and would fight to the death for us. In this case she won!....It's pure conjecture of course, but I've often wondered what would have happened to us if she hadn't fought as hard or if she'd eventually lost the battle? What I come up with scares me in ways that I can't describe. I'm almost positive that we would have lost my youngest brother, though! His learning disabilities would have been most likely completely overlooked without someone there, kicking and screaming for him. I'm sure, that the behaviours, and "chip-on-the-shoulder" attitude that came with the frustration of dealing with learning challenges that no one wanted to admit existed, would have surely sunk him! I have no doubt that he would have been labeled as nothing more than a behavioural problem, and likely a delinquent, instead of the quick minded, brilliant, funny and strong young man that he is today. And that's just him! I doubt 1 would have ended up graduating with one University degree and working towards a second (becoming a certified teacher). As I said though-pure conjecture on my part!

Mother:

I spent a lot of time at school. I knew every teacher my kids ever had. I visited each and every one of them on each and every parent/teacher night; I went to every interview; I attended all school plays and/or events; I helped/volunteered for every activity I could possibly schedule; I wrote many letters, and I made many, many phone calls!

Daughter:

Wow, she was always there! I remember sitting in my math class, looking out the door and seeing my mother making faces at me from the hallway! I started laughing and I'm not sure my teacher believed me when I told him why. Although, he'd met her previously that's for sure, so maybe he did believe me after all! I also remember leaving the classroom at one point and the Principal coming up to me. He was incredibly frustrated and looked like he'd had a heck of a day. I knew Mom was going to be at the school that day. Anyway, he came up to me and said that he hoped I knew how much my Mom loved us and how hard she fought for us. I was somewhat bewildered but told him that yes, that I knew she did and that she always would stick up for us. I remember, he smiled at me distractedly and then walked away muttering to himself. I remember feeling pretty darned good about this encounter!

Mother:

I supported the teachers and made it clear to my kids that I expected them to respect the teacher and the teacher's authority within the classroom. I also made it clear I was their advocate, that I expected them to be treated with respect by the adults in their lives and would stand behind them if they needed help in a dispute, but I demanded/required complete honesty from them in this respect.

Daughter:

Everyone knew it too. There were teachers who hated my mother with a passion. They knew that she would call them on their inappropriateness as quickly as she would us. She did it on more than one occasion too. She would do some of it in front of us so that we knew that she was on our side and would always support us. Then she would send us from the room and then finish the 'conversation' without us there. She insisted that we respect our teachers (and they respect us).

Mother:

I asked teachers to always consider a fund raising activity when they planned a class trip so that my kids could be part of it. I often provided (suggested) fundraisers and offered to help when I could. I could not afford to pay for class trips but I wanted them to be part of all class activities regardless of our financial situation. In this regard, most teachers tried to help out!

Daughter:

They were pretty good about it, even buying the muffins that we baked and set out for sale in the staff room as part of our fundraising for one event.   But they often created fundraising events for the whole class or school so as not to single us out.

Mother:

When needed, I created a list of money earning jobs that my kids could do for friends, neighbors and family.

Daughter:

No grass went unmowed, no leaves went unraked, and no garden went unweeded. Um .. okay, no garden until one of us mixed up which were weeds and which were the desired plants. Oops? But she found all kinds of stuff for us to do in order to raise the money for field trips. We cleaned out barns, garages, washed cars, started yard sales and bake sales, set up lemonade stands, everything ... You name it, we did it!

Mother:

The kids always had books. We went to the library frequently, once a week on average. Books were often part of birthday or Christmas presents. I read to them nightly!

Daughter:

Books had an appeal that very little else did. They were a great way to escape! For example, we couldn't afford for me to figure skate like I had used to love to do—but if I had a book about figure skating then I could easily imagine myself as being the one doing it. Actually, it wasn't just books. It's true that she read to us every night but we also created stories constantly. We'd be in the car or in the grocery store or pretty much anywhere and we'd always be telling stories. One of us would start it and then another would add something, then someone else would add something else, and on and on. It was a lot of fun but it also helped to develop our imaginations, our vocabulary, and in a way it also helped to develop skills related to writing because we were creating complex sentences and using words that we couldn't spell yet, but if we liked them we would learn how to! Through this Mom was also teaching us how to speak 'appropriately'. Proper grammar was always very important to her. Mom corrected us all the time. She was never punitive or mean about this, however, if we used the wrong word or phrased something incorrectly, she always gently corrected it. Again, we may not have had a lot of money, however, this fact was never going to be reflected in the way we looked or spoke!

Mother:

I went to school. My kids constantly saw me taking night courses and doing homework.

Daughter:

We also saw her working two jobs while going to school in order to still take care of us. She never complained, but we could certainly see how difficult this was for her. I once mentioned this fact to her but, as per usual, she just shrugged it off. She said that she did what she had to for us all to survive!..... I strongly disagree! She could have given up and let someone else take over. She could have given us to our Dad during one of the many times he tried to convince us to live with him. She didn't though! She knew that it was not in our best interest to live with Dad so she kept fighting. She fought for everything she/we had. She constantly talked hydro companies into not turning off the power during the winter when we were months behind in paying the bills. She convinced the men who filled our oil tank to do so anyways in February when it was freezing and we were out of oil to heat our home - but we didn't have the money to pay for the refill. She got us groceries, when we obviously couldn't pay for them. She learned how to fix bikes, patch holes in walls, and do minor plumbing. Basically, fixing anything that active children could break, and that was lots! She fought long and hard and never quit! Not once!

Mother:

My own mother graduated from University in her late 40's. Her graduation picture always hung proudly in our living room. I constantly talked about when the kids would go to college or university, not if, but always when! I always stressed it as an absolute fact, not as a dream. This was not an option in our household.

Daughter:

In my last years of high school I started talking about not going to University. At the time, Mom didn't get upset or argue with me. However, the next time she went out to complete some general errands, she made sure to take me with her. Well, the first place she took me was through a large government 'public' housing project. She talked about where we had come from, and how far we'd travelled as a family. She talked about some of the factors that qualified people to take advantage of subsidized housing. She stressed that although we didn't have stereotypes or misconceptions about the people who were forced to live there, many, many others did; and we talked about some of these stereotypes and misconceptions. But as we talked, she also subtly reminded me of all of the things I'd dreamed of having or doing and how I wouldn't be able to achieve those dreams if I didn't go to school. I must say, that ended the conversation fairly quickly—about not going to university!

Mother:

The kids participated in soccer and other low cost sports in the community. I hosted "hangout parties" with a couple bags of chips and a case of pop so their friends would "hang out" at our house. I chatted with many of their friends' parents.

Daughter:

And because she did we ended up getting invited by these same friends' parents to go places with them that we never would have otherwise. Or these parents became aware of our situation and helped *to* find donated equipment so we could play sports. And some of the fathers felt it was okay to include my brothers in 'guy activities' when they would take their sons places because they, or their wives, had become friends with Mom and knew we weren't seeing Dad all that much.

Mother:

Sleepover nights at our house were encouraged.

Daughter:

Our friends believed that we had the coolest parent that ever existed! (And ... we never had to tell our friends that we couldn't go to the movies or mini-golfing or whatever with them and then sleep over at their houses because we couldn't afford the price of admission). Instead, "sleepovers" were our exclusive domain, where everyone wanted to stay and hang out with our Mom and us.

Mother:

Television was restricted and usually supervised. I forbid TV programs like "Married with Children" and "The Simpson" that disrespected family, school or self. I watched with them and we discussed the situations we saw. I answered anything they asked. I took them to museums, plays, parks and churches. We watched video movies and discussed them. I played the devil's advocate and challenged them to see multiple sides of issues.

Daughter:

And because of that I have a hard time taking a stand on any issue (laughs). I can't help but see the other side. When I do take a stand I still recognize the opposing view and can often argue it as well as those who believe in it. This was part of her teaching us to respect others (and their opinions).... I think!

Mother:

One of my sons had a learning disability. He worked harder for a "D" than any of the other kids needed to in order to achieve an "A".

Daughter:

That kid had more guts and strength than any of us had. He constantly had to fight and struggle with things that he saw us doing with ease. Everyone helped where they could but ultimately it came down to him and his strength, stubbornness, and sheer will (on both his and Mom's part) to succeed.

Mother:

Each was applauded for work done, not necessarily grades achieved. Best efforts were rewarded. Each kid had a bragging book full of pictures, ribbons, certificates, badges and awards.

Daughter:

We still all have them too! When we were younger we could flip through them and get the immediate ego boost we might be needing. I think it was really important for my youngest brother though. He had so little traditional 'success' within school that he needed something that he could point to that showed he was good at something; that he had real value. He was a very active person so his sports awards definitely went into the books. He was very charming and could talk to people in a way that always got his point across, so newspaper articles that quoted him always went into his book. Pictures of him doing things he enjoyed or was good at were always included as well. School wasn't ignored in his book, but because he didn't have straight A's the way my other brothers and I did, stories, for example, that he had to work incredibly hard at creating, definitely went into his book.

Mother:

We cheered for each other and always celebrated as a family. Problems were supported as a family too. Individuals were definitely held responsible for their actions. No doubt, I expected them to "fix" any mistakes they made but stood behind them in case they needed some help somewhere along the way.

Daughter:

Apologies are not always easy to make! Emptying your piggy bank on the store counter so as to pay for something you broke was equally as difficult. But Mom insisted we do it! If we made a mistake it was up to us to fix it! If we broke something we had to replace it. That goes back to being responsible for your own actions, but also showing respect for other people.

Mother:

I hope my kids understood that they could make mistakes but remain loved.

Daughter:

We knew. We counted on it. Still do!!

Mother:

They were great kids! I made mistakes as I raised them but I had my family to help me along the way too.

Daughter:

She didn't make as many mistakes as she thinks she did. We learned a lot from her directly, but also indirectly by watching how she conducted herself. She worked for and demanded respect for herself regardless of our financial position- and she gave it back to everyone without a second thought. She also showed us that no matter how bad it gets, it can always get worse—so you need to be thankful for what you do have. In our house, growing up, Mom was constantly helping other people even when she didn't really have the resources to do so, especially the money. For example, she once moved a woman in with us who was leaving an abusive relationship, and then helped that woman find a Woman's Shelter when things got worse for her. When we got boxes of food at Christmas, she would generally turn around and pack a whole bunch of it back up and deliver it to someone she felt needed it even more than us.

Mother:

I love them as my kids but I really like the adults they have become.

Daughter:

We love her as our mother but also as one of our best friends. I can speak for my brothers on that point because they have told me that it's true for them as well.

Mother:

I don't know if any of this is what you were specifically looking for or if it helps as far as my daughter's assignment is concerned, but it made for some interesting reminiscing for me. Thanks!

Daughter:

In the end, when it comes to risk and resilience, where my story (my family's story is concerned) I can't say enough about the role my mother has played in it. She is the strongest, bravest woman I know. No, the strongest and bravest person that I know. She is smart, funny, and determined. And when it all comes tumbling down on you and your back is against the wall, she's the one you want on your side, fighting right alongside you!

Addendum

Daughter:

I've been a teacher for over a decade now, and risk and resilience mean a whole lot more to me now because I see it in action every day in my classroom. Some kids who shouldn't "make it"; who have all of the indicators going against them not only survive, some of them actually thrive. However, the majority, in my experience, do not!

I now have a better understanding of how remarkable it is that my brothers and I "made it". We shouldn't have! We did because of one adult who refused to quit and fought with everything she had. In fact, she fought so hard that we (her children) did too, as did other adults (teachers, etc.) that we came into contact with—if for no other reason, than to shut my mother up. Thank God, because it worked. We're still here, contributing! My brothers and I are successful in our chosen fields, have functional relationships, are incredibly close to one another, and all fight for what we want and/or believe in. Every bit of it can be attributed to our mother!

Am I a teacher because of or in spite of my family's experiences? I have a few theories. I do know, however, that it lets me relate to my students better; I see things that my co-workers miss. Not because they don't care, of course, but because I know what I'm seeing—I lived it, up close and personal! It also means that I am now well placed to advocate for them; to see that they all get a chance to become their possibilities. I can't save them—they have to do it for themselves—but I can fight just as hard alongside them as my Mom did for me. I owe it to her to at least try!

Mother:

As a teacher, with respect to her students, my daughter recognizes when their real life interferes with their academic life and advocates for them. She has learned that she cannot save them all but sometimes she can impact just one. Whether it was the kid living on the street and arriving late to class without eating, the young Mom missing an exam due to a sick baby, a family struggling with abuse, a kid coping with addicted parents, or an obnoxious "punk" who continually gets his ass kicked, she takes it on. She relates to them, understanding that their outside lives are more important than their school lives but that they need to succeed in the academic venue to overcome their living situations. She presents a no nonsense strategy to "her kids" who learn that she will work hard for them only if they work hard for themselves.....With humor, honesty and realism, she has become one of "those" teachers without knowing it. There is a generation of kids that will one day say, "I had a teacher once....!"

Chapter 44: Risk, Resiliency, and Narrative: Does It Really Matter?

"The world breaks everyone and afterward some are strong at the broken places."

(Ernest Hemingway, Farewell to Arms)

"I would like to ask you to remember only this one thing," said Badger. "The stories people tell have a way of taking care of them. If stories come to you, care for them. And learn to give them away where they are needed. Sometimes a person needs a story more than food to stay alive; that is why we put these stories in each other's memory. This is how people care for themselves."

(Lopez, 1990, p.48, in Chambers, 2004)

If one goes back to chapter one, where I describe the specifics of my risk/resiliency assignment, one may make the observation that, given the clear parameters of the assignment, some of my students clearly chose to go off in a radically different direction. Although this was never the case for those who chose to review a book within a risk/resiliency perspective, when it came to the personal submissions, I learned very early on to be incredibly more flexible. More specifically, when it came to the myriad personal approaches that a large number of my students brought to this assignment over a ten year period, I learned that whether or not I thought the narrative had met the explicit objectives of the assignment was completely irrelevant. What mattered most was that the students themselves, by telling their own stories, thought they had met the objectives of the assignment. In short, in filtering risk/resiliency characteristics through very personal lenses, if it was good enough for them, than it was definitely good enough for me. In essence, where the personal approach to the assignment was concerned, unlike the book review approach, for me, process took precedence over product every time, and in each and every case. In looking back at the design and delivery of this academic endeavour, sticking exclusively to a book review approach would have been far less problematic, however in hindsight, I'm certainly glad I decided very early on not to do that. Nevertheless, this is not to imply that there have not been some second thoughts along the way where this particular adventure has been specifically concerned.

About four years ago, having already done this assignment for the previous six years, I finally told my wife "enough was enough". I felt that I needed a break from this particular academic exercise because, for at least one month every year, it just wore me absolutely down. For a brief period annually, in reading, marking, talking to, and corresponding with my students related to their submissions, I would go into an absolute funk because, as previously alluded to in chapter one, and is certainly illustrated by some of the stories profiled in this book, when it comes to personal narratives sifted through a risk/resiliency paradigm, one has to wade (many times) through a whole lot of foulness at the beginning of some of the stories to eventually get to the magnificence at the end. For example, it was not uncommon to have some of my students completely go to pieces in my office while discussing their assignments with me, sobbing and, of course, breaking my heart in the process each and every time. And although we would always manage to muddle through, sometimes after many cups of coffee, meetings, telephone calls, and emails, and come out the other side celebrating the resiliency within their individual chronicles, and the impact they were going to have within our profession, I felt the process was taking years off my life.

My wife claims she could immediately note the onset of the assignment's reading and marking period, as she would see a discernable change in my overall demeanour. As she says, "there is a complete 180 degree change in your behaviour and mood; you become, for a time, sullen and cranky". However, with this being conceded, it was also my wife who strongly encouraged me to keep doing the assignment. As someone who also taught in the university, we would sometimes have students in common and she would consistently hear first hand accounts from some of them as to how valuable what we were doing together truly was. Looking in from the outside, my wife claimed that the assignment, and the general themes of risk and resiliency, seemed to be of profound significance to a fair number of my students so I needed to seriously consider all of the implications prior to abandoning it. Hence, I did, and in considering all of the implications, I quickly deduced that my primary motivation in abandoning the assignment had more to do with me than it did my students, so the decision was made (four years ago) to carry on as usual.

To end where I began, for ten years now, I have been lecturing on risk/resiliency and calling in an academically constructed assignment that provides an opportunity for my students to either review a book or share a personal narrative. The point of which was to illustrate that there are numerous examples of those who have transcended the most horrendous of circumstances and conditions and have gone on to live completely meaningful lives as adults (of course, looking especially closely at teachers and schools within this overall process). As Dorothy Fink Ungerleider suggests (1985, p. xv), "to understand the many, we have to look intensively at the few, or even one". Understanding this, I always truly appreciated the benefits of sharing a transcendent story with a wider audience, and that it is why the assignment was initially constructed exclusively around a review of a book, but it was not until I allowed personal perspectives to seep into the process that I also discovered just how important it was to those who actually constructed and told the story as well. As Blanchard and Casanova so astutely put it (1996: xi), and I now so fully understand.

> "People live in a world of stories. They are born into a world full of stories; their lives are stories and so are their deaths. Everyone listens to and tells stories, short ones and long ones, simple ones and complex ones, tragic ones and happy ones. Stories have been used throughout history to organize and communicate meaning, as well as to ponder the mysterious, the magical, and the unexplainable.....Stories help us to remember, to understand, to explain, and to find intellectual, social, and spiritual meaning".

To conclude, to attempt to address the question that was asked at the beginning of this final chapter, does it really matter when it comes to risk, resilience and the telling of stories? I have decided once again to turn back to some of my former students in search of a potential answer.

- I cried, I wrote, I cried some more, and then I wrote some more. I stopped, I started, and cried some more. But then I finished, drank two glasses of red wine, and truly celebrated. Thank you so much for this assignment!! Of all the things I've done this year; no, in my five-year academic life, this has been truly the most important. This rot was eating me up inside for many years now, and in the span of less than a month, you have initiated the healing process by providing a forum to think and write in a very personal way within a framework that offers nothing but hope! Thank-you, thank-you!
- I started to review a book, in fact, I'd spent many days reading it and documenting some of my thoughts. But something kept nagging at me. I kept thinking about your words in class. Then I reread some of my notes and looked at some of the assigned literature and decided to completely change directions – I decided to tell my own story......I think I selected the book I did because I could identify with many of the themes, as foul as some of them were, being described in the book. When it comes to some of these "unnatural things", I've always felt very alone. And what I did know about it generally suggested that it was only a matter of time before some of this foulness came back and got me, which somewhat depressed me. I could never let myself be really happy because it was only a matter of time before it all came crashing down around me. But that has all changed now. This course and this assignment has emphasized that I'm not alone, but most importantly that a great many people actually come through this stuff completely unscathed. I now have every reason to believe that I'll be one of these people.
- I found the writing experience and the forum to share something so very personal to be incredibly cathartic. I am more at peace with myself for having gone through this experience. Don't ever stop doing this

assignment as for some, me included, it's a life altering event, and one that I certainly didn't see coming when I signed up for the course. Thank you so much for everything.

- Writing my brief story for you was a cathartic experience, for sure! But, like everyone else that shares this 'wee dot of blue' called Earth... we are all very much a work in progress.... "Know Thy Self" and that is the truth of it. And when you wade through the bullshit of your own mind, you will eventually come up with the shining truth of it all—"I Am"... I most certainly give you permission to publish my story in your book. It will be of a benefit to others, ie. it is good Karma!

- I told my daughter that I had written the story as an assignment and the request to publish it. It was very emotional for her and myself. She cried through the entire story. In order to okay the publication of the story I needed to see how she would deal with the emotions of seeing her story in print. Unfortunately, I needed an honest reaction and it just about tore my heart out to stand back, not say a word, with only my hand on her shoulder for comfort. When she was finished reading it we hugged for a long time. She is an amazingly strong person and I am thankful for that. We are both saying 'Yes' to printing the story.

- I finally did it! I sat down this weekend and decided to write. I started and couldn't stop. It's long and not very polished in places, but it's done. I am giving it to you to read on your own time. I understand that you are busy, and I'm not even in your class, but hopefully you can read it when you have a spare moment. Thank you for taking the time to talk with me and encouraging me to write. I feel really good about this. It was very therapeutic for me.

- The way you've constructed the assignment and the way you speak to it in your lectures lulls people into sharing, and this has been an incredibly positive thing for me... Not just writing and sharing my story, but the way you responded to it in your emails, has left me feeling stronger as a person than I've ever felt for years. It's important to know that despite some incredibly early challenges, that you're not along in having faced these types of challenges, but more importantly that there are many examples of people rising above these challenges and going on to make real contributions with their lives. I feel that in finally documenting my story, you have provided an opportunity for me to better make a real contribution to the lives of others. I will definitely be a better teacher for having faced, for the first time, my innermost demons. Thank-you from the bottom of my heart for giving me this opportunity.

- I am honoured that you would like to include my story in your book. I am glad that you are putting together a book on resiliency as the pervasive stereotypes that exist in society and within the school system must be broken! Thank you for taking on such a worthy project.

- Thank you for the opportunity to share my story. Writing the essay was definitely a growth experience for me. I wrote it with my eyes closed and did not go over it again, to edit it, until after I had written it completely. I just wanted it to pour out of me and that was that. I have just now read it for the first time and have amazed myself with how truthfully it was written. It truly is me and my innermost thoughts and feeling... I have to say that this opportunity allowed me to finally put some closure on my past and embrace it to help others.

- Of course you can use my story for your book. You know, it is so amazing that you found such great importance in the stories of others. It must be real satisfying for people to be able to tell their stories. I know that in some strange way, I have found some final closure to pieces of me that I thought would never heal. I thank you for listening and for your words of wisdom. A pep talk can sometimes be the most helpful words one can hear during a difficult time. I appreciate your regards and wish you all the best and success with your work on risk and resiliency. This task could not have come at a better time for me as it helped me see my way through many issues. Thank you for those days in your class. You have changed my whole outlook on what teaching has to offer. It is those negative predictions that I will work to change for others. Everyone deserves to make it in this life.

- Thank you very much for giving me the opportunity to tell my story. Of course you have my permission to use it... It was so empowering typing my story in such a way that I could reflect on what had happened in my life almost through a third person lens. I think what you've done with this assignment is truly amazing, not just for the people writing, but for all those who'll now be reading!

- Wow! I would be honoured if you chose to publish my story. When I spoke to my husband about your course and your project, I told him about how I felt my piece wasn't really appropriate because it didn't necessarily have a teacher facilitating the resiliency. He said that it was indeed a teacher that helped him survive – namely me. It was one of the most touching moments of our relationship!

- Thanks so much for everything! I recall the first meeting for this Spec. Ed. class, when you began to speak about this assignment and how we would read a book etc. All I could think of was how I had my own story and wished I could share it and then, you said we could share our personal story of resilience. I was so glad to hear this. For me, although I have "dealt with it", it really is a celebration. Thank you for allowing me this opportunity. My goals are happening and I've always known that people connect with certain others at the right times and for particular purposes. I believe that you are one of those people. In hearing your stories, I am amazed at how you have helped transform the lives of others. One day, I hope I can say the same for me.

- If you think that sharing my story with others would be helpful, then by all means use it! The process of writing it, although trying by times, was a completely liberating experience for me. I certainly knew all about the risk shit, but by forcing me to look at the resiliency as well, has filled me with incredible hope... Everyone needs a little hope and that's what your class and this assignment have provided for me. What a great way to start a career!

- Thank you so much for allowing me a platform upon which I can share my personal triumphs. It has not been easy, however, in putting my thoughts to paper, especially in trying to rationalize some of the tremendous challenges I was forced to endure early in my life, has left me leaving this course with a tremendous amount of pride. I haven't felt this good about myself for quite some time ... Thank you for legitimating my story.

- Before leaving the city I just wanted to thank you for providing such a safe and structured environment for sharing my personal story and thoughts. I knew deep down in my heart that it needed to be done, and although it certainly was a struggle in piecing it together, it eventually got done. And it couldn't have come at a better time for me. I'm feeling very confident at the moment, and life is very good... Thanks again!

- I always knew there was something very precious in the sharing of one's life story. The triumphs and the failures, the happy and the sad, the nasty and the frilly. But as was driven home in this assignment, it's in the coming out on the other side – intact, that really matters... In my schooling experiences, teachers who offered life lessons as well as cover the curriculum, were the ones who mattered most to me and they were the ones I most wanted to be like. Now in finishing off with this course and this particular assignment, I can clearly see that for those most vulnerable – it's the individual that really matters, not the content. The content can definitely wait.

- I can't believe that I actually told you my personal story. I've only told one other person, and I'm married to him. Thanks for the opportunity to write this, as I never would have done it otherwise. I feel as though great weight has been lifted off of my shoulders. The way the assignment was structured, and supplemented with lectures and readings, provided a very safe environment to move forward from. I know it's an awful lot of marking, but you need to keep doing this with all of your students and not just those in Spec. Ed.

- You may not remember me but four years ago I was in your summer Spec. Ed. class, and I wrote a very personal resiliency story for you... I wanted to e-mail you just to let you know how much that experience has impacted my life. It changed my perspective on teaching and, most importantly, it changed my perspective on me. Since that time, I've confided in many others, and eventually sought out the help of a professional. After a few ups and downs along the way I feel as though I'm finally starting to heal...Thank you for initiating that process!

- Over the weekend I put to words my childhood story and it was an incredibly painful experience. However, it's now Monday morning and I feel like a new man. For too many years I saw myself as a victim, completely damaged by the things that were done to me in my youth. This course and this assignment have given me fresh insight into how people are able to survive bad experiences and not become bogged down by things that have happened in the past. It is encouraging to think that I have a repertoire of skills and character qualities that stand me in very good stead. What I've only thought about as being completely negative, has been turned into something completely positive. Thank you for that!

In direct response to the question that was asked at the beginning of this chapter, as the above sampling of correspondence collected over a ten year period in relation to this project clearly indicates, when it comes to risk, resilience and the telling of stories, it would appear to some that it matters a great deal!

> "I ask you right here please to agree with me that a scar is never ugly. That is what the scar makers want us to think. But you and I, we must make an agreement to defy them. We must see all scars as beauty. Okay? This will be our secret. Because take it from me, a scar does not form on the dying. A scar means, *I survived*".

> (Cleave, 2009, p. 9)

References

Barr, R. D. & Parrett, W. H. (2001). Hope fulfilled for at-risk and violent youth: K-12 programs that work. Boston: Allyn & Bacon Publishing.

Barriga, A. Q., Morrison, E. M., Liau, A. K., & Gibbs, J. C. (2001). Moral cognition: Explaining the gender difference in antisocial behaviour. Merill-Palmer Quarterly, *47*, pp. 532-562.

Beattie, M. (2001). The art of learning to teach: Preservice teacher narratives. Columbus, OH: Merrill Prentice Hall.

Benard, B. (August, 1991). Fostering resiliency in kids: Protective factors in the family, school, and community. Portland: Northwest Regional Educational Laboratory.

Benard, B. (1997). Turning it around for all youth: From risk to resilience. New York, New York: ERIC Clearinghouse on Urban Education, Institute for Urban and Minority Education.

Benard, B. (1998). How to be a turnaround teacher/ mentor. *Resiliency in Action.* Retrieved December 8, 2010, from http://www.resiliency.com/htm/turnaround.htm

Benard, B. (1999). The foundations of the resiliency framework: From research to practice. Resiliency in Action. Retrieved October 10, 2010, from http://www.resiliency.com/htm/research.htm

Benard, B. (1999). Applications of resilience: Possibilities and promise. In Meyer Glantz & Jeannette Johnson (Eds.), Resilience and development: Positive life adaptations, (pp. 269-277). New York: Kluwer Academic/Plenum Publishers.

Benard, B. (2004). Resiliency: What have we learned. San Francisco: WestEd Publishing.

Bennett, P., Elliott, M., & Peters, D. (2005). Classroom and family effects on children's behavioural problems. The Elementary School Journal, *5, pp.* 462-479.

Bersani, B. E. & Chapple, C. L. (2007). School failure as an adolescent turning point. Sociological Focus, 40, pp. 370-391.

Bevan, E. & Higgins, D. J. (2002). Is domestic violence learned? The contribution of five forms of child maltreatment to men's violence and adjustment. Journal of Family Violence, *17, pp.* 223-245.

Blanchard, J. S. & Casanova, U. (1996). Modern fiction about school teaching: An anthology. Boston: Allyn & Bacon.

Borland, M., Pearson, C., Hill, M., Tisdall, K., & Bloomfield, I. (1998). Education and care away from home, Edinburgh: Scottish Council for Research in Education.

Bradley, H. B. & Corwyn, R. F. (2000). Socioeconomic status and child development. Annual Review of Psychology, 53, pp. 371-399.

Bronfenbrenner, Urie, (1983). Beyond policies without people: An ecological perspective on child and family policy. In Children, families, and government: Perspectives on American social policy, ed. by Edward Zigler et al., New York: Cambridge University Press.

Brooks, R. & Goldstein, S. (2001). Raising resilient children: Fostering strength, hope, and optimism in your child. New York: McGraw-Hill.

Brown, J. H., D'Emidio-Caston, M., & Benard, B. (2001). Resilience education. Thousand Oaks, California: Corwin Press Inc.

Bruce, P. (2002) Resilience: Where does it come from? Early Childhood Today, 17, pp. 24-27.

Card, N. A., Stucky, B. D., Sawalani, G. M., & Little, T. D. (2008). Direct and indirect aggression during childhood and adolescence: A meta-analytic review of gender differences, intercorrelations, and relations to maladjustment. Child Development, 79, pp. 1185-1229.

Chambers, C. (2004). Research that matters: Finding a path with heart. Journal of the Canadian Association for Curriculum Studies, 2(1), pp. 1-19.

Chess, S. (1989). Defying the voice of doom. In T. Dugan & R. Coles (Eds.), The child in our times: Studies in the development of resilience, (pp. 179-199). New York: Brunner & Mazel Publishing.

Children's Defense Fund, (2005). The state of America's children yearbook. Washington, DC.

Clandinin, D. J. & Connelly, F. M. (1991). Narrative and story in practice and research. In D. Schön (Ed.), The reflective turn: Case studies in and of educational practice, (pp. 258-281). New York: Teachers College Press.

Clandinin, D. J. & Connelly, F. M. (2000). Narrative inquiry: Experience and story in qualitative research. San Francisco: Jossey-Bass.

Cleave, C. (2009). Little Bee. Toronto: Anchor Publishing.

Coburn, J. & Nelson, S. (1989). Teachers do make a difference: What Indian graduates say about their school experience. ERIC Document Reproduction Service # 306071, pp. 107-103.

Collishaw, S., Pickles, A., Messer, J., Rutter, M., Shearer, C., & Maughan, B. (2007). Resilience to adult psychopathology following childhood maltreatment: Evidence from a community sample. Child Abuse and Neglect, 31, pp. 211-229.

Craig, W. & Pepler, D. (1998). Observations of bullying and victimization in the school yard. Canadian Journal of School Psychology, Vol. 13, No. 2, pp. 41-59.

Dahlberg, L. L. (1998). Youth violence in the United States: Major trends, risk factors, and prevention approaches. American Journal of Preventative Medicine, 14, pp. 259-272.

Davis, H. A. (2003). Conceptualizing the role and influence of student-teacher relationships on children's social and cognitive development. Educational Psychologist, 38, pp. 207–234.

Department of Justice Canada Report, (2004). A one day snapshot of Aboriginal youth in custody across Canada. Phase II, (February).

Diamond, C. T. P. (1991). Teacher education as transformation: A psychological perspective. Milton Keynes, Philadelphia: Open University Press.

D,Haene, D. (2002). My father's touch. Danvers, MA: American Book Publishing.

Dryfoos, J. G. (1990). Adolescents at-risk: Prevalence and prevention. New York: Oxford University Press.

DuMont, K. A., Widom, C. S., & Czaja, S. J. (2007). Predictors of resilience in abused and neglected children grown-up. The role of individual and neighborhood characteristics. Child Abuse and Neglect, 31, pp. 255-274.

Dusenbury, L., Falco, M., Lake, A., Brannigan, R., & Bosworth, K. (1997). Nine critical elements of promising prevention programs. Journal of School Health, 67, pp. 127-132.

Fraser, S. (1989). My father's house. London: Virago Press.

Freiberg, H. J. (1993). A school that fosters resilience in inner-city youth. Journal of Negro Education, 62, pp. 364–376.

Furstenberg, F., Brooks-Gunn, J., & Morgan, S. (1987). Adolescent mothers and their children in later life. Family Planning Perspectives, 19, pp. 142-151.

Garmezy, N. (1971). Vulnerability research and the issue of primary prevention. American Journal of Orthopsychiatry, 141, pp. 101-116.

Garmezy, N. (1985). Stress-resitant children: The search for protective factors. In J. E. Stevenson (Ed.), Recent research in developmental psychopathology, (pp.213-233). Oxford, UK: Pergamon Press.

Garmezy, N. (1991). Resiliency and vulnerability to adverse developmental outcomes associated with poverty. American Behavioural Scientist. 34, pp. 416-430.

Garmezy N. (1993). Children in poverty: Resiliency despite risk. Psychiatry, (6), pp. 127–136.

Geary, P. A. (1988). Defying the odds: Academic success among at-risk minority teenagers in an urban high school. ERIC Document Reproduction Service # 296055.

Glantz, M. D. & Johnson, J. L. (1999). Resilience and development: Positive life adaptations. New York: Springer Publishing.

Graham, J. (1988). Schools, disruptive behaviour and delinquency. A review of research. Home Office Research Study (# 96). London: HMSO.

Henderson, N. & Milstein, M. (2003). Resiliency in school: Making it happen for students and educators. Thousand Oaks, California: Corwin Press Inc.

Henderson, N., Benard, B., & Sharp-Light, N. (2007). Resiliency in action: Practical ideas for overcoming risks and building strengths in youth, families, and communities, 2nd ed. Ojai, CA: Resiliency in Action, Inc.

Higgins, D. J. & McCabe, M. P. (2000). Multi-type maltreatment and the long-term adjustment of adults, Child Abuse Review, 9, pp. 6-18.

Higgins, G. (1994). Resilient adults: Overcoming a cruel past. San Francisco: Jossey-Bass.

Human Resources and Skills Development Canada (2000). Dropping out of high school: Definitions and costs. Applied Research Branch, October.

Hurlington, K. (2010). What works? Research into practice. The Literacy and Numeracy Secretariat: Ontario Ministry of Education (February). Retrieved February 8, 2014, from http://www.edu.gov.on.ca/eng/literacynumeracy/publications.html

Kaplan, H. B. (1999). Toward an understanding of resilience: A critical review of definitions and models. In Meyer Glantz & Jeannette Johnson (Eds.), Resilience and development: Positive life adaptations, (pp. 17-83). New York: Kluwer Academic/Plenum Publishers.

Kirby, D. (1999). Reflections on two decades of research on teen sexual behaviour and pregnancy. Journal of School Health, 69, pp. 89-94.

Krovetz, M. L. (2008). Fostering resilience: Expecting all students to use their minds and hearts well. Thousand Oaks, California: Corwin Press Inc.

Lerner, R. & Overton, W. F. (2008). Exemplifying the integrations of the relational developmental system: Synthesizing theory, research, and application to promote positive development and social justice. Journal of Adolescent Research, 23 (3), pp. 245-255.

Levine S. (2002). Against terrible odds: Lessons in resilience from our children. Palo Alto, California: Bull Publishing.

Loeber, R. & Hay, D. F. (1996). Key issues in the development of aggression and violence from childhood to early adulthood. Annual Review of Psychology, 48, pp. 371-410.

Losel, F. & Bliesener, T. (1990). Resilience in adolescence: A study on the generalizability of protective factors. In Klaus Hurrelmann & Freidrich Losel (Eds.), Health hazards in adolescence, (pp. 299-320). Berlin: Walter de Gruyter Publishing.

Luby, J., Belden, A., Botteron, K., Marrus, N., Harms, M., Babb, C., Nishino, T., & Barch, D. (2013). The effects of poverty on childhood brain development: The mediating effect of caregiving and stressful life events. JAMA Pediatrics, Vol. 167, No 12, pp. 1135-1142.

Luthar, S. S. & Cushing, G. (1999). Measurement issues in the empirical study of resilience. In Meyer Glantz & Jeannette Johnson (Eds.), Resilience and development: Positive life adaptations, (pp. 129-160). New York: Kluwer Academic/Plenum Publishers.

Luthar, S. S. (2000). The construct of resilience: A critical evaluation and guidelines for future work. Child Development, 71, pp. 543-562.

Luthar, S. S. (2003). Resilience and vulnerability: Adaptation in the context of childhood adversities. New York: Cambridge University Press

Manning, M. L. & Baruth, L. G. (1995). Students at-risk. Needham Heights, Massachusetts: Allyn & Bacon.

Mantley, P. (1999). Silent cries. Lockeport, Nova Scotia: Community Books.

Masten, A. S. (1994). Resilience in individual development: Successful adaptations despite risk and adversity. In M.C. Chang Wang & E.W. Gordon (Eds.), Educational resilience in inner-city America, (pp. 3-25). Hillsdale, NJ: Erlbaum.

Masten, A. S. & Coatsworth, J. D. (1998). The development of competence in favourable and unfavourable environments: Lessons from research on successful children. American Psychologist, 53, pp. 205-220.

Masten, A. S., Best, K. M., & Garmezy, N. (1990). Resilience and development contributions from the study of children who overcome adversity. Development and Psychopathology, 2, pp. 425-444.

Masten, A. S. (1999). Resilience comes of age: Reflections on the past and outlook for the next generation of research. In Meyer Glantz & Jeannette Johnson (Eds.), Resilience and development: Positive life adaptations, (pp. 281-296). New York: Kluwer Academic/Plenum Publishers.

Masten, A. S. (2001). Ordinary magic: Resilience processes in development. American Psychologist, 56 (3), pp. 227-238.

McCubbin H., McCubbin M., Thompson, A., Han, S.Y., & Allen, C. (1997). Families under stress: What makes them resilient. 1997 American Association of Family and Consumer Sciences Commemorative Lecture delivered by Hamilton McCubbin on June 22, 1997, in Washington, D.C.

McCubbin, H., Thompson, E. A., Thompson, A. I., & Futrell, J. A. (1998). Resiliency in African American families. Thousand Oaks, California: Sage Publishing.

McIlroy, A. (2010). How poverty shapes the brain. The Globe and Mail. Retrieved May 25, 2010 from http://www.theglobeandmail.com/news/national/how-poverty-shapes-the-brain/article:1579628

McIntyre J., Freeland J., Melville B., & Schwenke C. (1999). Early school leavers at risk. Australian National Training Authority, NCVER, South Australia.

McWhirter, J. J., McWhirter, B. T., McWhirter, E. H., & McWhirter, R. J. (2004). At-risk youth: A comprehensive response. Toronto: Brooks/Cole Publishing.

Meier, D. (1995). The power of their ideas: Lessons for America from a small school in Harlem. Boston: Beacon.

Milstein, M. M. & Henry, D. A. (2000). Spreading resiliency. Thousand Oaks, California: Corwin Press Inc.

Miller, A. (1990). The untouched key: Tracing childhood trauma in creativity. New York: Anchor Books.

Mireault, G. & Bond, L. (1992). Parental death in childhood: Perceived vulnerability, and adult depression and anxiety. American Journal of Orthopsychiatry, Vol. 62, (4), pp. 517-524.

Montgomery-Whicher, R. (2002). Aesthetic experiences. In M. van Manen (Ed.), Writing in the dark: Phenomenological studies in interpretive inquiry, (pp. 27-47). Langston, ON: The Althouse Press.

Neitzel, S. & Welzer, H. (2011). Soldaten: On fighting, killing, and dying. Toronto: McClelland & Stewart

Noddings, N. (1988). An ethic of caring and its implication for instructional arrangements. American Journal of Education, 96, pp. 215–230.

Noddings, N. (1992) The challenge to care in schools: An alternative approach to education. New York: Teachers College Press.

Noddings, N. (1999). Caring and competence. In G. Griffen (Ed.), The education of teachers, (pp. 205-220). Chicago: National Society of Education.

Noddings, N. (2003). Happiness and education. New York: Cambridge University Press.

Noddings, N. (2007). Philosophy of education. Boulder, Colorado: Westview Press.

O'Grady, D. & Metz, R. J. (1987). Resilience in children at high risk for psychological disorder. Journal of Pediatric Psychology, Vol. 12, No. 1, pp. 3-23.

Paolucci, A. & Richardson, W. J. (2009). Risk, resiliency, and a post-secondary cohort: Some preliminary findings. Child and Family Professional, Spring, pp. 61-76.

Parsley, K. & Corcoran, A. (2003). The classroom teacher's role in preventing school failure. Kappa Delta Pi Record. Retrieved December 7, 2009, from http://findarticles.com/p/articles/mi_qa4009/is_200301/ai_n9179139?tag=content;col1

Pelzer, D. (1995). A child called it. Deerfield Beach: Health Communications Inc.

Pelzer, D. (1997). The lost boy. Deerfield Beach: Health Communications Inc.

Pelzer, D. (1999). A man called Dave. Deerfield Beach: Health Communications Inc.

Richardson, G. E., Neiger, B. L., Jesnsen, S., & Kumpfer, K. L. (1990). The model. Health Education, 21, pp. 33-39.

Richardson, W. J., Richardson, C. A., & McCabe, M. J. (2004). The resilience of the human condition and the educational experience. The CAP Journal, Ethics, Morals, Values and Spirituality in Today's Schools. 12, pp. 12-14.

Richardson, W. J. (2005). Voices from the margins. Burnaby, BC: Aydy Press.

Richardson, C. A. (2008). Tuning our souls: Celebrating the courage to sing our own songs. In W. J. Richardson & C. A. Richardson (Eds.), Walking the talk. Putting theory into practice, (pp. 151-158). Calgary, Alta: Detselig Publishing.

Richardson, W. J. (2008). What's so "special' about special education?. In W. J. Richardson & C. A. Richardson (Eds.), Walking the talk. Putting theory into practice, (pp. 159-168). Calgary, Alta: Detselig Publishing.

Richardson, W. J., Paolucci, A., & Richardson, C. (2010). A descriptive analysis of risk and resiliency within a cohort of preservice teachers. The International Journal of Diversity in Organizations, Communities & Nations. Vol. 10. No. 3, pp. 49-72.

Ringwalt, C. L., Greene, J. M., & Robertson, M. J. (1998). Familial backgrounds and risk behaviours of youth with throwaway experiences. Journal of Adolescence, 21, pp. 241-252.

Rolf, J. & Johnson, J. (1990). Protected or vulnerable: The challenges of AIDS to developmental psychopathology. In J. Rolf, A. Masten, D. Nicchetti, K. Nuechterlein, & S. Weintraub, (Eds.), Risk and protective factors in the development of psychopathology, (pp. 384–404). Cambridge, U.K.: Cambridge University Press.

Rolf, J. & Johnson, J. (1999). Opening doors to resilience intervention for prevention research. In Meyer Glantz & Jeannette Johnson (Eds.), Resilience and development: Positive life adaptations, (pp. 229-249). New York: Kluwer Academic/Plenum Publishers.

Rutter, M., Maughan, B., Mortimore, P., Ouston, J., & Smith, A. (1977). Fifteen thousand hours. Cambridge, MA: Harvard University Press.

Rutter, M. (1979). Protective factors in children's responses to stress and disadvantagement. In M. W. Kent & J. E. Rolf (Eds.), Primary prevention of psycho- pathology: Social competence in children, (pp. 49-74). Oxford: Blackwell.

Rutter, M. & Garmezy, N. (1983). Developmental psychology. In E. M. Hetherington (Ed.), Handbook of child psychology: Social and personality development, (pp. 619-700). Chichester: Wiley.

Rutter, M. (1987). Psychosocial resilience and protective mechanisms. American Journal of Orthopsychiatry, 57, pp. 316-331.

Rutter, M. (1990). Psychosocial resilience and protective mechanisms. In J. Rolf, A. Masten, D. Cicchetti, K. Neuchterlein, & S. Weintraub (Eds.), Risk and protective factors in the development of psychopathology, (pp. 581-592). Cambridge: Cambridge University Press.

Rutter, M., Giller, H., & Hagel, A. (1998). Anti-social behaviour by young people. Cambridge: Cambridge University Press.

Rutter, M. (2000). Resilience reconsidered: Conceptual considerations, empirical findings and policy implications. In J. P. Shonkoff and S. J. Meisels (Eds.), Handbook of early childhood intervention, (pp. 651-682). New York: Cambridge University Press.

Rutter, M. (2012). Resilience: Causal pathways and social ecology. In M. Ungar (Ed.), The social ecology of resilience: A handbook of theory and practice, (pp. 33-42). New York: Springer.

Rutter, M. (2012). Resilience as a dynamic. Development and Psychology (24), pp. 335-344.

Sampson, R.J. & Laub, J.H. (1993). Crime in the making: Pathways and turning points through life. Cambridge, MA: Harvard University Press.

Sanders, M. G. (2000). Schooling students placed at risk: Research, policy, and practice in the education of poor and minority students. Mahwah, NJ: Lawrence Erlbaum Associates.

Scudder, L., Sullivan, K., & Copeland-Linder, N. (2008). Adolescent resilience: Lessons for primary care. Journal for Nurse Practitioners, 4, pp. 535-543.

Siegel, L. J., Welsh, B. C., & Senna, J. J. (2003). Juvenile delinquency: Theory, practice, and law. Toronto: Wadsworth Thompson.

Silliman, B. S. (1994). Resiliency research review: Conceptual & research foundations. Children and Youth Families Education and Research Network. Retrieved January 7, 2012, from http://www1.cyfernet.org/prog/fam/94-Silliman-resilreview.html

Spieker, S. J., Larson, N. C., Lewis, S. M., Keller, T. E., & Gilchrist, L. (1999). Developmental trajectories of disruptive behavior problems in preschool children of adolescent mothers. Child Development, 70, pp. 443-458.

Thomsen, K. (2002). Building resilient students: Integrating resiliency into what you already know and do. Thousand Oaks, CA: Corwin Press.

Thornberry, T., Huizinga, D., & Loeber, R. (1995). The prevention of serious delinquency and violence: Implications from the program of research on the causes and correlates of delinquency, (pp. 213-237). In James C. Howell, Barry Krisberg, J. David Hawkins, & John J. Wilson (Eds.). A sourcebook: Serious, violent and chronic juvenile offenders. New York: Sage Publishing.

Thornberry, T. & Krohn, M. (1997). Peers, drug use and delinquency. In D. Stoff, J. Breiling, & J. D. Maser (Eds.), Hand-book of anti-social behaviour, (pp. 218-233). New York: Wiley.

Tilleczek, K., Furlong, A., & Ferguson, B. (2010), Marginalized youth in contemporary educational contexts: A tranquil invitation to a rebellious celebration? Education Canada, 50(5), pp. 6-10.

Tomlinson, C. A. & Jarvis, J. (2006). Teaching beyond the book. Educational Leadership, 64 (1), pp. 16-21.

Toro, P. A., Urberg, K. A., & Heinze, H. J. (2004). Antisocial behaviour and affiliation with deviant peers. Journal of Clinical Child and Adolescent Psychology, 33, pp. 336-346.

Turner, M. G. (2000). Good kids in bad circumstances: A longitudinal analysis of resilient youth. United States Department of Justice: National Criminal Justice Reference Service, Document # 188263.

Ungar, M. & Teram, E. (2000). Drifting toward mental health: High-risk adolescents and the process of empowerment. Youth & Society, 32(2), pp. 228-252.

Ungar, M. (2004). A constructionist discourse on resilience: Multiple contexts, multiple realities among at-risk children and youth. Youth & Society, Vol. 35, No. 3, pp. 341-365.

Ungar, M. (2013). The impact of youth-adult relationships on resilience. International Journal of Child, Youth and Family Studies, (3), pp. 328-336.

Ungerleider, D.F. (1985). The terrible price paid to victims of school failure. Encino, CA: RWR Press.

Van Breda, A. D. (2001). Resilience theory: A literature review. Retrieved January 27, 2011 from, http://www.vanbreda.org/adrian/resilience.htm

van Manen, M. (1986). The tone of teaching. Portsmouth, NH: Heineman.

Wang, M. C. & Gordon, E. W. (1994). Resiliency in inner city America: Challenges and prospects. Hillside, New Jersey: Lawrence Erlbaum Press.

Waxman, H. C., Gray, J. P., & Padrón, Y. N. (2003). Review of research on educational resilience. Centre for Research on Education, Diversity and Excellence.

Waxman, H. C., Padrón, Y. N., and Gray, J. P. (2004). Educational resiliency: Student, teacher, and school perspectives. IAP.

Werner, E. (1989). High risk children in young adulthood: A longitudinal study from birth to 32 years. American Journal of Orthopsychiatry, 59, pp. 72-81.

Werner, E. & Smith, R. (1989). Vulnerable but invincible: A Longitudinal study of resilient children and youth. New York: Adams, Bannister, & Cox.

Werner, E. & Smith, R. (1992). Overcoming the odds: High-risk children from birth to adulthood. New York: Cornell University Press.

Werner, E. (1993). Risk, resilience, and recovery: Perspectives from the Kauai longitudinal study. Development and Psychopathology, 3, pp. 503-515.

Werner, E. (2000). Protective factors and individual resilience. In J. Shonkoff & S. Meisels (Eds.), Handbook of early intervention, (pp. 115-132). New York: Cambridge University Press.

Werner, E. & Smith, R. (2001). Journeys from Childhood to midlife: Risk, resilience, and recovery. Ithaca, New York. Cornell University Press.

West, W.G. (1984). Young offenders and the state. Toronto: Butterworths Canada Ltd.

Witherell, C. & Noddings, N. (1991). Stories lives tell: Narrative and dialogue in education. New York: Teachers College Press.

Wolin, S. J. & Wolin, S. (1993). The resilient self: How survivors of troubled families rise above adversity. New York: Villard Books.

Youth Justice Board Report (2005). Risk and protective factors. Communities that Matter, pp. 1-194.

Zimmerman, B.J. (2000). Self-efficacy: An essential motive to learn. Contemporary Educational Psychology, 25 (1), pp. 82-91.

CPSIA information can be obtained
at www.ICGtesting.com
Printed in the USA
LVOW01s2011150316

479315LV00006B/22/P